THE LAW AND PRACTICE OF PEACEKEEPING

In an increasingly complex world, it is more crucial than ever to have a full picture of how international peacekeeping can be a force for good, but can also have potentially negative impacts on host communities. After thirteen years of presence in Haiti, the highly controversial United Nations Stabilization Mission in Haiti has now withdrawn. The UN's legacy in Haiti is not all negative, but it does include sexual scandals, the divisive use of force to 'clean up' difficult neighbourhoods as well as a cholera epidemic, brought inadvertently by Nepalese peacekeepers, that killed more than 8,000 Haitians and infected more than 600,000. This book presents a unique multi-disciplinary analysis of the legacy of the mission for Haiti. It presents an innovative account of contemporary international peacekeeping law and practice, arguing for a new model of accountability, going beyond the outdated immunity mechanisms to foreground human rights.

Rosa Freedman is Professor of Law, Conflict and Global Development at the University of Reading. She has published widely on the UN and human rights, and serves on the UN Secretary-General's Civil Society Advisory Board for the prevention of sexual exploitation and abuse and as a Specialist Advisor to the UK Government.

Nicolas Lemay-Hébert is Senior Lecturer at the Department of International Relations, Coral Bell School of Asia Pacific Affairs, Australian National University.

Siobhán Wills is Professor of Law at the Transitional Justice Institute in the Law School of Ulster University. She has led two Arts and Humanities Research Council projects and held a British Academy Mid-Career Fellowship on peacekeepers' legal obligations and the impact of peacekeeping on marginalised communities. She co-directed the films *It Stays With You: Use of Force by UN Peacekeepers in Haiti* and *Right Now I Want to Scream: Police and Army Killings in Rio*.

The Law and Practice of Peacekeeping

FOREGROUNDING HUMAN RIGHTS

ROSA FREEDMAN
University of Reading

NICOLAS LEMAY-HÉBERT
Australian National University

SIOBHÁN WILLS
Ulster University

CAMBRIDGE
UNIVERSITY PRESS

University Printing House, Cambridge CB2 8BS, United Kingdom

One Liberty Plaza, 20th Floor, New York, NY 10006, USA

477 Williamstown Road, Port Melbourne, VIC 3207, Australia

314–321, 3rd Floor, Plot 3, Splendor Forum, Jasola District Centre, New Delhi – 110025, India

79 Anson Road, #06–04/06, Singapore 079906

Cambridge University Press is part of the University of Cambridge.

It furthers the University's mission by disseminating knowledge in the pursuit of education, learning, and research at the highest international levels of excellence.

www.cambridge.org
Information on this title: www.cambridge.org/9781108477529
DOI: 10.1017/9781108763776

© Rosa Freedman, Nicolas Lemay-Hébert and Siobhán Wills 2021

This publication is in copyright. Subject to statutory exception and to the provisions of relevant collective licensing agreements, no reproduction of any part may take place without the written permission of Cambridge University Press.

First published 2021

A catalogue record for this publication is available from the British Library.

ISBN 978-1-108-47752-9 Hardback

Cambridge University Press has no responsibility for the persistence or accuracy of URLs for external or third-party internet websites referred to in this publication and does not guarantee that any content on such websites is, or will remain, accurate or appropriate.

Contents

1 Introduction   1

  1.1 MINUSTAH – A Reflection of Wider Issues with Peacekeeping   1

  1.2 Peacekeeping in a Changing World   4

  1.3 The Rise of the Unintended Consequences Agenda   7

    1.3.1 Stabilisation and Robust Peacekeeping   8

    1.3.2 Sexual Exploitation and Abuse by Peacekeepers   10

    1.3.3 Cholera Outbreak   11

  1.4 Structure of the Book   11

2 A Political History of UN Involvement in Haiti   13

  2.1 Nature of the Haitian State: Beyond the Failed State Model   13

  2.2 Shared Sovereignty: Between Fragile States and Interventions   16

  2.3 Sovereignty in Practice   20

  2.4 UN Involvement in Haiti   24

  2.5 Conclusion: MINUJUSTH and Beyond   33

3 Integrating Human Rights Norms into UN Peacekeeping Practice   34

  3.1 Introduction   34

  3.2 Military Peacekeepers Are Members of National Armies   35

  3.3 The Basis of United Nations' Human Rights Law Obligations   40

  3.4 Conclusion   46

4 UN Immunities and Human Rights   48

  4.1 Introduction   48

4.2	Immunities		49
	4.2.1	UN Immunity	49
	4.2.2	Immunities of UN Personnel	51
4.3	A Victim-Centred Approach to Accountability		54
	4.3.1	Criminal Justice	55
	4.3.2	Truth and Reconciliation	57
	4.3.3	Human Rights	60
	4.3.4	Political Processes	64
4.4	Conclusion		65

5 The Cholera Epidemic: Unintended Consequences and Implications — 66

5.1	Introduction		66
5.2	Cholera in Haiti: An Overview		67
5.3	Un-accountable: The Fight for Justice		72
	5.3.1	The Legal Argument	75
5.4	How the Dispute Was (Not) Resolved by Politics		77
	5.4.1	Public Awareness	78
	5.4.2	UN Independent Experts on Human Rights	79
	5.4.3	Birmingham Initiative	81
	5.4.4	The Security Council	83
5.5	Conclusion		88

6 Sexual Exploitation and Abuse: Who Guards the Guardians? — 89

6.1	Introduction		89
6.2	Sexual Exploitation and Abuse in Peacekeeping		90
6.3	Laws and Frameworks		94
	6.3.1	Immunities and Jurisdictional Bars	94
	6.3.2	Civilian Staff	95
	6.3.3	Experts on Mission	97
	6.3.4	Military Personnel	97
6.4	Investigations and Prosecutions		99
	6.4.1	UN Internal Investigations	99
	6.4.2	Troop-Contributing Countries' Investigations	102
6.5	Peacekeeper Sexual Exploitation and Abuse in Haiti		104
	6.5.1	Children	107
	6.5.2	Transactional Sex	109
	6.5.3	'Consensual'/Survival Relationships	111
	6.5.4	Children Fathered by Peacekeepers	113
6.6	Conclusion		115

7	**UN Peacekeepers' Use of Deadly Force to Maintain Law and Order**		116
	7.1	Introduction	116
	7.2	Stabilization and Use of Force against 'Spoilers'	119
	7.3	Right to Life Obligations of UN Peacekeeping Troops	123
	7.4	'Collateral Damage' Caused by MINUSTAH in Cité Soleil the Years 2004–2007	126
	7.5	Rules of Engagement for UN Peacekeepers	134
	7.6	Conclusion	137
8	**Conclusion**		140
	8.1	Introduction	140
	8.2	Peacekeeping Expands to Protect Human Rights but Fails to Incorporate IHRL Standards into Its Practice	141
	8.3	Conclusion	145
Index			147

1

Introduction

1.1 MINUSTAH – A REFLECTION OF WIDER ISSUES WITH PEACEKEEPING

The United Nations (UN) Stabilisation Mission in Haiti (MINUSTAH) withdrew completely in October 2017 after thirteen years of deployment and was replaced by a smaller mission, the UN Mission for Justice Support in Haiti (MINUJUSTH), mandated under Chapter VII of the UN Charter but comprised of police units and police officers with no military component.[1] The draw down of MINUSTAH provides an opportunity to review the mission's significance and legacy and to provide a candid examination of the conduct and responsibilities of the mission without risk of exacerbating the challenges faced by UN troops on the ground.

Whilst MINUSTAH is praised for its role in improving security, within Haiti there is strong criticism of the mission for its human rights violations and lack of accountability. Pressure on the UN to address a perceived accountability gap is particularly acute in relation to the cholera outbreak of 2010 – for which the UN has since apologised but failed adequately to remedy – because the scale of the harm is so large: the epidemic has killed and injured many thousands.[2] But there is also pressure to address the mission's lack of accountability with regard to sexual exploitation and abuse (SEA) – the mission has one of the worst SEA records of any UN mission[3] – and the mission's use of

---

[1] S/RES 2350 13 April 2017; Security Council Grants Final Mandate Extension for United Nations Stabilization Mission in Haiti, Unanimously Adopting Resolution 2350 (2017) Delegations Question Language Added to Text, Reference to Chapter VII of Charter www.un.org/press/en/2017/sc12794.doc.htm (accessed 25 April 2020).

[2] R. Freedman and N. Lemay-Hébert, Haiti Report March 2017 http://blogs.reading.ac.uk/participation-lab/files/2017/05/Haiti-Report-Final-April-21.pdf (accessed 25 April 2020).

[3] UN Office of Internal Oversight Services (OIOS), 'Evaluation of the Enforcement and Remedial Assistance Efforts for Sexual Exploitation and Abuse by the United Nations and

excessive force in carrying out security operations that resulted in scores of deaths and injuries to people that were not involved in criminal activity.[4] In part the UN has relied on the immunity conferred on it by the Convention on the Privileges and Immunities of the UN[5] to deny any legal responsibility, especially regarding the cholera outbreak.[6] As of the time of writing, other than the UN Victims' Rights Advocate, senior UN personnel remain reluctant to meet with those that have been directly harmed by its operations even in cases, such as the cholera epidemic, where it acknowledges that it bears some responsibility.[7] These and other unintended consequences of MINUSTAH are central to the legacy that it leaves behind, whilst also providing a window into issues experienced by peacekeeping across the world.

MINUSTAH was unique as a UN mission in many respects, yet many of the challenges it faced, and many of the criticisms levelled against it, are paradigmatic of the challenges and criticisms facing current peacekeeping operations, particularly those missions with a stabilisation element. MINUSTAH was the first UN peacekeeping mission specifically to be designated as a stabilisation mission. Stabilisation usually entails support to the host state government in quelling threats to the stability of its rule. Today stabilisation has become a core function of peacekeeping, a rapid development that has taken place in less than fifteen years.

MINUSTAH is also the first mission in which none of its activities had any connection to armed conflict owing to there being no armed conflict in Haiti throughout the entire period of MINUSTAH's deployment.[8] The UN acknowledges that outside of armed conflict, the guiding principles governing

---

Related Personnel in Peacekeeping Operations', 15 May 2015, revised 12 June 2015 1434375935_1_IED_15_001.pdf.

[4] S. Wills and C. McLaughlin *It Stays With You*, a film and information website on the UN 'collateral damage' in Haiti https://itstayswithyou.com (accessed 25 April 2020).

[5] Convention on the Privileges and Immunities of the United Nations, 1 U.N.T.S. 15, 13 February 1946, New York.

[6] Briefing by Bureaux des Avocats Internationaux and Institute for Justice and Democracy in Haiti www.ijdh.org/cholera/cholera-litigation/ (accessed 25 April 2020); Interview with Haitian human rights lawyer Ezili Danto, World Brief Huffington Post Live 13 June 2015 www.youtube.com/watch?v=u3YJChM4U10 (accessed 25 April 2020).

[7] Freedman and Lemay-Hébert, Haiti Report March 2017 (n 2).

[8] International Crisis Group, 'Towards a Post-MINUSTAH Haiti: Making an Effective Transition: Latin America/Caribbean Report No 44', 2 August 2012, www.crisisgroup.org/latin-america-caribbean/haiti/towards-post-minustah-haiti-making-effective-transition, 16 (accessed 25 April 2020); C. Call and G. Sorensen, *U.N. Operations and State-building: A Case Study of Haiti* (New York: Center on International Cooperation 2009), 5. In researching the case study Call and Sorenson conducted interviews in Haiti and at UN headquarters with various units at DPKO, DPA, UNDOCO and UNDP, as well as with think tanks and some experts, which suggests that their view reflects a degree of consensus at the UN. Their case study is cited in UN

law enforcement should be informed by international human rights law (IHRL) standards – but has yet to formally incorporate these standards into its rules of engagement (ROE) for military forces carrying out law enforcement operations – such as providing security for elections, dealing with criminal gangs, and responding to riots. This is problematic given that much of peacekeepers' work is now concerned with law enforcement. This is true not only in Haiti – a paradigmatic example of a law enforcement oriented peacekeeping mission – but also in many other twenty-first-century missions, particularly those with a stabilisation element (notably the UN Organisation Stabilisation Mission in the Democratic Republic of the Congo (MONUSCO), the UN Multidimensional Integrated Stabilisation Mission in Mali (MINUSMA), the UN Multidimensional Integrated Stabilisation Mission in the Central African Republic (MINUSCA)).

According to the UN's own website, fifteen of the UN's current peacekeeping missions are mandated to carry out Rule of Law tasks; another fifteen to carry out tasks relating to Electoral Assistance; eleven to provide Support to State Institutions; and eleven to carry out Security Sector reforms.[9] Most of these missions are mandated under Chapter VII, and most are authorised to use force using the formula 'all necessary means' or 'all necessary measures',[10] which are euphemisms routinely used by the Security Council when discussing use of force.[11] This expansion of Chapter VII mandated peacekeeping activities to encompass law enforcement has not been matched by equivalent attention to the legal obligations and good practice standards that ought to be applied to operations that are not directed at parties to an armed conflict. The effects of this lag have been particularly noticeable in Haiti in relation to a number of key areas. The crisis in UN accountability triggered by the cholera epidemic has attracted worldwide attention and requires a change in approach – for Haiti and

---

DPKO's own report, *Second Generation Disarmament, Demobilization, and Reintegration Practices in UN Peacekeeping Operations* (New York: United Nations Department of Peacekeeping Operations, Office of Rule of Law and Security Institutions 2010), 67; A. Serafin, 'Urban Violence: War by Any Other Name' (2010) The Magazine of the International Red Cross and Red Crescent Movement, 1. www.redcross.int/EN/mag/magazi ne2010_1/20–23.html (accessed 25 April 2020); M. Schuberth 'A Transformation from Political to Criminal Violence? Politics, Organised Crime and the Shifting Functions of Haiti's Urban Armed Groups' (2015) 15 (2) *Conflict, Security & Development* 169, 176.

9 United Nations Security Council Field Missions Mandate Table, 30 June 2019 www.un.org /securitycouncil/file/122688 (accessed 25 April 2020).

10 Ibid.

11 Y. Dinstein 'The Right to Humanitarian Assistance' (2000) 53 (4) *Naval War College Review* 77, 87; N. Blokker, 'Ch. 9 Outsourcing the Use of Force: Towards More Security Council Control of Authorized Operations?' in M. Weller (ed.) *The Oxford Handbook of the Use of force in International Law* (Oxford: Oxford University Press 2015), 210.

for the reputation of the UN. But there are also serious issues to be resolved with regard to the legal standards applicable to use of force (and accountability for breaches of those standards) and accountability for SEA.

This book will provide an in-depth analysis of MINUSTAH's role and the implementation of its mandate and how it addressed, or otherwise, the challenges it faced and difficulties it encountered. The analysis will be key for making suggestions for reform with a view to enhancing the perceived legitimacy both of the UN in Haiti and of future stabilisation missions. We adopt a thematic approach when analysing the challenges faced by the mission, looking at (1) the cholera crisis, (2) SEA by peacekeepers, and (3) the use of force by peacekeepers. Those case studies enable in-depth analysis of human rights abuses within peacekeeping operations and how to improve accountability for such harms.

1.2 PEACEKEEPING IN A CHANGING WORLD

Peacekeeping has evolved as an international practice, from 'traditional' peacekeeping to more intrusive peacebuilding and peace enforcement practices, which has in turn opened up a gap between the law applicable and the practice of peacekeeping on the ground. These interventions have also led to a wide array of 'unintended' negative consequences on the ground, including SEA of the most vulnerable and deaths and injuries to civilians as a result of use of force for purposes other than self-defence. For Michael Doyle, who acted as assistant UN Secretary General and special adviser to Ban Ki-moon, when an international organisation is 'something like a trustee', then it needs to follow the basic norms of human rights, such as those embodied in the Universal Declaration of Human Rights.[12] Hence, 'peacebuilders in temporary sovereign authority should regard human rights standards as normative: to be fostered where feasible and not to be violated without cause'.[13]

It is useful to underline that peacekeeping missions do not appear in the UN Charter. These missions were initially included in the Chapter VI of the UN Charter, pertaining to 'pacific settlement of disputes'. In order to reflect this stretching of the original meaning of Chapter VI, the then Secretary General Dag Hammarskjöld famously coined the term 'Chapter six and a half'. The first missions have been described as 'traditional', 'classic', or 'straightforward',[14] probably in reference to the three principles that the

---

[12] M. W. Doyle, *The Question of Intervention* (Ithaca: Yale University Press 2015), 161–162.
[13] Ibid., 162.
[14] P. Wilkinson, 'Sharpening the Weapons of Peace: Peace Support Operations and Complex Emergencies' in O. Ramsbotham and T. Woodhouse (eds.) *Contemporary Conflict Resolution* (London: Frank Cass 2000), 63–64.

1.2 Peacekeeping in a Changing World

troops deployed on the ground were meant to observe in the course of their duty: impartiality, non-use of force, and respect of the consent of the parties. These three principles are in fact intertwined, making a coherent normative whole.

The first principle posits that the troops are generally not allowed to use force, except in self-defence and only as a last resort. Hammarskjöld himself provides a definition of the principle:

> a reasonable definition seems to have been established in the case of UNEF [United Nations Emergency Force], where the rule is applied that men engaged in the operation may never take the initiative in the use of armed force, but are entitled to respond with force to an attack with arms, including attempts to make them withdraw from positions which they occupy under orders from the Commander, acting under the authority of the Assembly and within the scope of its resolutions.[15]

The second core principle, consent, derives from the parties' 'perceptions of the peacekeepers' impartiality and moral authority'.[16] It basically refers to the agreement of a host government to a UN mission's presence. It was designed to protect the sovereignty of the host state, as well as reducing the risk to the peacekeepers. Finally, the third principle, impartiality, is for Shashi Tharoor, who acted as UN's Under-Secretary General, 'the oxygen of peacekeeping: the only way peacekeepers can work is by being trusted by both sides, being clear and transparent in their dealings, and keeping lines of communication open. The moment they lose this trust, the moment they are seen by one side as the "enemy", they become part of the problem they were sent to solve'.[17] These principles are considered by many as the cornerstones of the implementation of successful peacekeeping missions.[18]

---

[15] United Nations, *Report of the UN Secretary-General*, UN. Doc. A/3943, 9 October 1958, para. 178. The Peacekeeper's handbook also reaffirms this principle, stating that 'the degree of force [used] must only be sufficient to achieve the mission on hand and to prevent, as far as possible, loss of human life and/or serious injury. Force should not be initiated, except possibly after continuous harassment when it becomes necessary to restore a situation so that the United Nations can fulfil its responsibilities'. International Peace Academy, *Peacekeeper's Handbook* (New York: Pergamon 1984), 56.

[16] W. Durch, 'Introduction' in W. Durch (ed.) *The Evolution of UN Peacekeeping: Case Studies and Comparative Analyses* (New York: St. Martin's Press 1993), 12.

[17] S. Tharoor 'Should UN Peacekeeping Go Back to Basics?' (1995–1996) 37 (4) *Survival* 58.

[18] Olara Otunnu states that 'confusion between peacekeeping and enforcement action, including the tendency to slide from peacekeeping to enforcement action and then back again, has proved to be very dangerous [for the peacekeepers]'. O. Otunnu, 'The Peace-and-Security Agenda of the United Nations: From a Crossroads into the New Century' in O. Otunnu and M. Doyle (eds.) *Peacemaking and Peacekeeping for the New Century* (Lanham: Rowman & Littlefield 1998), 306. Marrack Goulding concurs, considering that 'creating this kind of grey area between peacekeeping and peace enforcement can give rise to considerable dangers. In

6   *Introduction*

Thus, lightly armed, neutral troops serving the UN are symbolically deployed between belligerents and could be retracted in case of a breach of peace.[19] The troops deployed in these missions are meant to defend a specific status quo – Peacekeeping in this sense is seen as a deterrent, in order to 'placate and refrigerate the conflict environment to allow formal negotiations to take place'.[20]

In contrast, peace enforcement or peacebuilding enters into a whole different category than 'traditional' peacekeeping. In fact, as its name suggests, peace enforcement implies operations that are meant to stop warring factions from sliding further into conflict. It has been defined as 'military intervention to compel compliance with international sanctions or resolutions designed to maintain or restore international peace and security'.[21] Peacebuilding missions 'demand that the UN intervene directly in the internal affairs of States, redefining the relationship between the government and its citizens and, in many cases, supporting popular legitimacy over traditional claims of state sovereignty'.[22]

political, legal and military terms, and in terms of the survival of one's own troops, there is all the difference in the world between being deployed with the consent and cooperation of the parties to help them carry out an agreement they have reached and, on the other hand, being deployed without their consent and with powers to use force to compel them to accept the decisions of the Security Council'. M. Goulding 'The Evolution of Peacekeeping' (1993) 69 (3) *International Affairs* 461. See also Paul Diehl, who advocates a return to traditional peacekeeping operations after some measure of conflict resolution has been implemented by other actors: P. Diehl, *International Peacekeeping* (Baltimore: John Hopkins University Press 1993), 106. For a more recent version of that thesis, see: A. Sitkowski, *UN Peacekeeping: Myth and Reality* (London: Praeger Security International 2006).

[19]   This is what happened to the first UN peacekeeping mission where 'blue helmets' where deployed, the first United Nations Emergency Force (UNEF) in the Suez Canal (1956–1967). Egypt requested the mission to withdraw in 1967, which led to the Arab–Israeli War (six-day war).

[20]   O. Richmond, *Maintaining Order, Making Peace* (Hampshire: Palgrave 2002), 44.

[21]   U.S. Office of the Secretary of Defence, *Report of the Bottom-Up Review* (Washington: Department of Defence October 1993) [quoted in T. Mays, *Historical Dictionary of Multinational Peacekeeping* (Lanham: The Scarecrow Press 2004), 121.]

[22]   E. Bertram, 'Reinventing Governments: The Promise and Perils of United Nations Peace Building' (1995) 39 (3) *Journal of Conflict Resolution* 392. The author defined peacebuilding missions as sharing most, if not all, of the following characteristics: (1) they deal with conflicts within rather than between States, (2) the host government is one of the parties to the conflict, (3) their aim is to develop and/or implement a political transition following or accompanying an end to military hostilities, and (4) a central component is the reform or establishment of basic state institutions. Out of the twenty-five UN peacekeeping operations undertaken between 1988 and 1995, twelve entailed peacebuilding in some measure according to the author. Ibid., 389-394. See also Annex 6 and maps 3 and 4 for more details on the current peacekeeping missions. Boutros-Ghali defines post-conflict peacebuilding as 'action to identify and support structures that will tend to strengthen and solidify peace in order to avoid a relapse into conflict'. An Agenda for Peace Preventive diplomacy, peacemaking and peace-keeping, Report of the Secretary General pursuant to the statement adopted by the Summit Meeting of the Security Council on 31 January 1992, UN.Doc. A/47/277-S/24111 17 June 1992, paragraph II. 21; Kofi Annan defines it as 'actions undertaken at the end of a conflict to

1.3 The Rise of the Unintended Consequences Agenda

They tend to redefine the three traditional pillars of peacekeeping. In fact, these operations, implying the use of force, necessitate a Chapter VII Resolution.[23] Thus, the troops deployed under the UN umbrella are generally allowed to use less strict ROE, in order to be more reactive to the harsher conditions in which these missions are deployed. Moreover, consent is no longer a prerequisite for the setting up of the mission, although it may constitute a legitimising asset for the intervening power. As Kofi Annan wrote, such missions use a combination of 'inducing consent' and 'coercive inducement'.[24] Contrary to the 'traditional' peacekeeping described earlier, peace enforcement and peacebuilding operations rest on a whole different understanding of sovereignty and intervention. For instance, Kofi Annan presented his 'conditional sovereignty'[25] doctrine in a provocative address to the General Assembly in 1999, stating that

> '[S]tate sovereignty ... is being redefined by the forces of globalization and international cooperation. The State is now widely understood to be the servant of its people, and not vice versa. . . . These parallel developments . . . demand of us a willingness to think anew – about how the UN responds to the political, human rights, and humanitarian crises affecting so much of the world'.[26]

1.3 THE RISE OF THE UNINTENDED CONSEQUENCES AGENDA

It is increasingly clear to all observers now that peacekeeping operations can intensify social divisions on the ground by creating unbearable situations for certain segments of the population, thus going against the 'do no harm'

---

consolidate peace and prevent the recurrence of armed confrontation. . . . Peace building may involve the creation or strengthening of national institutions, monitoring elections, promoting human rights, providing for reintegration and rehabilitation programmes, as well as creating conditions for resumed development'. United Nations, *Causes of Conflict and the Promotion of Durable Peace and Sustainable Development in Africa. Secretary General's Report to the United Nations Security Council*, UN Doc. A/52/871 and S/1998/318, 16 April 1998.

[23] Chapter VII specifies actions the UN can take with respect to threats to peace, breaches of peace, and acts of aggression. The Security Council can identify aggressors (Articles 39 and 40), decide what enforcement measures should be taken (Articles 41, 42, 48, and 49), and call on members to make military forces available, subject to special agreements (Articles 43, 44, and 45).

[24] Kofi Annan 'Peace Operations and the United Nations: Preparing for the Next Century' (1997) *Conflict Resolution Monitor* 1, 28. www.brad.ac.uk/acad/confres/monitor/crm1.html#comment (accessed 25 April 2020).

[25] J. Traub, *The Best Intentions: Kofi Annan and the UN in the Era of American World Power* (London: Bloomsbury 2014) 93.

[26] United Nations, *Annual Report of the Secretary-General to the General Assembly*, UN. Doc. SG/SM7136; GA/9596, 20 September 1999 [quoted in M. Karns and K. Mingst, *The United Nations in the 21st Century* (Boulder: Westview Press 2007), 125.]

principle.[27] The challenge for international peacekeepers in this context is 'to figure out how to do the good they mean to do without inadvertently undermining local strengths',[28] taking into account the unintended consequences of peacekeeping in the process. No one can deny that UN-led peacekeeping has made a positive contribution to the stabilisation and reconstruction of a number of war-torn countries and to broader peacebuilding objectives. However, in the context of peacekeeping interventions, certain consequences can be dire for the most vulnerable segments of local societies. Loose ROE by peacekeepers will affect some communities more than others. As it will be discussed in Chapter 7, the use of force by peacekeepers is not exempt of claims of politicisation, and poor communities will bear the brunt of the 'collateral damages' of clashes between belligerents. Peacekeepers who perpetrate SEA exacerbate the local culture of abuse of and violence against women and children, going against the normative agenda UN peacebuilding tries to promote. Finally, the presence of peacekeepers can bring about unintended consequences, such as bringing a disease to a country, or distorting local economies.[29]

This new-found interest in unintended consequences of peacekeeping also mirrors international practice, with the mitigated legacy of past peacekeeping interventions leading to a new era of doubt in policy circles. After the certainties of the 1990s and the early 2000s, which operated following simple causation logics ('intervention A' responding to 'problem B' and leading to 'outcome C'), interveners are now increasingly familiar with complexity theories and (sometimes instinctively) understand the full reach of possible unintended outcomes for each intervention ('intervention A' is meant to respond to 'problem B' but can lead to a multiple set of outcomes – from C to Z – as well as potentially creating new problems. As intervenors came to accept that all peacekeeping interventions entail unintended consequences, certain consequences came to have more prominence than others.

1.3.1 *Stabilisation and Robust Peacekeeping*

It has been suggested by some scholars that stabilisation as a concept entered the realm of peacekeeping with the establishment in January 1996 of the

---

[27] M. Anderson, *Do No Harm: How Aid Can Support Peace – Or War* (Boulder: Lynne Rienner 1999).

[28] Ibid., 2.

[29] N. Lemay-Hébert and S. M. Murshed 'Rentier Statebuilding in a Post-Conflict Economy: The Case of Kosovo' (2016) 47 *Development and Change* 517; N. Lemay-Hébert et al., 'The Internal Brain Drain: Foreign Aid, Hiring Practices, and International Migration' (2020) 44 *Disasters* 621.

1.3 The Rise of the Unintended Consequences Agenda

NATO Stabilisation Force for Bosnia and Herzegovina,[30] and that similar ambitions and practices later migrated to UN operations, for instance in Haiti in 2004. Others suggest that the contemporary focus and agenda of stabilisation evolved from the shared experience of France, the United Kingdom, and the United States in Afghanistan and in Iraq in the 2000s, with the doctrines and policies around stabilisation missions developed by these countries in these contexts later permeating the work of the UN operations in Mali (MINUSMA), Central African Republic (MINUSCA) and, of course, Haiti.[31] This stabilisation agenda is in turn linked to the rise of the 'social' in counter-insurgency doctrines.[32] The most well-known example of this is the human terrain system (HTS) programme of hiring anthropologists to serve with American military units as a mechanism to improve the image and effectiveness of intervenors.

There is a constant back and forth in the UN between more people-centred approaches, such as the one advocated in the 2015 High-Level Independent Panel on Peace Operations (HIPPO),[33] and more militaristic rhetoric. The recent Cruz Report, led by Lieutenant General Carlos Alberto dos Santos Cruz, Force Commander in the MINUSTAH between 2007 and 2009 is a good indication of the latter.[34] The report clearly indicates that 'unfortunately, hostile forces do not understand a language other than force' and that 'missions should go where the threat is, in order to neutralise it'. The use of force by peacekeepers is still highly debated, especially regarding how applicable the

---

[30] R. Mac Ginty 'Against Stabilisation' (2012) 1 (1) *Stability: International Journal of Security & Development* 23; J. Karslrud 'The UN at War: Examining the Consequences of Peace-Enforcement Mandates for the UN Peacekeeping Operations in the CAR, the DRC and Mali' (2015) 36 (1) *Third World Quarterly* 42.

[31] These countries are penholders on almost all of the resolutions related to UN peacekeeping missions. See: C. De Coning, 'Is Stabilisation the New Normal? Implications of Stabilisation Mandates for the Use of Force in UN Peace Operations' in P. Nadin (ed.) *Use of Force in UN Peacekeeping* (London: Routledge 2018), 85, 87, also available at: https://cedricdeconing.net /2016/10/04/is-stabilisation-the-new-normal-implications-of-stabilisation-mandates-for-the-use-of-force-in-un-peace-operations/ (accessed 25 April 2020).

[32] L. Wiuff Moe and M. Muller, 'Introduction: Complexity, Resilience and the "Local Turn" in Counterinsurgency' in L. Wiuff Moe and M. Muller (eds.) *Reconfiguring Intervention: Complexity, Resilience and the 'Local Turn' in Counterinsurgency Warfare* (Basingstoke: Palgrave 2017), 1–27.

[33] Report of the Independent High-Level Panel on Peace Operations, UN Doc. A/70/95/-S/2015/ 446, 17 June 2015 https://peacekeeping.un.org/en/report-of-independent-high-level-panel-peace-operations (accessed 26 April 2020).

[34] Lt. Gen. (Retired) C. A. dos Santos Cruz, Col. (Retired) W. R. Philips, and S. Cusimano, *Improving Security of United Nations Peacekeepers: We need to change the way we are doing business*, 19 December 2017 https://peacekeeping.un.org/sites/default/files/improving_securi ty_of_united_nations_peacekeepers_report.pdf (accessed 26 April 2020).

1.3.2 *Sexual Exploitation and Abuse by Peacekeepers*

More than twenty years ago, UNICEF noted that in six out of twelve country studies on sexual exploitation of children in situations of armed conflict, the arrival of peacekeeping troops was associated with a rapid rise in child prostitution.[35] Systematic patterns of SEA have emerged around UN peacekeeping missions over the course of many years[36] and represent one of the key issues linked with the international peacekeepers' presence. Despite the numerous pledges to tackle these issues[37], peacekeeping is still struggling to effectively mitigate SEA by peacekeepers. The recent 'Code Blue' campaign, launched in 2015 and aimed at ending immunity for sexual violence by UN peacekeeping personnel by encouraging UN personnel to leak compromising documents, has further increased the pressure on the UN to take into account the impacts of its presence on vulnerable segments of the local population.[38]

António Guterres personally promised to 'end impunity for those guilty of sexual exploitation and abuse' at a September meeting on peacekeepers' conduct. However, the legacy of past missions still cast their shadows on contemporary peacekeeping. The mothers of Haiti's 'peacekeeper babies' have filed the first legal action against both the UN and individual peacekeeping soldiers in paternity and child support claims.[39] That is after lawyers tried to obtain financial assistance for ten women who gave birth to children of departed peacekeepers say UN has ignored requests for information.[40] Sexual

[35] United Nations 'Promotion and Protection of the Rights of Children', UN Doc. A/51/306, 26 August 1996.

[36] C. Lutz, M. Gutmann, and K. Brown 'Conduct and Discipline in UN Peacekeeping Operations: Culture, Political Economy and Gender', Watson Institute Report submitted to the Conduct and Discipline Unit, Department of Peacekeeping Operations, United Nations, 2009.

[37] See for instance: United Nations, 'A Comprehensive Strategy to Eliminate Future Sexual Exploitation and Abuse in United Nations Peacekeeping Operations', UN Doc. A/59/710, 24 March 2005.

[38] Paula Donovan, director of the Code Blue campaign, interviewed by N. Lemay-Hébert in P. Donovan 'JISB Interview: Immunity, Sexual Scandals and Peacekeeping' (2015) 9 (3) *Journal of Intervention and Statebuilding* 408–417.

[39] K. McVeigh, 'Haitian Mums Seek Support from UN Troops for Peacekeeper Babies', The Guardian, 15 December 2017, www.theguardian.com/global-development/2017/dec/15/peace keeper-babies-mums-haiti-support-un-troops?CMP=share_btn_fb (accessed 26 April 2020).

[40] R. Ratcliffe, 'Haitian Mothers Claim UN Unresponsive Over Support for Peacekeeper Children', *The Guardian*, 21 April 2017, www.theguardian.com/global-development/2017/a pr/21/haiti-mothers-claim-un-unresponsive-over-support-for-peacekeeper-children (accessed 26 April 2020).

exploitation and abuse by peacekeepers is still a very prominent and sensitive topic, especially in Haiti.

1.3.3 Cholera Outbreak

The UN's involvement in Haiti will long be remembered by the introduction of cholera by peacekeepers in the aftermath of the 2010 earthquake. In December 2016, Ban Ki-moon apologised to the Haitian people for the organisation's role in the cholera outbreak in the country that has killed more than 10,000 Haitians. That apology was the first time that he, or the UN, publicly acknowledged its role in bringing cholera to Haiti. The decision to apologise directly to the Haitian people is the first time an acting Secretary General apologised directly to a population subject to a peace operation. It is important that Ban Ki-moon did so in Haitian Creole, of the official languages of Haiti.

The country has now been cholera-free for more than a year, with the last confirmed case of cholera in Haiti being a boy under age five in the Artibonite department of Haiti during the last week of January 2019.[41] However, the issue of reparations to the victims is still open and ongoing. UN missions are now acutely aware of the danger they may pose to host populations, and this also takes a new dimension in the context of the novel coronavirus.[42]

1.4 STRUCTURE OF THE BOOK

What this evolution of peacekeeping entails will be explored in the following chapters. This book is divided in two separate parts. In the first part, we explore the complex relationship between peacekeeping and sovereignty, as well as how this is linked with the expansion of IHRL. In Chapter 2, we chart a brief history of the UN involvement in Haiti, going beyond the 'failed state' lens to apprehend the complex nature of the sovereign arrangement, especially under MINUSTAH. In Chapter 3, we discuss the sharp contradistinction between the extensive legal and academic material documenting the applicability of IHRL to UN peacekeeping operations and the UN's inadequate attempts to entrench those standards into its operations. In Chapter 4, we set out the laws governing UN immunities, why the UN in its practice of peacekeeping is

---

[41] UN News, Haiti cholera outbreak 'stopped in its tracks'; 24 January 2020 https://news.un.org /en/story/2020/01/1056021 (accessed 26 April 2020).

[42] C. de Coning (2020) *The Impact of COVID-19 on Peace Operations*, IPI Global Observatory https://theglobalobservatory.org/2020/04/impact-covid-19-peace-operations/ (accessed 26 April 2020).

bound by fundamental human rights, and how those rights are violated by current practices.

Over the past decade there have been key publications by leading experts and by international organisations setting out the theoretical aspects of the applicability of IHRL to peacekeeping operations. Our analysis is in line with theirs. However, many of those texts focus on theory rather than practice, and have not included in-depth analysis of the implementation and integration of IHRL frameworks into peacekeeping practice. In the second part of this book, we explore three specific issues which combined bring a new and innovative light to the challenges faced by contemporary peacekeeping. In Chapter 5, we look at the cholera epidemic that was imported from Nepalese peacekeepers in 2010 as an emblematic case underlining the rise of the unintended consequences agenda in the peacekeeping world. It looks at the UN's legal strategy to hide behind immunity, as well as the legal fight that ensued in New York when legal representatives of the victims of cholera decided to sue the UN for reparations. In Chapter 6, we take an in-depth look at the series of sexual exploitation and abuse scandals that has dogged the UN in Haiti. We will look at the current legal framework for dealing with SEA cases as well as the various proposals made by scholars to tackle these issues in order to suggest our own framework for dealing with these issues. In Chapter 7, we examine the approach taken by the UN to the use of deadly force by UN Stabilisation Mission in Haiti and assess the extent to which the UN's theoretical approach, as well as its practice in the field in the twenty-first century, complies with international legal standards protecting the right to life. It will look at the highly militarised operations against criminal gangs in the period 2004 and 2007, and the social implications these operations have had in Haiti. Finally, we conclude with Chapter 8 on the possible ways forward from there.

2

A Political History of UN Involvement in Haiti

2.1 NATURE OF THE HAITIAN STATE: BEYOND THE FAILED STATE MODEL

The United Nations (UN) Stabilisation Mission in Haiti's (MINUSTAH) official mandate as set out in UN Security Council Resolution 1542 (2004) is to 'build state capacity' by 'extending state authority throughout Haiti' and by 'ensur[ing] a stable and secure environment'. In order to understand the state-building mandate, it is important first to understand the specific nature of the Haitian state. The Haitian state has long been considered a perennial 'failed state' and has been described variously as a nightmare, predator, collapsed, failed, failing, parasitic, kleptocratic, phantom, virtual, pariah state, or even 'a basket-case'. This discourse of Haiti as a failed state is both reductive and simplistic, and more importantly passes over, through its silence, the role of international actors in the Haitian state-building process. While it may appear intuitive to label Haiti 'failed' – after all, everyone, local politicians included, recognises that the Haitian state is not up to the task – semantics has tangible implications and, maybe more importantly, specific limitations.[1] We suggest four limitations here as applied to the specific case of Haiti, which will inform the theoretical stance of this book.

First, as already hinted, the *failed state* discourse tends to underplay international factors in the *failed state-building* process. When the 'failed state' discourse meets the 'empty shell approach' – where infrastructural destruction is equated with societal bankruptcy[2] – it suddenly legitimises all forms of

---

[1] N. Lemay-Hébert, N. Onuf, and V. Rakic, 'Introduction: Disputing Weberian Semantics' in N. Lemay-Hébert et al. (eds.) *Semantics of Statebuilding: Language, Meanings, and Sovereignty* (London: Routledge 2014), 1–15.

[2] N. Lemay-Hébert 'The "Empty-Shell" Approach: The Setup Process of International Administrations in Timor-Leste and Kosovo, Its Consequences and Lessons' (2011) 12 *International Studies Perspectives* 190–211.

international intervention. While this discourse has offered a convenient legitimisation basis for the setting up of international administrations in the past – including in Kosovo and Timor-Leste – the same discourse has also emerged in the context of Haiti, with pleas for the setting up of an international trusteeship as the solution to 'Haiti's misery'.[3] There is no way around the fact that international factors played and still play an integral role in the *failed state-building* process in Haiti; actually Haiti's failed state status is not only a story of lack of governance but also the product of 'too much governance'.[4]

Second, the failed state discourse adopts the Organization for Economic Cooperation and Development's (OECD) list of 'developed countries' as the standard against which other states are measured, in the process ignoring the specificities of the state formation process. 'Failed states' are thus understood as falling short of specific standards of social, political, and economic performance. In this context, the expressions 'failed' or 'failing state' seem to be a convenient neologism describing nothing more than a state with low standards of living, a country that has not attained the same level of development – measured as the public goods provision of state institutions – as the 'developed world'.[5] Haiti went through a very specific process of state formation – one could argue that it is the case for every political community – which will be quickly summarised later, and thus understanding Haiti only in terms of indicators of state capability obscures more than it reveals.

Third, the failed state discourse, by isolating local factors of fragility from structural and international ones and by focusing almost exclusively on state capacity (or the lack thereof), encourages and promotes a technocratic approach to state-building. Success for an international intervention is defined through various technical benchmarks, which results in David Malone and Sebastian von Einsiedel making claims such as that 'the case of Haiti presents an instance in which UN operations were broadly successful – yet the patient failed to recover'.[6] The 'technocratisation' of international state-building in

---

[3] C. Black, 'A Plan for Haiti', *National Post*, 6 February 2010; D. Bohning, 'An International Protectorate Could Bring Stability to Haiti', *Miami Herald*, 23 November 2004; L. Brooks, 'The Underlying Tragedy', *The New York Times*, 14 January 2010; J. Mendelson-Forman 'Security Sector Reform in Haiti' (2006) 13 *International Peacekeeping* 14, 15.

[4] C. Kivland 'Unmaking the State in "Occupied" Haiti' (2012) 35 *Political and Legal Anthropology Review* 248, 261.

[5] N. Lemay-Hébert, 'Peace, Intervention, and State Fragility' in G. Visoka and O. Richmond (eds.) *Oxford Handbook of Peacebuilding, Statebuilding, and Peace Formation* (Oxford: Oxford University Press 2021); S. Grimm, N. Lemay-Hébert, and O. Nay '"Fragile States": Introducing a Political Concept' (2014) 35 *Third World Quarterly* 197.

[6] S. Von Einsiedel and D. Malone 'Haiti' in D. Malone (ed.) *The UN Security Council: From the Cold War to the 21st Century* (Boulder: Lynne Rienner 2004), 467.

2.1 Nature of the Haitian State: Beyond the Failed State Model

turn leads to cases of attention-deficit disorder for international actors and undue compartmentalisation of programmes, focusing on specific benchmarks (number of police officers trained at the academy, number of arrests, etc.) without taking into account the broader picture of Haiti's political evolution.

Fourth and finally, the failed state discourse through the objectivisation of state fragility promotes, consciously or unconsciously, a 'one size fits all' approach. Following diverse and numerous 'lessons learned' from various humanitarian interventions in the world and successful examples of development, plans for Haiti have been tailored following Taiwan's ('Taiwan of the Caribbean' discourse in Duvalier's time), post-tsunami Indonesia's, or the Dominican Republic's experiences.[7] However, too few of these plans are truly specific to the Haitian context and endogenous in their elaboration and application. We advance the position that it is impossible, or at the very least significantly limiting, to attempt to understand the challenges, difficulties, and accomplishments of MINUSTAH without viewing the mission as part of the wider context of the complex web of interrelations between international and national actors.

Rather than reading Haitian politics through the failed state prism, we can understand the Haitian state-building process to be driven by three specific features of class struggles that permeate Haitian history from colonialism to the postcolonial state and that help us to understand its specificity: (1) a hierarchical social order – marked by racial tensions between white colonisers and African slaves and 'free people of colour' in the colonial period, then between mulattos and blacks after independence, and, more generally, social tensions between a privileged few and an impoverished majority; (2) an autocratic and militarised political system, built on the colonial heritage, reinforced by international encroachment and outright occupations, and crystallised in the development of the Haitian predatory state and the predominance of the military establishment throughout most of Haitian history; and (3) an export-oriented economy, from the plantation system to the free-trade regulations, clashing with the subsistence agriculture model (subsistence farmers represent two-thirds of the population). Taken together, these features tell a specific story made up of local and international factors meshing together, producing a more nuanced account of the logics often associated with the simplistic discourse of Haiti as a 'failed state' needing 'fixing' or rescuing by international actors.

---

7 P. Farmer, *Haiti after the Earthquake* (New York: Public Affairs 2011), 151–152.

The struggle between Haiti's impoverished majority (*pèp la* in Haitian Creole) and the wealthy few has been at the centre of Haitian politics before and after independence. Politics has constantly been a zero-sum game, orchestrated by 'predatory elites', a term coined by Robert Maguire to describe the peculiar blend of gangsterism and populism that has defined the country's political superstructure for most of its history.[8] Haiti became independent in 1804, but the colonial legacy far outlasted the French colonial regime. Isolation on the international scene – the Haitian state was unevenly recognised by the international community between 1804 and 1862, and there was also a looming and constant threat of military invasion by France up until 1825 – made Haiti's independence so insecure that early regimes devoted significant state resources to safeguarding sovereignty to the detriment of the population's overall welfare.[9] To support the costs associated with the military build-up, the plantation system was retained and the new Haitian rulers began to place former slaves back on the plantations where they had to work under military supervision. The temporary solidarity that had developed among members of diverse ethnic backgrounds, classes, and status during the war of liberation dissipated and was replaced by the 'emergence of opportunistic factions who exploited racial and class differences to maximize profits and self-interest'.[10] As Robert Fatton, Jr articulates, virtually all Haitian rulers looked at political power 'as a brutal, indivisible quantity that could be won collectively, but that had to be kept individually and exercised absolutely'.[11]

2.2 SHARED SOVEREIGNTY: BETWEEN FRAGILE STATES AND INTERVENTIONS

If the state can take various forms depending on the complex nature of the state-building process, the same can be said about the changing nature of sovereignty claims. International practice has always recognised that claims and practices of sovereignty can take various forms. One recent example is the UN, under then Secretary General Kofi Annan, suggesting a new understanding of state sovereignty: 'redefined by the forces of globalization and

---

[8] R. Maguire, *Demilitarizing Public Order in a Predatory State: The Case of Haiti* (Coral Gables: North-South Center Press 1995).

[9] M. Gélin-Adams and D. Malone, 'Haiti: A Case of Endemic Weakness' in R. Rotberg (ed.) *State Failure and State Weakness in a Time of Terror* (Washington, DC: Brookings Institution Press 2003), 290.

[10] Ibid., 291.

[11] R. Fatton, Jr. 'The Saturnalia of Emancipation and the Vicissitudes of Predatory Rule' (2006) 27 *Third World Quarterly* 115, 118.

2.2 Shared Sovereignty: Between Fragile States and Interventions 17

international cooperation ... the State is now widely understood to be the servant of its people, and not vice versa'.[12] Annan's doctrine came to be christened 'conditional sovereignty'[13] and builds on the human security doctrine developed a few years earlier and on the humanitarian intervention doctrine,[14] while foregrounding the development of the Responsibility to Protect (R2P) doctrine a few years later. Through these developments, intervention became – or as always been[15] – co-constitutive of the principle of sovereignty.

However, some still think that the principle of sovereignty acts – and acted – as a barrier for interventions, even though there is little basis on which to support this argument.[16] That claim has been exaggerated, particularly by 'sovereigntists' who would like to believe that absolute sovereignty – seen as unalterable and indivisible – precludes any forms of intervention, but also by scholars criticising the principle of sovereignty in order to buttress their own argument in support of humanitarian interventions. They tend to present the argument in very stark terms: a choice between sovereign inviolability and great power domination, or again to either side with global ethics or to reward tyrants and be complicit in the worse human rights violations. [17] Both discourses fixate sovereignty in time and space, and do not account for the fluid nature of the concept[18] or of practices associated with sovereign power.

A crucial contribution on the subject has been made by Stephen Krasner,[19] who suggests breaking down sovereignty in three different and not necessarily complementary ways: international legal sovereignty, domestic sovereignty, and Westphalian or Vatellian sovereignty. International legal sovereignty is linked to international recognition and the general ability of state authorities

---

[12] United Nations (1999) Annual Report of the Secretary-General to the General Assembly, UN. Doc. SG/SM7136; GA/9596, 20 September.

[13] J. Traub, *The Best Intentions: Kofi Annan and the UN in the Era of American World Power* (New York: Farrar, Straus, and Giroux 2006), 93.

[14] M. Bettati, *Le Droit d'Ingérence* (Paris: Odile Jacob 1996).

[15] B. Badie, *Un Monde sans Souveraineté* (Paris: Fayard 1999).

[16] See: A. Hehir, *The Responsibility to Protect: Rhetoric, Reality, and the Future of Humanitarian Intervention* (Basingstoke: Palgrave 2012), 185.

[17] Ibid., 180–208.

[18] J. Bartelson, *A Genealogy of Sovereignty* (Cambridge: Cambridge University Press 1995); F. Kratochwil, 'Sovereignty as Dominium: Is There a Right to Humanitarian Intervention?' in G. Lyons and M. Mastanduno (eds.) *Beyond Westphalia?* (Baltimore: The Johns Hopkins University Press 1995), 21–42; N. Onuf, 'Intervention for the Common Good' in G. Lyons and M. Mastanduno (eds.) *Beyond Westphalia?* (Baltimore: The Johns Hopkins University Press 1995), 43–58; R. B. J. Walker, *Inside/Outside: International Relations as Political Theory* (Cambridge: Cambridge University Press 1993).

[19] S. Krasner, *Sovereignty: Organized Hypocrisy* (Princeton: Princeton University Press 1999).

to enter into relations with its neighbours; domestic sovereignty is the ability to regulate and control activities within the territory of the state; and a state has Westphalian or Vatellian sovereignty when its authority structures are determined autonomously. Departures from 'conventional sovereignty' have always been present and will persist, and possibly become more frequent,[20] particularly in the context of weak or fragile states. In this context, international legal sovereignty is not usually the main issue, unless, that is, states fall in the 'frozen conflict' or unrecognised state category (e.g. Northern Cyprus, Abkhazia, South Ossetia, or Transnistria). After all, many states persist as a legal fiction even when they make little sense empirically.[21] However, the ability to enforce rules on the territory (domestic sovereignty) and autonomous structures of power (Westphalian or Vatellian sovereignty) is generally seen as the main issues facing 'failed' or 'fragile' states.[22]

This focus brings us back to the somewhat classic internal and external dimensions of sovereignty,[23] where the state and its sovereignty are understood through state's capacity, on the one hand, and through its autonomy, on the other. The first, defined as 'the formal organisation of the political authority within the state and the ability of public authorities to exercise effective control within the borders of their own polity'[24] explicitly draws on Weberian semantics. For Thomas Risse, drawing heavily from Krasner, limited statehood closely follows Max Weber's conceptualisation of statehood and can thus be defined as areas where states partially control the instruments of force and are only partially able to enforce decisions, mainly for reasons of insufficient political and administrative capacities.[25] In a classical neo-Weberian fashion, the state apparatus is understood as a separate entity clearly distinguishable from society,[26] which enables all forms of institutional invention from the outside.[27]

---

[20] S. Krasner, 'The Persistence of State Sovereignty' in O. Fioretos, T. Falleti, and A. Sheingate (eds.) *The Oxford Handbook of Historical Institutionalism* (Oxford: Oxford University Press 2016), 521–537.

[21] R. Jackson, *Quasi-States: Sovereignty, International Relations and the Third World* (Cambridge: Cambridge University Press 1993).

[22] Krasner, 'The Persistence of State Sovereignty' (n 20).

[23] Walker, *Inside/Outside* (n 18).

[24] Krasner, *Sovereignty* (n 19), 4.

[25] T. Risse, 'Governance in Areas of Limited Statehood' in D. Levi-Faur (ed.) *The Oxford Handbook of Governance* (Oxford: Oxford University Press 2012), 703.

[26] P. Lottholz and N. Lemay-Hébert 'Re-reading Weber, Redefining State-Building? From Neo-Weberian to Post-Weberian Approaches to State, Legitimacy, and State-Building' (2017) 29 (4) *Cambridge Review of International Affairs* 1467–1485.

[27] N. Lemay-Hébert, 'Rethinking Weberian Approaches to Statebuilding' in D. Chandler and T. Sisk (eds.) *Routledge Handbook of International Statebuilding* (London: Routledge 2013), 3–14.

2.2 *Shared Sovereignty: Between Fragile States and Interventions* 19

Regarding the second aspect, authority goes back to the Vatellian understanding, proclaimed in 1758, that 'Nations are free and independent of each other as men are by nature'. If sovereignty is conceived as an ordering principle within the state – one that locates authority in a single high office, thereby rationalising and regulating the state's organisational apparatus – then this principle dates back to Jean Bodin and Thomas Hobbes, writing in the last decades of the Renaissance. To be sovereign is to be subject to no higher authority (from the French, *souverain*). This so-called Westphalian model holds that all sovereigns are equal; however, non-European states have been characterised by international law as non-sovereign for several centuries.[28] Haiti itself was only recognised in 1825 by England, in 1838 by France, and only in 1862 by the United States, despite having won their independence from France in 1804. But in any case, what is needed is a different kind of history of sovereignty – as Nicholas Onuf suggested more than twenty-five years ago – one that avoids 'undue texturing of histories of ideas and the artificiality of histories of political thought'.[29] Autonomy, as a concept, seems to make little empirical sense as a benchmark for sovereignty, especially if understood as a 'high degree of insulation from societal pressures'.[30]

Finally, the logical extension of Krasner's thesis is that the world needs new international solutions to meet the challenges of what he calls 'troubled societies', defined by Robert Keohane as 'unable, due to political conflicts, to create well-ordered domestic regimes'.[31] In a context of profound international mutation, where the trajectories of political development that characterised most of history will not repeat themselves according to Krasner, 'statebuilding is now more externally than internally driven'.[32] Given the limitations of foreign assistance to improve governance and transitional administrations to face the issue of failing states,[33] Krasner advocates two 'new' options: de facto trusteeships and shared sovereignty schemes. The former consists of reviving 'the idea of trusteeship or protectorate', while the

---

[28] A. Anghie, 'Western Discourses on Sovereignty' in J. Evans et al. (eds.) *Sovereignty: Frontiers of Possibility* (Honolulu: University of Hawai'i Press 2013), 21.

[29] N. Onuf 'Sovereignty: Outline of a Conceptual History' (1991) 16 *Alternatives* 425–446; see also Kratochwil, 'Sovereignty as Dominium' (n 18), 22.

[30] S. Krasner, *Defending the National Interest* (Princeton: Princeton University Press 1978).

[31] R. Keohane, 'Political Authority After Intervention: Gradations in Sovereignty' in J. L. Holzgrefe and R. Keohane (eds.) *Humanitarian Intervention: Ethical, Legal, and Political Dilemmas* (Cambridge: Cambridge University Press 2003), 279.

[32] S. Krasner 'Building Democracy after Conflict: The Case for Shared Sovereignty' (2005) 16 (1) *Journal of Democracy* 74.

[33] S. Krasner, 'Troubled Societies, Outlaw States, and Gradations of Sovereignty', paper presented at a conference on failed states, Stanford University, 20 July 2002.

latter would be to explore 'possibilities for shared sovereignty in which national rulers would use their international legal sovereignty to legitimate institutions within their states in which authority was shared between internal and external actors'.[34] It is important to note that Haiti does appear broadly to fall into this category. If this was first suggested as a possible policy development arising from the need to deal with these issues, Krasner later clarified that governance in 'areas of limited statehood' is in fact of a 'multilevel' nature (linking multiple 'scales' – local, national, regional, global) and already based on shared sovereignty.[35] The functions that have traditionally been associated with the state are assumed by external actors.[36] It is interesting to note that logics of 'shared sovereignty' are increasingly recognised as a social reality across very divergent communities of scholars, from conventional approaches to state fragility to approaches rooted in social constructivism.

2.3 SOVEREIGNTY IN PRACTICE

Beyond conventional approaches to sovereignty, which are quite limiting as we have argued already, there is a plurality of theoretical and conceptual perspectives on sovereignty that can help highlight the fluid and shared nature of sovereignty in Haiti, and the specific role external actors play in the sovereignty arrangement in Haiti. Without trying to reconcile the various ontological stances or trying to create an integrated theory of sovereignty, we will highlight a few key theoretical contributions and link them to Haiti.

A general starting point is the recognition that power is no longer constrained by the parameters of sovereignty, as Michel Foucault argued. Hence, understandings of 'sovereignty' restrict our view of power, making us unable to think about the problem of domination, and Foucault aims to displace sovereignty as the principle of intelligibility of power. For Giorgio Agamben, building on Foucault's work, the sovereign is the decision-maker in situations of exception or in states of emergency,[37] which is a definition based on the work of Carl Schmitt. It is important to highlight that for Schmitt (and indeed for Agamben), building on Foucault's work, the sovereign does not need to be

---

[34] S. Krasner 'Sharing Sovereignty: New Institutions for Collapsed and Failing States' (2004) 29 (2) *International Security* 105. See also Jackson's revival of 'colonies, protectorates, mandates, and condominia' in Jackson, *Quasi-States* (n 21), 33.

[35] T. Risse, 'Governance in Areas of Limited Statehood: Introduction and Overview' in T. Risse (ed.) *Governance without a State? Policies and Politics in Areas of Limited Statehood* (New York: Columbia University Press 2011), 3.

[36] S. Krasner and T. Risse 'External Actors, State-Building, and Service Provision in Areas of Limited Statehood: Introduction' (2014) 27 (4) *Governance* 546.

[37] G. Agamben, *State of Exception* (Chicago: Chicago University Press 2005).

2.3 Sovereignty in Practice

a particular entity bounded by territoriality. Indeed, whoever decides de facto is sovereign, if one accepts a revised, and more precise, translation from the original German.[38] Situations of exception blur the inside and the outside of the juridical order through its suspension,[39] and the sovereign operates as the threshold of order and exception. For Agamben, the predominant form of power in the contemporary world is sovereign power, which operates through the production of 'bare' or 'naked life' (the life of the home or domestic sphere), deprived of any rights and stripped of its political significance (a life that can be killed). In Haiti, there is no doubt that external actors have this power over bare life. After all, a president elect (Jean-Bertrand Aristide) was reinstated in power in 1994 by a coalition of international partners after he had been pushed out of the country in 1991, only to be forced into exile again in 2004 by a new coalition of international partners (Aristide himself described the event as a kidnapping by the United States, France, and Canada). More recently, after the 2010 earthquake (which clearly falls into the category of 'situations of exception'), René Préval claimed that the Special Representative of the Secretary General of the United Nations wanted to remove him from office and 'put him on a plane' giving him an ultimatum of forty-eight hours. This helps with the question of who is truly the sovereign in Haiti.

Some scholars encourage us to think of the conditions for realising concrete sovereignty, especially when the control of resources necessary for such expression is beyond the state's authority. This brings them to question the historical effects of the capitalist global division of labour on sovereignty, and how the wealth-creating division of labour can operate as a type of external authority that limits and challenges the state.[40] As will be discussed in the next section, the new ruling elite after Haiti's hard-fought independence in 1804 feared a military invasion by France to reclaim the territory, which contributed to the decision to keep the extractive plantation system in place. Additionally, in return for recognising Haiti as a sovereign republic, France requested payment of 150 million francs in 1825 and also that Haiti halve its import and export taxes. The debt was later reduced to 90 million francs, which is approximately $21 billion in today's money, and was paid to France until 1947. This massive transfer of wealth from Haiti to France helps to explain the conditions structuring sovereignty in Haiti and Haitian

---

[38] V. Erlenbusch 'The Concept of Sovereignty in Contemporary Continental Political Philosophy' (2002) 7 (6) *Philosophy Compass* 373.

[39] Agamben, *State of Exception* (n 37) 23.

[40] N. Inayatullah, 'Beyond the Sovereignty Dilemma: Quasi-States as Social Construct' in T. Biersteker and C. Weber (eds.) *State Sovereignty as Social Construct* (Cambridge: Cambridge University Press 1996), 51–52.

dependency upon external actors. Other examples also include the African swine flu crisis of 1978–1982, introduced from the Dominican Republic, which led actors (local and international) to eradicate more than one million animals with the fear that the illness might reach the United States. The Creole pig has traditionally constituted the 'peasant bank', a source of wealth in difficult times or in celebratory times, and represented a massive loss of wealth for the peasant community. In general, the very candid apology by Bill Clinton for forcing Haiti to drop tariffs on imported subsidised US rice during his time in office, wiping out rice farming and seriously damaging Haiti's ability to be self-sufficient, is a useful reminder of the economic position of power enjoyed by external actors in Haiti and that contributes to the shared sovereignty arrangement.

Another strand of scholarship, coming from development or peace studies and drawing on cultural studies, highlights the hybrid nature of state-building processes.[41] Studies on hybridity have led to a new wave of insightful contributions on spaces of interventions, helping to move away from the unhelpful binaries of 'local' versus 'international', 'bottom-up' versus 'top-down', 'modern' versus 'traditional', 'internal' versus 'external', 'centre' versus 'periphery', or 'Western' versus 'Non-Western'. This scholarship focusses on the interplay between international and local practices, norms, and institutions,[42] as a way to emphasise local agency in its interaction with outside forces,[43] and/or to engage with local actors beyond the nation-state.[44] However, this scholarship has been criticised for emphasising the binary it first wanted to challenge.[45] To be helpful, this theoretical approach needs to situate every analysis of hybridity in a specific context where the conditions that shape hybridity(ies) are

---

[41] N. Lemay-Hébert and R. Freedman, 'Critical Hybridity: Exploring Cultural, Legal, and Political Pluralism' in N. Lemay-Hébert and R. Freedman (eds.) *Hybridity: Law, Culture and Development* (London: Routledge 2017), 3–14.

[42] R. Mac Ginty 'Hybrid Peace: The Interaction between Top-Down and Bottom-Up Peace' (2010) 41 (4) *Security Dialogue* 391–412; O. Richmond and A. Mitchell, 'Introduction – Towards a Post-Liberal Peace: Exploring Hybridity Via Everyday Forms of Resistance, Agency, and Autonomy' in O. Richmond and A. Mitchell (eds.) *Hybrid Forms of Peace: From Everyday Agency to Post-Liberalism* (Basingstoke: Palgrave 2012), 1–38; G. Visoka 'Three Levels of Hybridisation Practices in Post-conflict Kosovo' (2012) 7 (2) *Journal of Peacebuilding and Development* 23–36.

[43] R. Belloni 'Hybrid Peace Governance: Its Emergence and Significance' (2012) 18 *Global Governance* 21–38; Mac Ginty, 'Hybrid Peace' (n 42).

[44] F. Colona and J. Rivke 'Hybrid Governance Arrangements' (2016) 28 (2) *European Journal of Development Research* 175–183.

[45] Especially the local vs international dimension; see: S. Hameiri and L. Jones 'Beyond Hybridity to the Politics of Scale: International Intervention and "Local" Politics' (2017) 48 (1) *Development and Change* 54–77; E. Randazzo 'The Paradoxes of the "Everyday": Scrutinising the Local Turn in Peace Building' (2016) 37 (8) *Third World Quarterly* 1351–1370.

2.3 Sovereignty in Practice

addressed.[46] Hybridity is not parity – a sort of revenge of the subaltern or the 'weak' against the powerful boundary-creating forces at play; on the contrary, it is hegemonically constructed in the interest of dominant societal actors.[47] It does not imply a 'peaceful coexistence of the vis-à-vis, but rather a violent hierarchy',[48] hierarchy that needs to be identified in order to be overturned. This is something we will strive to emphasise in this book, especially with regards to how dynamics of intervention reinforces structures of domination in Haiti. This also opens up new perspectives on the need for new mechanisms of accountability to keep in check intervenors in state-building processes.

Drawing explicitly or implicitly from the theoretical and conceptual discussions above, and without pretending to reconcile the divergent ontological stances, we will both understand state-building as 'bundle of practices and meanings'[49] and state sovereignty as a set of practices, a social product of the 'actions of powerful agents and the resistances to those actions by those located at the margins of power'.[50] All the above mentioned theoretical strands shed a different light, each in their own way, on the complex arrangement underpinning state-building processes, highlighting the interplay between external and internal actors across different boundaries. This helps to reframe international politics beyond the unhelpful sovereignty/intervention boundary:[51] breaking away from the notion of sovereignty as synonymous with sovereign statehood. Rather than being stuck within the limiting legal and political category of statehood – which does not fully enable us to understand either the complex state-building within Haiti or the issue of responsibilisation of international actors in that context – we agree with Jenny Edkins and Véronique Pin-Frat that we need to focus on how power relations or grammars of power persist and how they operate.[52] We hence call for a shift from a discussion around state capacities, or abstract discussions of 'autonomy', to how actors negotiate sovereignty in practice within a state-building context.

---

[46] M. Kraidy, *Hybridity, of the Cultural Logic of Globalization* (Philadelphia: Temple University Press 2005), vi.

[47] Ibid., p. 67.

[48] J. Derrida, *Positions* (London: Athlone Press 1981), 41.

[49] D. Chandler, *International Statebuilding: The Rise of Post-liberal Governance* (Abingdon: Routledge 2010), viii.

[50] T. Biersteker and C. Weber, 'The Social Construction of State Sovereignty' in T. Biersteker and C. Weber (eds.) *State Sovereignty as Social Construct* (Cambridge: Cambridge University Press 1996), 3.

[51] C. Weber, *Simulating Sovereignty* (Cambridge: Cambridge University Press 1995); W. Connolly, *A World of Becoming* (Durham: Duke University Press 2011).

[52] J. Edkins and V. Pin-Frat, 'Introduction: Life, Power, Resistance' in J. Edkins, V. Pin-Frat, and M. Shapiro (eds.) *Sovereign Lives: Power in Global Politics* (London: Routledge 2004), 3.

Understanding sovereignty in terms of 'authority relations which are worked out in practice'[53] in turn helps to highlight the constitutive nature of intervention and sovereignty through historical practices.

2.4 UN INVOLVEMENT IN HAITI

Haiti's democratic transition formally began in 1986 after Jean-Claude Duvalier went into exile. Indeed, the rise to power of the 'popular movement' in 1991 (The *Lavalas* coalition, meaning 'the flood' – a word popularly used for the deluge of water and mud which descends into the capital after a storm) has clearly been one of the most potent symbols for progressive political change in Haiti, and even arguably, in the entire world.[54] However, this period was still marked by constant social struggles between the political and economic elites and the *moun andeyo* (or outsiders), those who are not considered part of the nation and are excluded from its benefits and recognition.[55] After an immediate period marked by a transitional military government ('Duvalierism after Duvalier'), Jean-Bertrand Aristide was triumphantly elected president in 1991. The initial goal of Aristide was to challenge the hierarchical fabric of Haitian society, an approach encompassed in his slogan *tout moun se moun* ('every human being is a human being'). However, less than eight months after Aristide's inauguration, a group of army officers organised a coup, replacing the elected president with a military junta and sending him into exile in the United States. Aristide's reforms of the armed services and his steps to create a distinct police force clearly led to unease in the army.[56] It also has to be said that, from the first day of the post-Duvalier era, Haiti's dominant classes never ceased to oppose, undermine, and challenge Lavalas' rule.[57] The 'international community' responded with an embargo and international sanctions on the leader of the military junta, Raul Cédras, which inadvertently reinforced the dependency of the country on international economic aid. Aristide returned to the presidency in 1994, with the backing of US troops and the UN, and one of his first decisions was to dissolve the *Forces Armées*

---

[53] Weber, *Simulating Sovereignty* (n 51), 11; see also Kratochwil, 'Sovereignty as Dominium' (n 18) for a call to understand sovereignty on the level of actual practice.

[54] P. Hallward, *Damming The Flood: Haiti and The Politics of Containment* (London: Verso 2010), xxvi.

[55] R. Fatton, Jr., *The Roots of Haitian Despotism* (Boulder: Lynne Rienner 2007), 75; G. Barthélémy, *L'Univers Rural Haïtien: Le Pays en Dehors* (Port-au-Prince: Henri Deschamps 1989).

[56] D. Nicholls, *From Dessalines to Duvalier: Race, Colour, and National Independence in Haiti* (New Brunswick: Rutgers University Press, 1996).

[57] Fatton, Jr., *The Roots of Haitian Despotism* (n 55), 123.

2.4 UN Involvement in Haiti

d'Haiti (FADH – Haitian Armed Forces). Another member of the Lavalas coalition, René Préval, was voted in as his successor in 1996, and Aristide returned for another term in 2001. However, a small group of former military officers took up arms against Aristide, and this time the United States did not support the elected president – on the contrary, Aristide himself described the event as a kidnapping by the United States, France, and Canada.[58]

In this context, the UN and other international actors have constantly been drawn into Haitian politics and have thus become principal actors in local politics. A succession of security sector reform (SSR) missions – UNMIH, UNSMIH, UNTMIH, MIPONUH, and MICAH – were deployed to Haiti to help the development of the new *Police Nationale d'Haiti* (PNH), as well as to support prison and judicial reform. These missions were an integral part of the Haitian *failed state-building* process, insisting for example on the inclusion of former FADH personnel in the new police force, which not only undermined the legitimacy of the new police force in the eyes of large parts of the civilian population but also fuelled corruption. The series of UN interventions following the reinstatement of Aristide were all framed in a very technocratic way, 'outside of development programming'.[59] Furthermore, the missions were inherently limited by their insufficient understanding of the country's history, society, and culture.[60]

Following the second (forced) exile of Aristide, the international community imposed a government of technocrats, headed by Gérard Latortue, to assure the transition to the elections of 2006. MINUSTAH was deployed in June 2004 to assist the transitional government in this process, but taking into account the historical process of state formation in Haiti, the central question remains: what was the UN supposed to stabilise in Haiti? The approach of the Latortue government, and its domestic and foreign supporters (including the UN) was to use a military solution to what is fundamentally a social problem, anchored in profound social, economic, and cultural inequalities.[61] MINUSTAH relied on the same SSR practices that failed in the first instance. MINUSTAH oversaw the same policy of incorporating ex-army paramilitaries

---

[58] CNN (2004) 'Aristide says U.S. deposed him in "coup d'etat"', 2 March, https://edition.cnn.com/2004/WORLD/americas/03/01/aristide.claim/; A. Buncombe and A. Gumbel (2004) 'Aristide Marines Forced me to Leave', *The Independent*, 2 March, www.independent.co.uk/news/world/americas/aristide-marines-forced-me-to-leave-71698.html.

[59] Mendelson-Forman, 'Security Sector Reform in Haiti' (n 3), 15.

[60] International Peace Academy, 'Lessons Learned: Peacebuilding in Haiti', *IPA Seminar Report*, 23–24 January 2002; T. Donais 'Back to Square One: The Politics of Police Reform in Haiti' (2005) 7 *Civil Wars* 270.

[61] A. Dupuy, *The Prophet and Power: Jean-Bertrand Aristide, the International Community, and Haiti* (Plymouth: Rowman & Littlefield Publishers 2007), 179–180.

into the police force,[62] thus contributing once again to the disputed process of state formation. In general, police reform in Haiti since 2004 has followed a relatively narrow, technical agenda, emphasising training and vetting; an agenda that has been challenged by structural constraints and on-the-ground realities.[63] Hence, there was no vision of a holistic SSR approach within MINUSTAH,[64] which set the UN on a course to reinforce the same dynamics that had caused tensions in the first place.

MINUSTAH's mandate differs from preceding UN missions in Haiti in two ways. First, it has a greater emphasis on security exemplified by the contributing countries' lasting commitment in terms of troops and police since the set-up of the mission. Second, there is a greater importance given to human rights with Security Council resolutions placing these issues at the heart of the UN's presence in Haiti. At the same time, as it will be discussed in the following chapters, MINUSTAH came to be criticised locally and internationally precisely for its tendency to focus too much on security (through the securitisation of social issues) and its track record on human rights.

MINUSTAH was mandated under Security Council resolution 1542 of 30 April 2004, which made no reference to armed conflict but noted 'the existence of challenges to the political, social and economic stability of Haiti and determin-[ed] that the situation in Haiti continues to constitute a threat to international peace and security in the region'.[65] Topping the list of MINUSTAH' s mandated tasks was 'in support of the Transitional Government, to ensure a secure and stable environment within which the constitutional and political process in Haiti can take place'.[66] The accompanying Secretary General's report described the security environment as uncertain, in particular:

> 'The community-organized armed groups and gangs are highly fragmented, located primarily in impoverished urban areas and pose the greatest threat to security. Moreover, many of these groups also turned to banditry and other criminal activities in order to sustain themselves. The absence of the rule of law has reinforced a climate of impunity and other crimes, such as kidnapping,

---

[62] J. Sprague, *Paramilitarism and the Assault on Democracy in Haiti* (New York: Monthly Review Press 2012), 15.

[63] T. Donais, 'Reforming the Haitian National Police: From Stabilization to Consolidation' in J. Heine and A. Thompson (eds.) *Fixing Haiti: MINUSTAH and Beyond* (Tokyo: United Nations University Press 2011), 101.

[64] E. Mobekk, 'MINUSTAH and the Need for a Context-Specific Strategy: The Case of Haiti' in H. Hänggi and V. Scherrer (eds.)*Security Sector Reform and UN Integrated Missions: Experience from Burundi, the Democratic Republic of Congo, Haiti, and Kosovo* (Geneva: DCAF 2008), 125.

[65] S/RES 1542, 30 April 2004.

[66] Ibid.

2.4 *UN Involvement in Haiti*

robberies and rape, are on the rise. In addition, politically motivated intimidation now mainly targets Fanmi Lavalas supporters'.[67]

MINUSTAH's presence and mandate can be divided into three phases.[68] In the first phase of its deployment, from 2004 to 2006, MINUSTAH focussed exclusively on restoring stability following Aristide's exile and on providing security for the 2006 elections. The second phase (2006–2010) was characterised by a focus on securing difficult neighbourhoods of Port-au-Prince as well as on SSR. This phase also involved reconciliation and political dialogue in preparation for the 2010 parliamentary and presidential elections. The third phase which started with the 2010 earthquake put the security agenda back to the top of the priority list, along with support of recovery and reconstruction programmes. Since around 2011 decisions on MINUSTAH's operations have been accompanied by debates over how to support an effective transition to a post-MINUSTAH Haiti.[69] In 2013, the Haitian Senate unanimously adopted a resolution requesting MINUSTAH to leave by May 2014 at the latest, which Secretary General Ban Ki-moon briefly acknowledged in his report of August 2013.[70] MINUSTAH's mandate subsequently was renewed five times until the mission finally ended in October 2017, replaced by a smaller, Chapter VII mandated police mission, MINUJUSTH.

In the context of social struggle between Haiti's impoverished majority and the wealthy few, a struggle exacerbated by Aristide's controversial 'exile' and a transitional government perceived as siding with the elite, MINUSTAH's approach to strengthening security institutions and its disarming of 'rebels' could be seen as partisan and a continuation of past policies. The Latortue government (2004–2006) and its domestic and foreign supporters (including the United Nations) opted for a military solution to address what was fundamentally a social, economic and cultural problem. While MINUSTAH hesitantly challenged the presence of the disbanded Haitian army in a few localities, it used significantly more repressive means to curb the power of the pro-Aristide *Chimères* ('chimeras') in Cité Soleil.[71] In the first twenty-two

---

[67] Report of the Secretary-General on Haiti/2004/300, 16 April 2004 para. 23.

[68] N. Lemay-Hébert, 'United Nations Stabilization Mission in Haiti (MINUSTAH)' in J. Koops, N. MacQueen, T. Tardy, and P. Williams (eds.) *The Oxford Handbook of United Nations Peacekeeping Operations* (Oxford: Oxford University Press 2015), 720–730.

[69] International Crisis Group, 'Towards a Post-MINUSTAH Haiti: Making an Effective Transition,' *Latin America/Caribbean Report N°44*, 2 August 2012.

[70] Report of the Secretary General on the UN Stabilisation Mission in Haiti, S/2013/493, 19 August 2013, para. 8. The report also notes that the Senate had adopted a similar resolution in 2011 – though the Secretary General's report of 2011 did not address it.

[71] J. Sprague, *Paramilitarism and the Assault on Democracy in Haiti* (New York: Monthly Review Press 2012), 212.

months following Aristide's forced departure, an estimated 8,000 people were murdered and 35,000 women were sexually assaulted.[72] Identified perpetrators included criminals from pro- and anti-Aristide groups, the national police – and UN peacekeepers as well. In 'Operation Baghdad', the name given to the ghetto uprising by the interim government in an attempt to label the people fighting as terrorists,[73] MINUSTAH and the police proceeded to 'clean' the 'difficult' urban areas of Cité Soleil and Bel Air in Port-au-Prince. These actions by MINUSTAH were in line with the requirements of the UN Security Council, and especially Resolution 1743 (2007), which demanded strong measures against the 'armed gangs'. But the heavily militarised approach adopted by MINUSTAH to clearing the gangs from densely populated neighbourhoods is difficult to reconcile with the international law framework that governs use of force outside of a hostilities-in-armed-conflict context – which is international human rights law.

Military peacekeepers are soldiers and their primary training is in law of armed conflict or international humanitarian law (IHL). The law is applicable to hostilities in an armed conflict and authorises much higher levels of force (e.g. shooting at enemy forces) than would be permissible in a law enforcement operation against criminal gangs or rioters. The directions for use of force (DUF) for UN police peacekeeping units require them to comply with human rights obligations – particularly the Basic Principles on the Use of Force and Firearms by Law Enforcement Officials adopted by the General Assembly in 1990 – but there is no specific reference to human rights in the UN Master List of Rules of Engagement for military peacekeeping personnel[74] or in the specific rules of engagement (ROE) for MINUSTAH troops.[75] Currently, the ROE for military contingents of all UN peacekeeping missions are based primarily on modified principles of IHL, regardless of the context in which the mission is operating. If peacekeepers are to be deployed to carry out security operations

---

[72] A. Kolbe and R. Hutson 'Human Rights Abuse and other Criminal Violations in Port-au-Prince, Haiti: A Random Survey of Households' (2006) 368 *The Lancet* 9538.

[73] However, the term was later adopted by the demonstrators themselves. See H. Lunde, *The violent lifeworlds of young Haitians Gangs as livelihood in a Port-au-Prince ghetto*, Haiti Youth Project (2012) Fafo Paper 3, 16–17.

[74] UN Guidelines for the Development of Rules of Engagement and Sample ROE for UN Peacekeeping Operations, Jean-Marie Guehenno, 1 December 2000; see also United Nations, Guidelines for the development of ROE for UNPKO, UN document MD/FGS/0220.0001, May 2002 (provisional), Attachment 1, published in T. Findlay, *The Use of Force in Peace Operations* (Oxford University Press 2002), 425.

[75] Rules of Engagement for the Military Component of the UN Stabilisation Mission in Haiti, 28 June 2004, signed by Jean-Marie Guehenno, Under-Secretary General for Peacekeeping Operations.

2.4 UN Involvement in Haiti

against criminals and other spoilers – as distinct from parties to an armed conflict – they will need training in use of force in accordance with human rights law standards, in the same way as police, and appropriate ROE. This was the first mission to face this problem on a large scale – but it will not be the last.

Stabilisation activities are an integral part of the renewal of international interventions since the 1990s, and as such are co-constitutive of a reliance on the use of force by international actors such as the United Nations to accomplish the mandate of the missions. Besides MINUSTAH, the UN Organisation Stabilisation Mission in the Democratic Republic of the Congo (MONUSCO; 1999-present), the UN Multidimensional Integrated Stabilisation Mission in Mali (MINUSMA; 2013-present) and the UN Multidimensional Integrated Stabilisation Mission in the Central African Republic (MINUSCA; 2014-present) are good examples of this trend. In addition to these, several missions that are not explicitly designated as stabilisation missions are nevertheless mandated to carry out stabilisation objectives,[76] but the question remains as to what these stabilisation interventions are effectively stabilising.

It has been suggested by some scholars that stabilisation as a concept entered the realm of peace and conflict with the establishment in January 1996 of the NATO Stabilisation Force for Bosnia and Herzegovina,[77] and that similar ambitions and practices later migrated to UN operations, such as in Haiti in 2004.[78] Stabilisation's contemporary focus and agenda – as an internationally promoted enterprise to restore and maintain order in conflict-affected and post-conflict contexts – evolved, however, in particular from the shared experience of France, the United Kingdom, and the United States in Afghanistan and in Iraq in the 2000s, with the doctrines and policies around stabilisation missions developed by these countries in these contexts later permeating the work of the UN operations in Mali (MINUSMA), Central African Republic (MINUSCA) and elsewhere.[79]

---

[76] S/RES 1701 11 August 2006, para. 12; S/RES 2226 25 June 2015, para. 19 c.

[77] R. Mac Ginty 'Against Stabilisation' (2012) 1 *Stability: International Journal of Security & Development* 20, 23; J. Karslrud 'The UN at War: Examining the Consequences of Peace-Enforcement Mandates for the UN Peacekeeping Operations in the CAR, the DRC, and Mali' (2015) 36 *Third World Quarterly* 40, 42.

[78] J. Fisher and N. Lemay-Hébert, *More Ambition, Less Commitment? Stabilisation and Peacebuilding Efforts Since the 1990s*, (2018) EDA Working Paper, 6, https://eda.ac.ae/docs/default-source/Publications/eda-working-paper_stabilisation-efforts_en.pdf?sfvrsn=2 (accessed 26 April 2020).

[79] C. De Coning, 'Is Stabilisation the New Normal? Implications of Stabilisation Mandates for the Use of Force in UN Peace Operations' in P. Nadin (ed.) *Use of Force in UN Peacekeeping* (London: Routledge, 2018), 85, 87, also available at: https://cedricdeconing.net/2016/10/04/is-stabilisation-the-new-normal-implications-of-stabilisation-mandates-for-the-use-of-force-in-un-peace-operations/ (accessed 25 April 2020).

This stabilisation agenda is in turn linked to the rise of the 'social' in counter-insurgency doctrines.[80]

The UN peacekeeping website lists '[s]upport for the restoration and extension of State authority' as one of the activities in which 'UN peacekeepers are often mandated to play a catalytic role'.[81] Thus, although, MINUSTAH was the first Chapter VII mandated peacekeeping mission to be deployed to support a host state government in enforcing stability through law enforcement operations – the pattern is now a commonplace.

One of the most controversial aspects of MINUSTAH's role in its early years of deployment was that it was mandated to support a government (and its police force) that were committing serious and widespread human rights violations, a fact acknowledged by the UN Secretary General, Kofi Annan. In his February 2005 report on Haiti, he stated that he was 'concerned about the human rights situation, including allegations of human rights abuses attributed to Haitian National Police (HNP) officers, which have not yet been properly investigated by the authorities'.[82] A Security Council Mission visited Haiti in April 2005 and reported that it

> received reports that a culture of impunity remained pervasive, marked by arbitrary arrest, wrongful detention, inhumane prison conditions, excessive use of force, and extrajudicial executions. As a result, the population continues to view the national police with fear and lack of respect. The mission learned that the commission that should investigate allegations against the police had yet to be established.[83]

Similar problems subsequently arose in the Democratic Republic of the Congo and resulted in the adoption of the Human Rights Due Diligence Policy (2013) that applies to all UN entities. The policy states that before UN forces provide support to a host state, an assessment must take place of 'the risk of the recipient entity committing grave violations of international humanitarian law, human rights law or refugee law' and 'procedures for monitoring the recipient entity's compliance with international humanitarian, human rights and refugee law' must be established as part of an effective

---

[80] See: L. Wiuff Moe, 'Clear, Hold, Build . . . a "Local" State: Counterinsurgency and Territorial Orders in Somalia' in N. Lemay-Hébert (ed.) *Handbook on Intervention and Statebuilding* (Cheltenham: Edward Elgar 2020), 151–160.

[81] United Nations Peacekeeping, *Mandates and the Legal Basis for Peacekeeping* https://peacekeeping.un.org/en/mandates-and-legal-basis-peacekeeping (accessed 26 April 2020).

[82] S/2005/124 25 February 2005, para. 58.

[83] Report of the Security Council mission to Haiti, 13–16 April 2005 S/2005/302 6 May 2005, para. 24.

2.4 UN Involvement in Haiti

implementation framework.[84] If 'the United Nations receives reliable information that provides substantial grounds to suspect that the recipient entity is continuing to engage in grave violations of international humanitarian, human rights, or refugee law, then the UN entity must suspend or withdraw support from the recipient.'[85] Had this policy been in place in 2004, MINUSTAH would have been required to respond to the human rights violations being committed by the interim host state government and may have been required to withdraw its support had the government failed to respond positively.

As of 2010, MINUSTAH's post-earthquake agenda concentrated on the security of displaced persons, support for national elections, and the establishment of a government that could accelerate reconstruction. MINUSTAH has also promoted a rule of law compact with the Haitian authorities, the private sector and other international actors to integrate the stabilisation and economic development agendas. However, this initiative was dogged by political bickering between the executive and the parliament.[86] Another impediment to SSR has been the lack of effective coordination among different donor countries (a recurring theme in Haiti). This led MINUSTAH's then Special Representative of the Secretary General (SRSG), Edmond Mullet, to state that 'the Haiti National Police [HNP] is an example of the international community's failure to work in concert'.[87] Police reform has followed a relatively narrow and technical agenda that emphasised training and vetting, an approach challenged by structural constraints and realities on the ground.[88] As a consequence, despite many achievements, an overarching vision of SSR that would integrate state-building and SSR was absent within MINUSTAH.[89] This set the UN on a course that reinforced the dynamics that had caused social tensions in the first place.

A string of sexual abuse and exploitation scandals by the military components of MINUSTAH fuelled the anti-UN sentiment. In 2007, 111 Sri Lankan

---

[84] Annex to 'Identical Letters Dated 25 February 2013 from the Secretary General Addressed to the President of the General Assembly and to the President of the Security Council' (5 March 2013), UN Doc. A/67/775–S/2013/110.

[85] Ibid., para. 27.

[86] International Crisis Group, 'Keeping Haiti Safe: Police Reform', Briefing 26 Latin America/ Caribbean, 8 September 2011, 5. www.crisisgroup.org/latin-america-caribbean/haiti/keeping-haiti-safe-police-reform (accessed 26 April 2020).

[87] Ibid., page 3.

[88] D. Coughlin, 'WikiLeaks Haiti: US Cables Paint Portrait of Brutal, Ineffectual and Polluting UN Force', The Nation, 6 October 2011.

[89] T. Donais, 'Reforming the Haitian National Police: From Stabilization to Consolidation' in J. Heine and A. Thompson (eds.) Fixing Haiti (Tokyo: United Nations University Press 2011), 101.

soldiers were repatriated after allegations of sexual exploitation and abuse of minors.[90] In January 2011, Pakistani troops were accused of the rape of a boy in Gonaïves and of having sexual relations with minors in the capital; three of them were later found guilty of sexual exploitation and abuse and were condemned to a one-year jail sentence.[91] In July 2011, Uruguayan troops were accused of sexually assaulting a young man in the southern town of Port-Salut (while only being charged with 'coercion' offences). There was an 'amplification factor' at work, with each scandal building on the narrative of occupation in Haiti and feeding latent hostility towards international troops in certain segments of the society (especially in highly politicised student circles in Port-au-Prince).[92]

A few months after the 2010 earthquake, a cholera outbreak began in Mirebalais, in the Artibonite region. Local support for the UN mission, while never high, decreased dramatically after the outbreak of cholera in October 2010, and the allegations of sexual assaults. In this atmosphere, within weeks after the first cases there was stoning of UN vehicles and clashes, some fatal, between locals and UN forces.[93] Similarly, following the news of sexual exploitation and abuse, protests spread around Haiti, as people took to the streets demanding that the United Nations leave the country.

Since its establishment in June 2004, the UN's presence in Haiti has 'at times been problematic, even divisive', as one observer put it.[94] Many Haitians interviewed felt that it was a return to international occupation under a new guise (a complaint to a certain extent recognised by international officials following the earthquake of 2010).[95] At the same time and throughout the evolution of the mission, many prominent international officials voiced their opposition to the security emphasis of MINUSTAH, feeling that the mission

[90] B. K. N. Gaye et al., 'Haiti's Renewal of MINUSTAH's Mandate in Violation of the Human Rights of the Haitian People', 24 March 2011, submission to the UN Universal Periodic Review (UPR), Twelfth Session of the Working Group on the UPR Human Rights Council, October 2011.

[91] J. Vaccarello, 'Three Pakistani Police Officers Found Guilty of Sex Exploitation of 14-Year-Old in Haiti', CNN, 13 March 2012.

[92] D. Valet, Editor-in-Chief, *Le Matin Newspaper*, interview by N Lemay-Hébert, 1 February 2011, Port-au-Prince.

[93] P. Farmer, *Haiti after the Earthquake* (New York: Public Affairs 2011), 196; D. Coughlin, 'WikiLeaks Haiti: US Cables Paint Portrait of Brutal, Ineffectual and Polluting UN Force', *The Nation*, 6 October 2011.

[94] J. Heine and A. Thompson, 'Introduction: Haiti's Governance Challenges and the International Community' in J. Heine and A. Thompson (eds.) *Fixing Haiti* (n 89), 15.

[95] As Kevin Kennedy, Deputy Special Representative of the UN Secretary General noted in a personal interview, it might be an occupation, but 'with a lesser case "o"'. Kevin Kennedy, MINUSTAH D-SRSG, interviewed by N Lemay-Hébert, 2 February 2011, Port-au-Prince.

should reorient itself towards a more developmental agenda.[96] MINUSTAH's 'capital of legitimacy' quickly floundered. In this context, local actors started to openly criticise the United Nations, referring to it as a 'force of occupation', sensing perhaps that there was gain to be made at the expense of the international organisation. Quite tellingly, in his last speech to the UN Security Council President Préval criticised MINUSTAH for not adapting quickly enough to the new situation, stating that the international intervention in Haiti has 'practically led to eleven years of military presence in a country that has no war'.[97]

2.5 CONCLUSION: MINUJUSTH AND BEYOND

In April 2017, the UN Security Council passed Resolution 2350 (2017) in which it set out that MINUSTAH would close on 15 October 2017, and that there would be a transition to a smaller follow-up peacekeeping Mission that would support Government efforts to strengthen rule-of-law institutions; further develop the Haitian National Police; and engage in human rights monitoring, reporting, and analysis. This smaller mission was MINUJUSTH, with a mandate set out in the Security Council Resolution 2350 (2017), which was adopted on 13 April 2017. MINUJUSTH's mandate was to assist the Government of Haiti in further developing HNP; to strengthen Haiti's rule of law institutions, including the justice and prisons; and to promote and protect human rights – all with a view to improving the everyday lives of the Haitian people. The mission was short-lived however, and MINUJUSTH completed its mandate on 15 October 2019, putting an end to fifteen consecutive years of peacekeeping operations in the country. The UN family has vowed to continue supporting Haiti with a new configuration, through the nineteen agencies, funds, and programmes present in the country and the United Nations Integrated Office in Haiti (BINUH), established by the Security Council resolution 2476 (2019).

---

[96] R. Dumas, *An Encounter with Haiti: Notes of a Special Adviser* (Port of Spain: Medianet 2008); Farmer, *Haiti after the Earthquake* (n 93); interviews by N. Lemay-Hébert with MINUSTAH officials in 2011.

[97] E. Lederer, 'Departing Haiti Leader Faults UN', *Associated Press*, 7 April 2011.

3

Integrating Human Rights Norms into UN Peacekeeping Practice

3.1 INTRODUCTION

Peacekeeping today commonly involves large numbers of heavily armed troops mandated to use 'all necessary means' to carry out a wide range of tasks, often in densely populated and poorly resourced urban neighbourhoods. One function of international human rights law (IHRL) is to ensure that those who exercise power do so in accordance with the international standards established to protect human rights; however, it remains a relatively new development in international law that has advanced gradually, and as a result its integration into UN law and practice has been incremental and piecemeal. This chapter will discuss the development of human rights protection as a core UN goal and the Organisation's inadequate attempts to entrench IHRL standards into peacekeeping theory and practice.

The Universal Declaration of Human Rights (UDHR) was adopted in 1948, three years after the UN was created and it took over twenty years before the Declaration was codified in treaties. The pace of IHRL development within the UN picked up significantly from the 1960s with the expansion of UN membership to include decolonised states, with a further boost again after the end of the Cold War. The UN's Office of the High Commissioner for Human Rights (OHCHR)[1] was established in 1993 with the aim of promoting and securing 'all human rights for all people'.[2] OHCHR is tasked with mainstreaming human rights within the UN which means 'injecting a human

---

[1] General Assembly Resolution 'High Commissioner for the Promotion and Protection of All Human Rights' A/RES/ 48/141, 7 January 1994.

[2] Webpage of the Office of the High Commissioner for Human Rights (OHCHR) www .ohchr.org/EN/AboutUs/Pages/WhoWeAre.aspx (accessed 26 April 2020); J. P. Thérien and P. Joly '"All Human Rights for All": The United Nations and Human Rights in the Post-Cold War Era' (2014) 36 *Human Rights Quarterly* 373–396, 374.

rights perspective' into all UN programmes.[3] As part of this goal, it is committed to the 'integration of human rights in peacekeeping'[4] so as to ensure that the 'three pillars of the UN system' peace and security, development, and human rights 'are interlinked and mutually reinforcing'.[5]

To date OHCHR's commitment to integrating human rights into peacekeeping has largely been concerned with strengthening UN mission obligations to respond to serious human rights violations by host state actors and armed groups – clearly an important objective, but one that falls short of establishing IHRL as a foundational principle that should inform all mission decisions, actions, and policies. The UN Department of Peace Operations (DPO, formerly DPKO) has published various guidelines on aspects of peacekeeping, several of which include single sentence assertions that peacekeepers must comply with applicable IHRL; however, with the exception of those relating to UN Police, they do not provide any detail on what IHRL obligations may be applicable and in what circumstances. The UN has not yet adopted any document specifically addressing the applicability of IHRL to its peacekeeping operations and setting out the nature and scope of the IHRL obligations that peacekeepers must observe.

To some degree inconsistency between the UN's goal of 'all human rights for all' and its failure to address the applicability of IHRL to its peacekeeping missions, despite the unequal power relationships between the mission and host state communities and their residents, is not all that surprising: neither IHRL nor peacekeeping were developed, at least formally, in 1945 when the UN Charter was adopted. Both IHRL and peacekeeping have since become key components of the UN system, but they have developed ad hoc and not in tandem.

3.2 MILITARY PEACEKEEPERS ARE MEMBERS OF NATIONAL ARMIES

One of the reasons for the piecemeal incorporation of IHRL into the UN's regulation of its peacekeeping activities is that peacekeeping has traditionally been viewed through a military lens. UN troops are 'first and foremost members of their own national armies' seconded to work under the command and

---

[3] www.ohchr.org/EN/AboutUs/Pages/WhatWeDo.aspx (accessed 26 April 2020).

[4] USG OHCHR, DPKO, USG DPA, USG DFS *Human Rights in United Nations Peace Operations and Political Missions Policy*, Ref. 2011.20 1 September 2011.

[5] General Assembly Resolution 'World Summit Outcome' A/RES/60/1, 2005 (New York, 2005), para. 9.

36   *Integrating Human Rights Norms into UN Peacekeeping Practice*

control of the UN;[6] therefore, the main focus of their previous training, as regards their legal obligations, is likely to have been in the law of armed conflict or international humanitarian law (IHL) and military law. More than 90,000 soldiers are deployed in current UN peacekeeping missions, as compared with approximately 9,000 police.[7]

International Humanitarian Law is of limited relevance to peacekeeping since, with very limited exceptions, UN troops do not serve as parties to an armed conflict. Even when heavily armed and mandated to use force, they serve as peacekeepers not as combatants. If IHL were to become applicable to their operations, peacekeepers would lose their right to civilian status and protection from attack under IHL. This is undesirable and so is generally avoided even in robust operations mandated under Chapter VII and authorised to use 'all necessary means'. Consequently, the international laws most relevant to peace-keeping operations are not the Geneva Conventions and their Protocols but those relating to law enforcement, primarily IHRL.[8] However, during the early decades of UN peacekeeping most of the legal debate on this question focussed on the UN's reluctance to recognise the potential applicability of IHL to peacekeeping operations,[9] with very little discussion of the applicability or relevance of IHRL. At this time, the question of whether IHRL remained applicable during armed conflict was still an emerging debate; it was not until 1996, in its landmark Advisory Opinion on the *Legality of the Threat or Use of Nuclear Weapons*, the International Court of Justice (ICJ) stated, for the first time, that the protection of the International Covenant on Civil and Political Rights (ICCPR) does not cease in times of war.[10]

---

[6]   United Nations website https://peacekeeping.un.org/en/military (accessed 27 April 2020).

[7]   United Nations websites https://peacekeeping.un.org/en/military; https://peacekeeping.un.org/en/un-police (accessed 27 April 2020).

[8]   Nigel D. White, 'Peacekeeping and International Law' in J. A. Knoops, Thierry Tardy, Norrie MacQueen, Paul D. Williams (eds.)*The Oxford Handbook of United Nations Peacekeeping Operations* (Oxford University Press 2015), 43–55; *Leuven Manual on the International Law Applicable to Peace Operations* eds. T. Gill, D. Fleck, W. Boothby, and A. Vanheusden (Cambridge University Press 2017, pages 150 and 152); ICRC, *Violence and the Use of Force*, 1 January 2015, 37 www.icrc.org/en/publication/0943-violence-and-use-force; D. Murray, D. Akande, F. Hampson, C. Garraway, N. Lubell, E. Wilmhurst,*Practitioner's Guide to Human Rights Law in Armed Conflict* (Chatham House Royal Institute of International Affairs and Oxford University Press 2016), page 260.

[9]   Institut de Droit International 'Conditions of Application of Humanitarian Rules of Armed Conflict to Hostilities in which United Nations Forces May Be Engaged' Session of Zagreb — 1971; D. Shraga, 'UN Peacekeeping Operations: Applicability of International Humanitarian Law and Responsibility for Operations-Related Damage' (2000) 94 *American Journal of International Law* 406.

[10]   *Legality of the Threat or Use of Nuclear Weapons*, Advisory Opinion of 8 July 1996, ICJ Reports (1996) 240, para. 25.

3.2 Military Peacekeepers Are Members of National Armies 37

For the first half-century of peacekeeping, DPO did not formally integrate either IHRL or IHL into peacekeeping operational standards and guidance, and instead adopted a sui generis approach that combined a commitment to compliance with the 'principles and spirit' of IHL together with adherence to the three basic principles of peacekeeping: consent of the parties; impartiality; and non-use of force except in self-defence and defence of the mandate.[11] During the 1990s, following serious allegations of human rights abuses committed by peacekeepers in Somalia and Bosnia Herzegovina, this respecting the 'principles and spirit' approach was heavily criticised for being too vague and unenforceable.[12] Therefore, in 1999 the then Secretary General Kofi Annan promulgated the *Bulletin on the Observance by UN Forces of International Humanitarian Law*, which acknowledged that the fundamental principles and rules of IHL 'are applicable to United Nations forces when in situations of armed conflict they are actively engaged therein as combatants, to the extent and for the duration of their engagement'.[13] In all other circumstances, peacekeepers retain the right to protection from attack afforded to non-combatants, and therefore IHL is not applicable to their operations.[14] The bulletin says nothing about what laws apply when IHL does not. The promulgation of the bulletin broadly coincided with a change in UN practice towards the routine use of Chapter VII mandates in a bid to prevent a repetition of the failures of UN missions to prevent genocide in Rwanda and Bosnia–Herzegovina.[15]

---

[11] United Nations, General Assembly 50th Session (1995), Fourth Committee, Agenda item 86, 16 November 1995, statement by the International Committee of the Red Cross; R. D. Glick, 'Lip Service to the Laws of War: Humanitarian Law and United Nations Armed Forces' (1995) 17 *Michigan Journal of International Law* 53, 54; Shraga, 'UN Peacekeeping Operations' (n 9), 406.

[12] There was strong criticism of decisions by military courts in Canada and Italy exculpating peacekeepers' conduct on the grounds that IHL was not applicable: Fréderic Mégret and Florian Hoffman, 'The UN as a Human Rights Violator? Some Reflections on the United Nations Changing Human Rights Responsibilities' (2003) 25 (2) *Human Rights Quarterly* 314, 327.

[13] Secretary General's Bulletin on Observance by UN Forces of International Humanitarian Law (date of promulgation 6 August 1999, entered into force 12 August 1999) UN Doc ST/SGB/1999/13, Article 1.

[14] This is in order to ensure that both the obligations and privileges of IHL apply to all combatants regardless of whom they fight for: Adam Roberts notes that if this principle were to be undermined 'all respect for the 1949 Geneva Conventions may be destroyed'. Adam Roberts and Richard Guelff, *Documents on the Laws of War* (3rd ed., Oxford: Oxford University Press 2000), 625.

[15] On 22 October 1999, a few weeks after the promulgation of *Bulletin on Observance by United Nations Forces of International Humanitarian Law*, the Security Council adopted Resolution 1270 on the situation in Sierra Leone first Security Council resolution explicitly mandating

38   *Integrating Human Rights Norms into UN Peacekeeping Practice*

The controversy over whether IHRL applies in armed conflict has now been largely resolved. In 1996, three years before the promulgation of the *Bulletin on the Observance by UN Forces of International Humanitarian Law*, the ICJ stated that the protection of the ICCPR, including the right to life, 'does not cease in times of war'; the 'test of what is an arbitrary deprivation of life, however, then falls to be determined by the applicable *lex specialis*, namely, the law applicable in armed conflict which is designed to regulate the conduct of hostilities'.[16] The Court reaffirmed that IHRL conventions remain applicable during armed conflict in its Advisory Opinion on the *Legal Consequences of the Construction of a Wall in the Occupied Palestinian Territory*, in the *Case Concerning Armed Activities on the Territory of the Congo*.[17] Regional human rights courts and tribunals also hold that IHRL remains applicable in armed conflict and this is now accepted by nearly all states, and almost all international legal opinion.[18] This consensus is reflected in Human Rights Council resolution 9/9, which states that 'the protection provided by human rights law continues in armed conflict situations, taking into account when international humanitarian law applies as a *lex specialis*'.[19]

It is accepted that customary IHRL applies extraterritorially, but the question of whether IHRL conventions apply to operations conducted outside the

---

a peacekeeping mission under Chapter VII of the UN Charter, and authorising it to use force to protect civilians. The close proximity in timing of the resolution authorising a peacekeeping mission under Chapter VII and the promulgation by the Secretary General of the *Bulletin on Observance by United Nations Forces of International Humanitarian Law* may be one reason why some peacekeepers might regard IHL rather than IHRL as their applicable legal framework.

[16] *Legality of the Threat or Use of Nuclear Weapons*, Advisory Opinion of 8 July 1996, ICJ Reports (1996) 240, para. 25.

[17] *Legal Consequences of the Construction of a Wall in the Occupied Palestinian Territory*, Advisory Opinion of 9 July 2004, ICJ Reports (2004), para. 106; *Case Concerning Armed Activities on the Territory of the Congo: Democratic Republic of the Congo v Uganda* ICJ, 19 December 2005, [217]; See also *Application of the International Convention on the Elimination of All Forms of Racial Discrimination, Order Indicating Provisional Measures*, ICJ, 15 October 2008.

[18] F. Hampson 'The Relationship between International Humanitarian Law and Human Rights Law from the Perspective of a Human Rights Treaty Body' (2008) 90 *International Review of the Red Cross* 549, 551. The United States rejects the view that the ICCPR is applicable extraterritorially; see Human Rights Committee, 'Concluding Observations on the Fourth Periodic Review of the United States of America' (2014) UN Doc CCPR/C/USA/CO/4, para. 4. But note also that in its report to the Human Rights Committee in 2011, the United States stated that 'determining the international law rule that applies to a particular action in the context of an armed conflict is a fact-specific action which cannot be easily generalized' UN Human Rights Committee, 30 December 2011, CCPR/C/USA4 at para. 47.

[19] Human Rights Council, Resolution 9/9, 'Protection of the Human Rights of Civilians in Armed Conflict' A/HRC/RES/9/18.

3.2 Military Peacekeepers Are Members of National Armies   39

state party's territory has proved more controversial. The Human Rights Committee, in General Comment No. 31, states that parties to the ICCPR must ensure the human rights of persons 'within the power or effective control' of the forces of a State Party acting outside its territory 'such as forces constituting a national contingent of a State Party assigned to an international peacekeeping or peace-enforcement operation'.[20] Francoise Hampson suggests that for most international human rights courts and tribunals, whether or not a state has effective control for the purposes of jurisdiction depends on whether it has 'control over the effects said to constitute a violation, subject to a foreseeable victim being foreseeably affected by the act'.[21] The approach of the European Court of Human Rights (ECtHR) has been somewhat different because of its 2001 decision in *Banković and Others v. Belgium and Others*, in which it held that jurisdiction is 'essentially territorial' and explicitly rejected the applicant's claim that the fact that a victim is foreseeably affected by an act of the contracting party is sufficient to bring that person within jurisdiction of the contracting party.[22] However, in 2004, in *Issa and Others v. Turkey*, the Court held that the Article 1 jurisdictional provisions of the European Convention on Human Rights 'cannot be interpreted so as to allow a State party to perpetrate violations of the Convention on the territory of another State, which it could not perpetrate on its own territory'.[23] Since then the Court has found contracting parties to have jurisdiction outside their own territories in many cases including in armed conflict contexts.[24] In the *Al-Skeini* case, the Court held that 'in certain circumstances, the use of force by a State's agents operating outside its territory may bring the individual thereby brought under the control of the State's authorities into the State's Article 1 jurisdiction'.[25]

---

[20] Human Rights Committee, General Comment No. 31, 'Nature of the General Legal Obligation on States Parties to the Covenant', UN Doc CCPR/C/21/Rev.1/Add.13 (2004), para. 10.

[21] Hampson 'The Relationship between International Humanitarian Law and Human Rights Law from the Perspective of a Human Rights Treaty Body' (n 18), 570.

[22] European Court of Human Rights, *Banković and Others v. Belgium and Others* Application No 52207/99, Admissibility, 12 December 2001, paras. 61 and 75. The court reiterated this view in *Medvedyev and Others v. France* Application No 3394/03, Judgement 29 March 2010, para. 64.

[23] European Court of Human Rights, *Issa and Others v. Turkey* Appl. No. 3182/96 Judgment, 16 November 2004, para. 71.

[24] Examples include *Al-Saadoon and Mufdhi v. UK*, Application no. 61498/08, Admissibility Decision, 30 June 2009; *Jaloud v. The Netherlands* Appl. No. 47708/08, Judgment, 20 November 2014.

[25] European Court of Human Rights, *Al-Skeini and Others v. UK*, Appl. No. 55721/07, Judgment, 7 July 2011, para. 139.

Integrating Human Rights Norms into UN Peacekeeping Practice

Today most states and the majority of international legal opinion hold that IHRL remains applicable in armed conflict, that customary IHRL applies extra-territorially, and that in certain circumstances IHRL conventions also apply extraterritorially. However currently peacekeeping guidance on operational standards remain heavily premised on IHL principles. Language based on IHL, and drawn directly from the *Bulletin on the Observance by UN Forces of International Humanitarian Law*, is now routinely incorporated into UN peacekeepers' Rules of Engagement (ROE), including prohibitions on the use of asphyxiating, poisonous, or other gases and biological methods of warfare; bullets which explode, expand, or flatten easily in the human body; and certain explosive projectiles; non-detectable fragments, anti-personnel mines, booby traps, and incendiary weapons; methods of warfare, which may cause superfluous injury or unnecessary suffering, or which are intended, or may be expected to cause widespread, long-term, and severe damage to the natural environment; methods of warfare to attack, destroy, remove, or render useless objects indispensable to the survival of the civilian population, such as foodstuff, crops, livestock, and drinking-water installations and supplies.[26] The routine inclusion in peacekeeping ROE of prohibitions on war crimes, including the most extreme and inhumane methods of warfare, with no reference at all to any of the fundamental customary laws rule of IHRL, is at best imbalanced and certainly implies a very different conception of peacekeeping from Hammarskjold's creation.

3.3 THE BASIS OF UNITED NATIONS' HUMAN RIGHTS LAW OBLIGATIONS

The UN has long accepted that the 'international responsibility of the United Nations for the activities of United Nations forces is an attribute of its international legal personality and its capacity to bear international rights and obligations'.[27] In 2004, the UN's legal counsel noted: 'As a subsidiary organ of the United Nations, an act of a peacekeeping force is, in principle, imputable to the Organization, and if committed in violation of an international obligation entails the international responsibility of the Organization and its liability in compensation.'[28] That acceptance of responsibility, however, is

---

[26] United Nations' Guidelines for the Development of ROE for United Nations Peacekeeping Operations, Rule 1.5, U.N. Doc. MD/FGS/0220.0001 (2002).

[27] Secretary-General's report, *Administrative and budgetary aspects of the financing of the United Nations peacekeeping operations*, A/51/389, 1996, para. 6.

[28] Unpublished letter of 3 February 2004 by the United Nations Legal Counsel to the Director of the Codification Division. Quoted in *Report of the ILC, General Assembly Official Records, 56th session, Supplement No. 10 A/59/10* (2004), at 111.

3.3 *The Basis of United Nations' Human Rights Law Obligations*   41

based on compensation for harms caused rather than a wider acceptance of responsibility for upholding and implementing human rights. It is widely accepted that the UN is subject to norms of jus cogens and is bound by at least some parts of general international law.[29] It is also widely accepted that customary international law and the general principles of responsibility can apply to international organisations,[30] but the extent of UN IHRL obligations remains a contested topic.

A straightforward reading of the Charter is that the UN must promote human rights (Articles 1(3), 55 and 56), but those provisions direct an Organisation that was intended to be a forum within which member states agree upon actions that must be taken. As the UN has developed, it is clear that the Organisation serves different purposes at different times. As such, there is significant scope for arguing that the Charter provisions indicate that the UN must also promote human rights when acting externally rather than as a forum. Any actions that violate human rights would therefore contradict the UN's purposes and certainly would not be 'necessary' for their achievement. It appears contradictory, at best, that the UN would hold immunity with regard to such acts. However, that in itself does not demonstrate that the UN is bound by IHRL.

The UN is not party to human rights conventions. Although it is able to ratify treaties, it has not done so where it comes to international human rights conventions. However, that does not mean the UN is not bound by IHRL. States are only bound by those obligations to which they consent, but the rules are different for international organisations. Mégret and Hoffman set out three main ways in which the UN is bound: the external conception, the internal conception, and the hybrid conception.[31]

The external conception relies on the UN having legal personality. Legal personality confers rights and duties, including from customary international

---

[29] For further discussion see R. Higgins, *Problems and Processes: International Law and How We Use It* (Oxford: Oxford University Press 1994), 181; F. Morgenstern, *Legal Problems of International Organizations* (Cambridge: Cambridge University Press 1986), 32; A. Orakhelashvili, *Collective Security* (Oxford: Oxford University Press 2011), at 56; A. Orakhelashvili 'The Acts of the Security Council: Meaning and Standards of Review' (2007) 11 *Max Planck Yearbook of United Nations Law* 143–195; S. Maus, 'Human Rights in Peacekeeping Missions' in H. J. Heintz and A. Zwitter (eds.) *International Law and Humanitarian Assistance* (Berlin Heidelberg: Verlag-Springer 2011), 103.

[30] S. Sheeran and J. Bevilaqua, 'The UN Security Council and International Human Rights Obligations: Towards a New Theory of Constraints and Derogations' in S. Sheeran and N. Rodley (eds.) *Routledge Handbook of International Human Rights Law* (London: Routledge 2013), 371.

[31] Mégret and Hoffman, 'The UN as a Human Rights Violator?' (n 12), 314.

law,[32] which includes certain human rights.[33] The ICJ has made it clear that the UN has legal personality, firstly in the *Reparations* Advisory Opinion (1949)[34] and then again in a later Advisory Opinion (1980).[35]

The internal conception focusses on the UN Charter and its constitutional mandate on human rights.[36] Alongside the provisions to promote, respect, or encourage human rights, (Preamble, Articles 1(3), 55 and 56),[37] Article 56 further mandates that UN member states have a positive duty to enforce the Charter's human rights obligations over and above any other international law.[38] That position has been affirmed by the ICJ[39] and the UN Human Rights Committee.[40] The hybrid conception focusses on the obligations of both the Organisation and on those of its member states, reaching the conclusion that the UN is bound by a broad range of obligations.[41]

The scope of the UN's rights and duties depend on its purposes, functions, and practices.[42] The extent to which UN bodies are governed by human rights obligations depends on their mandates, roles, and composition. Mégret and

---

[32] See, for example, Sheeran and Bevilaqua, 'The UN Security Council and International Human Rights Obligations' (n 30), 371.

[33] T. Dannenbaum 'Translating the Standard of Effective Control into a System of Effective Accountability' (2010) 51 *Harvard International Law Journal* 301, at 323.

[34] The ICJ stated that the UN 'is at present the supreme type of international organization and it could not carry out the intentions of its founders if it was devoid of international personality': International Court of Justice 'Reparation for Injuries Suffered in the Service of the United Nations', Advisory Opinion, 1949 I.C.J. 174 (April 11) at 179.

[35] Where the court stated: 'are subjects of international law and, as such, are bound by any obligations incumbent upon them under general rules of international law, under their constitutions or under international agreements to which they are parties'. International Court of Justice 'Interpretation of the Agreement of 25 March 1951 Between the WHO and Egypt', Advisory Opinion, 1980 I.C.J. 73, (December 20) at para. 37.

[36] Dannenbaum, 'Translating the Standard of Effective Control into a System of Effective Accountability' (n 33), at 324.

[37] Ibid., 301.

[38] See, generally, G. L. Rios and E. P. Flaherty 'Legal Accountability of International Organization: Challenges and Reforms' (2010) 16 *ILSA Journal of International & Competition Law* 433.

[39] The Court stated that human rights violations are 'a flagrant violation of the purposes and principles of the [UN] Charter', International Court of Justice 'Legal Consequences for States of the Continued Presence of South Africa in Namibia (South West Africa) notwithstanding Security Council Resolution 276' (1970), 1971 I.C.J. 12, (January 21) at 57.

[40] 'There is a United Nations Charter Obligation to Promote Universal Respect for, and Observance of, Human Rights and Fundamental Freedoms', UN Human Rights Committee, General Comment No. 31 (26 May 2004) UN Doc. CCPR/C/21/Rev.1/Add.13, para. 2.

[41] Mégret and Hoffman, 'The UN as a Human Rights Violator?' (n 12).

[42] International Court of Justice 'Reparation for Injuries Suffered in the Service of the United Nations', Advisory Opinion, 1949 I.C.J. 174 (April 11) at 178–179.

3.3 The Basis of United Nations' Human Rights Law Obligations 43

Hoffman insist that there is a difference between the UN negatively affecting the realisation of human rights or contradicting human rights principles, and actual human rights violations.[43] A distinction is made between situations when the UN exercises its functions and powers as an international organisation, and when the UN acts like a sovereign power within a state's territory.[44] A further distinction is made between UN acts that are overwhelmingly controlled by member states, and those acts that the organisation itself controls.

Member states control resolutions, which countries draft, sponsor, and vote upon. Some of those resolutions create a situation in which the UN becomes an external actor rather than a forum for member states. It is at this point that the UN, rather than the member states, is bound by IHRL and responsible for violations that arise through its external activities. One key example concerns the resolutions creating UN missions to states, as those missions are run by the UN and even though troops remain under the control of their home states, the UN is responsible for human right violations committed by the mission.[45] This responsibility has a clear parallel to the responsibility of the UN for private law claims arising from peacekeeping missions. The difference between private law claims and human rights violations is who commits the wrongful acts. Private law claims arise from acts of peacekeepers, with the UN then having a duty under Section 29 of the Convention on Privileges and Immunities of the United Nations (CPIUN) to provide dispute mechanisms. Human rights violations arise from UN actions and the organisation is then responsible for remedying any violations.

Since the 1990s UN peacekeeping activities have increasingly involved the UN assuming the functions of a sovereign or hybrid-sovereign power, including through state-building activities and exercising powers of governance, as discussed in Chapter 2. Such activities ought then to be governed by human rights obligations in much the same way as a state exercising such functions would be bound by those laws.[46] The UN has increasingly shown that it accepts that peacekeeping missions have some human rights obligations. 'We are United Nations Peacekeeping personnel' a brochure given to all new staff members states that all mission members comply with 'the applicable portions of the Universal Declaration on Human Rights as the fundamental basis of our standards'[47] and

---

[43] Mégret and Hoffman, 'The UN as a Human Rights Violator?' (n 12).

[44] See, for example, J. Chopra 'The UN's Kingdom of East Timor' (2000) 42 (2) *Survival* 29.

[45] See, generally, K. M. Larsen, *The Human Rights Treaty Obligations of Peacekeepers* (Cambridge: Cambridge University Press 2012).

[46] Mégret and Hoffman, 'The UN as a Human Rights Violator?' (n 12), at 327–328.

[47] 'We are United Nations Peacekeeping Personnel' www.un.org/en/peacekeeping/documents/un_in.pdf

44   *Integrating Human Rights Norms into UN Peacekeeping Practice*

the Model 'Memorandum of Understanding between the United Nations and personnel contributing States' specifies that the 'Government shall ensure that all members of the Government's national contingent are required to comply with the United Nations standards of conduct'.[48]

To understand which peacekeeping missions are bound by which human rights and in what circumstances, it is important to distinguish between the situations where the UN is mandated to take over the entire administration of a state[49] and when it is given some legislative and administrative powers to be exercised in conjunction with local actors.[50] Traditionally, when a UN mission becomes an interim state, it will be bound by IHRL. Examples occurred in Kosovo and Timor-Leste where the UN was the sole and sovereign power since the UN assumed the role of the state and held sovereign powers both *de jure* and *de facto*.[51] In those circumstances it is accepted that the UN is bound by the IHRL treaties that it ratifies when acting as the sole sovereign power in the state,[52] alongside those that already exist within the state.[53] That position, however, does not take into account the UN's existing human rights obligations. Adopting the internal, external or hybrid conception leads to the same conclusion that when the UN exercises external functions as a sovereign state

[48]   Letter dated 22 February 2008 from the Chairman of the 2008 Working Group on Contingent-Owned Equipment to the Chairman of the Fifth Committee, (29 January 2009) (A/C.5/63/18) Chapter 9, Article 7 bis, 165.

[49]   Security Council Resolution 1244 establishing the 'United Nations Interim Administration Mission in Kosovo (UNMIK)' mandated UNMIK to perform basic civilian administrative functions, support the reconstruction of key infrastructure, maintain civil law and order, promote human rights, and assure the safe return of all refugees: UN. Doc. S/Res 1244, 10 June 1999; Similarly, Security Council Resolution 1272 establishing the 'United Nations Transitional Authority in East Timor (UNTAET)' gave UNTAET overall responsibility for the administration of East Timor including all legislative and executive authority, as well as the administration of justice: UN Doc. S/Res 1272, 25 October 1999.

[50]   For example, The United Nations Transitional Authority in Cambodia (UNTAC), the second United Nations Operation in Somalia (UNOSOM II), the United Nations Mission in Bosnia and Herzegovina (UNMIBH) in combination with a United Nations International Police Task Force (IPTF), and the 'United Nations Transitional Administration for Eastern Slavonia (UNTAES)'.

[51]   N. Lemay-Hébert 'The "Empty-Shell" Approach: The Setup Process of International Administrations in Timor-Leste and Kosovo, Its Consequences and Lessons' (2011) 12 *International Studies Perspectives* 190.

[52]   In Timor-Leste an early regulation stated that 'all persons undertaking public duties or holding public office in East Timor shall observe internationally recognized human rights standards' (UNTAET Regulation No. 1999/1). In Kosovo, Section 2 of Regulation 1991/1 set out that UNMIK shall comply with international human rights standards when discharging its functions (S.C. Res. 1244. Art. 11(j) UN Doc. S/RES/1244 (10 June 1999)). UNMIK later expressly submitted to existing Council of Europe monitoring mechanisms.

[53]   Human Rights Committee (HRC), General Comment No. 26, 8 December 1997, U.N. Doc. CCPR/C/21/Rev.1/Add.8/Rev.1, para. 4.

3.3 *The Basis of United Nations' Human Rights Law Obligations*   45

it bears responsibility for any violations directly attributable to its actions. Therefore, when the UN assumes sovereign or hybrid-sovereign powers within a state it is bound by a range of human rights. That responsibility is separate to the responsibility that member states have for UN actions, as set out by the ECtHR.[54]

Where the UN shares sovereign powers with local actors, it will be bound by any human rights treaties to which that country is party. However, when a violation occurs it is less clear as to which entity bears responsibility. In each case, and at each stage of a peacekeeping mission, it is too simplistic to ascribe responsibility based solely on the sovereign power being held de jure by the government; instead it is crucial to look to whether the government or the UN has de facto control. The idea of effective authority and control is, for instance, central to Krasner's theory of sovereignty in the contemporary world, as discussed in Chapter 2.[55] Krasner insists that determining which actor holds authority and control enables determination of which actor bears responsibility in circumstances where there is hybrid-sovereign power-sharing within a state. This draws parallels with the 'effective control' test that has been adopted when considering the extraterritorial scope of application of human rights.[56] Adopting that approach provides a logical method to determine responsibility, because only the entity with authority and control has the power to prevent and to remedy human rights violations. Adopting this approach, the UN would bear responsibility for human rights violations

---

[54] European Court of Human Rights, *Behrami and Behrami* v. *France*, App. No. 71412/01 (2007) and *Saramati* v. *France, Germany and Norway*, App. No. 78166/01 (2007), paras. 144–152 in which the Court held that 'UNMIK was a subsidiary organ of the UN created under Chapter VII and KFOR was exercising powers lawfully delegated under Chapter VII of the Charter by the UNSC. As such, their actions were directly attributable to the UN'; see also paras. 144 and 152. See, further, C. Bell 'Reassessing Multiple Attribution: The International Law Commission and the Behrami and Saramati decision' (2010) 42 *New York University Journal of International Law and Politics* 501. Other relevant decisions include: *Kasumaj* v. *Greece*, App. No. 6974/05 (2007); *Gajić* v. *Germany*, App. No. 31446/02 (2007); *Berić and others* v. *Bosnia and Herzegovina*, App. Nos. 36357/04; 36360/04; 38346/04; 41705/04; 45190/04; 45578/04; 45579/04; 45580/04; 91/05; 97/05; 100/05; 101/05; 1121/05; 1123/05; 1125/05; 1129/05; 1132/05; 1133/05; 1169/05; 1172/05; 1175/05; 1177/05; 1180/05; 1185/05; 20793/05; 25496/05 (2007); *Mothers of Srebrenica/Netherlands and United Nations*, District Court of the Hague, 10 July 2008, De Rechtspraak BD6795 (Neth.).

[55] S. D. Krasner, *Sovereignty: Organized Hypocrisy* (Princeton: Princeton University Press 1999); N. Lemay-Hébert 'Exploring the Effective Authority of International Administrations from the League of Nations to the United Nations' (2017) 11 *Journal of Intervention and Statebuilding* 468.

[56] See, for example, European Court of Human Rights, *Al-Skeini and Others* v. *the United Kingdom*, App. No. 55721/07, 53 Eur. H.R. Rep. 589 (2011).

46 Integrating Human Rights Norms into UN Peacekeeping Practice

arising from its actions wherever it has domestic authority and control even if is not acting alone and therefore is not a sole and sovereign power.

3.4 CONCLUSION

The spirit and purpose of the UN project is to protect humans and humanity from grave atrocities. At the heart of that project is ensuring peace and security through preventing conflicts and building environments in which conflicts do not occur. To that end, the UN's two largest activities are peacekeeping and development, with both in principle aimed at ensuring individuals have their human rights realised.

Over the past decade, the UN has adopted a number of initiatives aimed at advancing human rights protection within the UN system. The Human Rights Due Diligence Policy adopted in July 2011, requires all United Nations entities to carry out a risk assessment evaluating the potential risks and benefits of providing support to non-UN forces and to withdraw support if the risks to human rights protection outweigh the benefits of continued support.[57] The Human Rights Up Front initiative adopted in 2013, asserts that protecting human rights 'is a core purpose of the United Nations and defines our identity as an organization'[58] and requires UN staff to take timely and effective action to prevent and respond to serious violations of IHRL or IHL.[59] These are necessary initiatives and major milestones in the development of UN's overarching goal of human rights' protection and advancement, but they are focused on responding to human rights violations by other actors, for example host state forces or armed groups, rather than on ensuring UN actors themselves comply with IHRL.

The UN's 'Capstone Doctrine', which sets out the principles and guidelines that should govern peacekeeping operations and was adopted in 2008, states that 'peacekeeping personnel – whether military, police or civilian – should act in accordance with international human rights law and understand how the implementation of their tasks intersects with human rights'.[60] The UN's 2017

---

[57] Human Rights Due Diligence Policy on UN Support to Non-UN Security Forces Guidance Note (United Nations Sustainable Development Group, October 2015) https://unsdg.un.org/resources/guidance-note-human-rights-due-diligence-policy-un-support-non-united-nations-security (accessed 27 April 2020).

[58] Aide-Memoire to the Human Rights Up Front Plan of Action, 2014, on file with authors.

[59] 'Rights Up Front' (May 2014) United Nations Secretary General, www.refworld.org/pdfid/54 9141f84.pdf; The Rights Up Front Initiative is designed primarily for settings where the UN does not have a peacekeeping mission, however 'its spirit can and should also be applied to "mission settings"'; Ibid.

[60] United Nations Peacekeeping Operations Principles and Guidelines ('the Capstone Doctrine'), approved by J. M. Guéhenno, USG/DPKO, 18 January 2008.

Guidelines on *Use of Force by Military Components in United Nations Peacekeeping Operations*, also state that peacekeepers must comply with applicable IHRL. Neither of these doctrines specifies *which rules of IHRL bind UN military personnel or in what circumstances.*[61] But they do reflect the fact there exists a broad consensus within the UN, as well as outside it, that IHRL applies during armed conflict, that it also applies extraterritorially in some – if not many – circumstances, and that it applies to UN peacekeeping operations. We should expect DPO to be able to draw on such resources to develop a bulletin setting out the practical implications for peacekeepers conducting operations to which IHL is not applicable and affirming that where IHL is not applicable peacekeepers must comply with, at a minimum, customary IHRL. The UN has not produced such a bulletin.

In the following chapters, we look at the gap between law and practice where it comes to human rights in peacekeeping, identifying why human rights need to be integrated throughout. We use examples from Haiti to explore the grave violations that occur owing to the human rights obligations owed by the UN and its agents being ignored in law and practice, and to demonstrate how and why human rights must be foregrounded in future operations and activities.

---

[61] United Nations Department of Peacekeeping Operations/ Department of Field Support, *Use of Force by Military Components in United Nations Peacekeeping Operations* Ref: 2016.24, approved by Hervé Ladsous, USG DPKO; Atul Khare, USG DFS Effective date: 1 February 2017, para. 8.

4

UN Immunities and Human Rights

4.1 INTRODUCTION

In order to discuss the legacy of MINUSTAH and the lack of accountability for civil and criminal wrongs, it is first necessary to understand the current system of immunities and of the UN and of its personnel. The system of immunities for the UN and its personnel was created in 1946, and as the Organisation has grown and its activities have developed, there have been increasing criticisms of and challenges to the application of those laws, particularly from a human rights perspective. In 1946 the system reflected understandings of state and diplomatic immunity, and those laws were enshrined in a Convention that has remained unchanged for more than seven decades despite state and diplomatic immunity evolving since that time. As such, the system is criticised for being unfit for purpose, particularly where it prevents individuals from being able to realise their fundamental rights to access a court and a remedy. In Haiti there have been many examples of when UN immunities have prevented justice for victims, including use of force and criminal wrongs perpetrated by peacekeepers. In the following two chapters we will explore in-depth two of the most egregious and prominent examples: the Haiti Cholera Claims and sexual exploitation and abuse (SEA) by peacekeepers. In order to understand those case studies, we must first explore the system of UN immunities. In this chapter, we first explain the system, the laws, and how they operate in practice, before deploying a human rights perspective to understand whether the UN is bound by international human rights law (IHRL) and how the system of immunities can violate those obligations. This chapter provides the foundations for analysing accountability in the context of our case studies of the UN Stabilisation Mission in Haiti in three areas: the Cholera Claims (Chapter 5); Sexual Exploitation and Abuse (Chapter 6); and Use of Force (Chapter 7).

4.2 IMMUNITIES

There are two types of immunities that we must understand before discussing whether the current interpretation and application of UN immunities violate individuals' human rights. The first is the immunity that the UN holds as an international organisation, and the second is the immunities granted to its personnel.

4.2.1 UN Immunity

The United Nations may be viewed as a quasi-state in terms of its functions and internal legal systems,[1] yet it is granted absolute immunity rather than the 'restrictive' immunity that is mostly afforded to states nowadays. Of course, international organisations' immunity can be distinguished from that of states in terms of sources and rationale. State immunity has been an evolving concept now codified within the 2004 UN Convention on State Immunities, while international organisations' immunity is usually enshrined within treaties specific to an organisation or within its constituent instrument, and usually is based on the UN's immunities, which were enshrined in 1946. This has restricted the extent to which such immunity can be interpreted or evolved. Absolute immunity was the prevailing theory up until the second half of the twentieth century. As such, when the UN was created, it was afforded absolute immunity, which was subsequently enshrined in the Convention on Privileges and Immunities of the United Nations (1946) (Hereafter CPIUN). Moreover, some would insist that even if that treaty was easy to amend, the UN needs to hold immunity from national courts' jurisdiction in order to prevent inconsistencies that would occur across different national courts.[2] Some scholars even have insisted that national courts or tribunals are 'totally unsuited' for disputes involving international organisations.[3] While there is a clear need for the UN to have immunity in order to carry out its work, we insist that such immunity may only be upheld where the UN has ensured that an individual's fundamental rights to access a court and a remedy, and to truth, are not violated. In other words, the UN has an obligation to provide alternative dispute resolution mechanisms in order that its immunity does not violate individuals' fundamental human rights.

---

[1] A. Reinisch 'The Immunity of International Organizations and the Jurisdiction of their Administrative Tribunals' (2008) 7 *Chinese Journal of International Law* 285–306.

[2] Compare *Broadbent v. Organization of American States*, 628 F.2d 27, 35 (D.C.Cir. 1980).

[3] M. B. Akehurst, *The Law Governing Employment in International Organizations* (Cambridge: Cambridge University Press 1967), 12.

The UN's immunity is based on the Charter of the United Nations: Article 105 (1) sets out that 'The Organization shall enjoy in the territory of each of its Members such privileges and immunities as are necessary for the fulfilment of its purposes'.[4] That provision does not set out absolute immunity,[5] leading some commentators to insist that the UN was intended only to be granted functional immunity,[6] but it has been interpreted as absolute immunity by states and by courts. A straightforward reading of the Charter indicates that the UN's immunity is restricted by its human rights obligations under Articles 1(3), 55 and 56. Any actions that violate fundamental human rights to access a court and a remedy, and to truth, would contradict the UN's purposes and certainly would not be 'necessary' for their achievement; it appears contradictory, at best, that the UN would hold immunity with regard to such acts. However, when the Charter provisions were elaborated upon in the CPIUN, the immunity was interpreted as being absolute.

Section 2 of the CPIUN establishes that

'The United Nations, its property and assets wherever located and by whomsoever held, shall enjoy immunity from every form of legal process except insofar as in any particular case it has expressly waived its immunity'.[7]

Courts have generally interpreted section 2 as granting absolute immunity to the United Nations.[8] This approach is based on the UN Charter and the General Convention pre-dating the move to restrictive immunity,[9] meaning that even if the UN's immunity was conceived of as functional, it was codified as absolute. That approach can be seen, for example, in the early case of *Manderlier v. Organisation des Nations Unies et l'Etat Belge*[10] (1966) and

---

[4]   UN Charter, Article 105 (1).
[5]   See, for example, J. J. Paust 'The UN Is Bound By Human Rights: Understanding the Full Reach of Human Rights, Remedies, and Nonimmunity' (2010) 51 *Harvard International Law Journal* 1, 9.
[6]   A. Reinisch, 'Convention on the Privileges and Immunities of the United Nations 196, Convention on the Privileges and Immunities of the Specialized Agencies 1947', 1, in United Nations (eds.) *Audiovisual Library of International Law*, https://legal.un.org/avl/ha/c piun-cpisa/cpiun-cpisa.html (accessed 27 April 2020).
[7]   UN General Assembly Resolution 22(1), 'Convention on the Privileges and Immunities of the United Nations', 13 February 1946, section 2.
[8]   A. Reinisch, *International Organizations Before National Courts* (Cambridge: Cambridge University Press 2000), 332.
[9]   G. L. Rios and E. P. Flaherty 'Legal Accountability of International Organization: Challenges and Reforms' (2010) 16 *ILSA Journal of International & Competition Law* 437.
[10]   *Manderlier v. Organisation des Nations Unies et l'Etat Belge (Ministre des Affaires Etrangeres)*, Brussels Civil Tribunal, 11 May 1966, (1966) Journal des Tribunaux 72; (1972) 45 ILR 446.

subsequently in cases ranging from employment disputes[11] to damages arising from peacekeeping operations.[12] Traditional justification for the UN's absolute immunity is that it would be undesirable for national courts to determine the legality of the UN's acts because (1) those courts would have very different interpretations to one another; and (2) it may be open to prejudice or frivolous actions within some countries.[13]

The wording in section 2 is unambiguous, yet there remains the key problem that the UN's absolute immunity can and does give rise to violations of individuals' human rights. Even though a potential counterbalance is provided in section 29 of the CPIUN, which requires the UN to set up alternative dispute resolution mechanisms, courts have ruled that section 2 is not dependent on section 29 being implemented. Judges to date have determined that they are bound to grant immunity to the UN,[14] but judicial comments within some cases demonstrate that this is not unproblematic especially where there are no other avenues for alternative dispute resolution through which an individual may exercise her/his right to access a court and a remedy.[15] This is something that will be explored in-depth in our case study on the *Haiti Cholera Claims* (Chapter 5) in order to demonstrate that a new human rights-based approach is necessary.

4.2.2 *Immunities of UN Personnel*

When considering the position of UN personnel, it is important to distinguish between three key categories, all of whom have different immunities or jurisdictional bars set out under different treaty provisions. First, there are

---

[11] For example, *Radicopoulos* v. *United Nations Relief and Works Agency*, Egyptian Court, 1957, *Annual Report of the Director of UNWRA*, 13 UN GAOR, Supp. (No. 14) 41, UN Doc. A/391 (1958); *Boimah* v. *United Nations General Assembly*, US District Court EDNY, 24 July 1987, 664 F. Suppl. 69 (EDNY 1987).

[12] For example, *Abdi Hosh Askir* v. *Boutros Boutros-Ghali*, US District Court, Southern District, New York, 29 July 1996, 933 F. Suppl. 368 (SDNY 1996).

[13] P. Sands and P. Klein, *Bowett's Law of International Institutions* (5th ed., London: Sweet & Maxwell 2001), section 15–045, 491.

[14] E. Gaillard and I. Pingel-Lenuzza 'International Organisations and Immunity from Jurisdiction: To Restrict or To Bypass' (2002) 51 *International and Comparative Law Quarterly* 1, 2.

[15] See for example, *Abdi Hosh Askir* v. *Boutros Boutros-Ghali*, US District Court, Southern District, New York, 29 July 1996, 933 F. Suppl. 368 (SDNY 1996), in which a Somali citizen brought a claim against the UN seeking damages for unlawful possession of property during UN operations in Somalia in April 1992. See also Johnson, 'Introductory Note to Brzak v. United Nations (2D CIR.) and Mothers of Srebrenica v Netherlands & United Nations (Neth. App. Ct.)', (2010) 49 *International Legal Materials* 1, 1012.

UN civilian staff who are directly employed by the UN. Then there are experts on mission, who may be part-time, unpaid, or contractors. Finally, there are military soldiers whom the UN contracts in for peacekeeping missions but who remain under the control of their national militaries. These categories are crucial for understanding how current laws and practices result in human rights violations of victims of crimes committed by UN personnel, as will be explored in our case study on sexual exploitation and abuse (later).

First, UN civilian personnel are granted immunity from the jurisdiction of any national court under Article V of the CPIUN.[16] There are two types of immunity in relation to UN civilian staff: personal or functional. Personal immunity protects an individual from all legal processes at any time, and is given to the highest level UN staff. All other civilian staff are given functional immunity, which protects them from legal processes in relation to any act that forms part of their official functions.

Officially, the UN agrees that most civilian personnel have functional immunity, stating that no immunity will operate in respect to actions that are not part of a person's official functions. Whether an act forms part of official functions is not about whether the person was 'on duty' at that time, but rather whether the act was part of that person's job. It is clear then, that some crimes such as driving whilst drunk or unlawful killing may be covered by functional immunity, whereas others such as sexual exploitation or abuse will never fall within that sphere.[17] Where there is a question as to whether or not functional immunity applies, the UN must make such a determination based on internal investigations into whether the context within which it occurred was part of the person's official duties.

The two main problematic areas are as follows: (1) UN investigations into whether or not functional immunity applies, and (2) whether local mechanisms meet international standards. Despite a lack of mandate to do so, the UN conducts its own internal investigations into all allegations of crimes irrespective of whether the act committed is able to form part of an individual's official functions and irrespective of whether the context in which the crime was part of a person's official duties. Those investigations typically go beyond looking at whether functional immunity applies, and instead focus on whether there is sufficient evidence to cooperate with local investigations.[18] This is deeply

---

[16] Convention on the Privileges and Immunities of the United Nations', General Assembly Resolution 22(1), 13 February 1946, (United Nations 1 *Treaty Series* 15), Article V.

[17] See, for example, A. J. Miller 'Legal Aspects of Stopping Sexual Exploitation and Abuse in UN Peacekeeping Operations' (2006) 39 *Cornell International Law Journal* 92.

[18] This has been exposed most recently in terms of UN investigations into allegations against personnel in Haiti and Central African Republic, as evidenced in UN Office of Internal Oversight Services reports (e.g. 2015).

problematic and undermines the foundations of functional immunity that require a person to be handed over to local investigatory bodies where an act falls outside of their official functions. Even where the UN agrees that functional immunity does not apply, personnel cannot be handed over to local mechanisms if they do not meet international standards in relation to human rights and rule of law, which frequently is the case in conflict zones and failed states.

Second, similar provisions (Article VI CPIUN) and practices govern UN experts on missions as they do for UN civilian staff.[19] Those experts on mission have functional immunity in relation to acts committed whilst on mission. In addition, those individuals are deemed to be inviolable whilst on mission. Inviolability goes beyond immunity from legal processes in relation to an act, and protects the person from any interference with their integrity whilst on mission. Inviolability attaches directly to the person, and prevents an individual from being arrested or detained until after their mission finishes. Therefore, even if an act falls outside of their official functions nothing can be done whilst the expert remains on mission. This is an important additional aspect to understand given that many police deployed on peacekeeping missions are experts on mission.

Third and last, military personnel are not afforded the same immunities as their civilian counterparts.[20] Soldiers are not directly employed by the UN, instead remaining under the control of their home country, which in turn has a contract with the UN. Those individuals are covered by bilateral agreements[21] between their sending state (the 'Troop Contributing Country') and the UN; and those bilateral agreements set out jurisdiction over such personnel if they commit crimes whilst on peacekeeping operations.[22] Military personnel operate under a system where the host state is barred from exercising jurisdiction in relation to crimes committed by those individuals. That is not an immunity,

[19] A. J. Miller 'United Nations Experts on Mission and their Privileges and Immunities' (2007) 4 (1) *International Organizations Law Review* 11.

[20] For an in-depth discussion, see Z. Deen-Racsmány 'Exclusive Criminal Jurisdiction over UN Peacekeepers and the UN Project(s) on Criminal Accountability: A Self-Fulfilling Prophecy' (2013) 53 (2) *Military Law & Law of War Review* 247.

[21] These are based on the model memorandum of understanding between the United Nations and [participating State] contributing resources to [the United Nations Peacekeeping Operation] in 'Manual on Policies and Procedures Concerning the Reimbursement and Control of Contingent-Owned Equipment of Troop/Police Contributors Participating in Peacekeeping Missions', UN Doc. A/C.5/66/8, 27 October 2011.

[22] The bilateral agreements between the UN and the host states (UN Model SOFA, 'Report of the SG, Model Status-of-Forces Agreement for Peace-Keeping Operations', UN Doc A/45/594, 9 October 1990), further underscore that jurisdiction over military personnel belongs exclusively to the troop-contributing countries.

per se, as the troop-contributing country retains exclusive jurisdiction over its own soldiers and commits to exercise that jurisdiction to prosecute troops who commit criminal offences whilst on missions.[23] However, it operates as an absolute immunity from the jurisdiction of the host state. The troop-contributing country is obligated to investigate and prosecute such crimes, with the UN being limited to administrative investigations and even then only if the troop-contributing country fails to undertake its own investigations within ten days of an allegation being handed over to its authorities. Prosecutions may occur by the host state if a soldier is court-martialled in situ and handed over to local authorities, or may be done through military courts or national courts in the soldier's home state. The decision as to how to proceed belongs exclusively to the troop-contributing country.[24]

There are two main problems with this system. First, troops frequently are not held accountable by their own countries, for legal and for political reasons. Not all troop-contributing countries are able to exercise extraterritorial jurisdiction over acts committed by their soldiers whilst on peacekeeping operations. Even where they are able to do so, the reality is that such states rarely if ever prosecute their soldiers. That may be because there is insufficient evidence gathered to do so – a key problem of investigating crimes committed abroad and in fragile or conflict zones. Or it may be because of the national political implications of doing so, and the likelihood that such prosecutions would undermine national support for contributing troops to UN peacekeeping operations. Second, the removal of host state jurisdiction results in a lack of access to justice for victims that highlights the problem with the legal frameworks centring on perpetrators and state sovereignty rather than on victims and human rights.

4.3 A VICTIM-CENTRED APPROACH TO ACCOUNTABILITY

To date, the UN approach to accountability has constantly placed the Organisation, perpetrators, and state sovereignty at the heart of all laws and frameworks. In order to adopt a more holistic and appropriate approach to accountability for the UN and its personnel, there needs to be a shift away from this approach and towards one that centres the victims.

---

[23] UN General Assembly, 'Model Status-of-Forces-Agreement for Peacekeeping Operations,' report of the Secretary General, A/45/594, 9 October 1990.

[24] On these matters, see R. Burke, *Sexual Exploitation and Abuse by UN Military Contingents: Moving Beyond the Current Status Quo and Responsibility under International Law* (Leiden: Brill/Martinus Nijhoff 2014).

A number of scholars in recent years have examined UN human rights obligations in the context of immunity,[25] and some argue that members have a positive duty to enforce the Charter's human rights obligations 'over and above any other international law granting immunity',[26] with Paust insisting that the proposition that the UN has immunity even where that would violate human rights is 'counter-intuitive'.[27] But those discussions largely remain at the theoretical level. More practical discussions of accountability largely focus on criminal offences and laws of war, which are informative but do not address the human rights violations that occur when victims are denied access to a court and a remedy and to truth.[28] There are limited reported cases,[29] reflecting the difficulties in bringing the UN or its personnel before courts, and the jurisprudence that does exist from national and regional courts focusses either on broader issues of immunity or on private law claims arising from criminal acts. As we shall see, the evolving line of case law discussing issues of immunity and human rights, as well as the UN's use of human rights mechanisms to address harms caused, provides a strong basis for adopting a human rights-based approach.

Ensuring a holistic and victim-centred approach means placing relevant aspects of criminal justice, truth and reconciliation, human rights and political processes at the heart of responses to allegations of SEA by peacekeepers. This section explores these approaches, drawing upon theory and practices to understand how different aspects of those models may be appropriate when designing a system to deal with UN peacekeeping personnel.

4.3.1 Criminal Justice

The use of criminal justice to hold accountable actors in the international arena began with the Nuremberg Trials following the Second World War.[30]

---

[25] J. Wouters and P. Schmitt, 'Challenging Acts of Other United Nations' Organs, Subsidiary Organs and Officials', *Leuven Centre for Global Governance Studies*, Working Paper No. 49, April 2010.

[26] Rios and Flaherty, 'Legal Accountability of International Organization' (n 9), 433.

[27] Paust, 'The UN Is Bound By Human Rights' (n 5).

[28] Freedman however, has taken these theoretical foundations and applied them in the practical context of the UN's operations. R. Freedman 'UN Immunity or Impunity? A Human Rights Based Challenge' (2014) 25 (1) *European Journal of International Law* 239; R. Freedman 'UNaccountable: A New Approach to Peacekeepers and Sexual Abuse' (2018) 29 (3) *European Journal of International Law* 961.

[29] The UN CDU maintains a database of SEA cases at http://cdu.unlb.org/.

[30] P. Sands, *From Nuremberg to the Hague: The Future of International Criminal Justice* (Cambridge: Cambridge University Press 2003).

Those trials focussed on war crimes, crimes against humanity, and genocide, and are the foundations of the modern system of international criminal law (ICL). Yet, it was not until the early 1990s, in relation to the Former Republic of Yugoslavia and to Rwanda, that ICL was once again enforced through an international tribunal[31] and since has been in relation to crises in Cambodia (1997), Sierra Leone (2002), Iraq (2003), and Lebanon (2009). Those courts and tribunals have been created alongside the International Criminal Court (ICC) that was established by the 1998 Rome Statute.[32]

Despite these mechanisms existing to tackle what are seen as the most pernicious harms at the international level, of which SEA by peacekeepers is undoubtedly one, there are two main reasons why ICL mechanisms in isolation are inappropriate for holding accountable peacekeepers who commit serious crimes. First, those courts and tribunals focus on international crimes, which is not the same as ordinary crimes committed within the international arena.[33] And second, those mechanisms only prosecute those most responsible for international crimes, which includes military and political leaders.[34] In those scenarios, the perpetrators of individual crimes if brought to justice are done so by national courts rather than by these international mechanisms.

International crimes are those crimes committed as part of a systemic pattern seeking to oppress, subjugate, or destroy local populations. While those crimes may include murder, rape, looting, arson, and many other criminal acts, the basis for ICL is the context within which those crimes are committed and the purpose for which those crimes are perpetrated. As such, where sexual violence is used to persecute or strike terror into a population, it may form the basis of a war crime or crime against humanity, or where rape is used to prevent the future birth of children accepted by a particular religion or ethnicity then it may even form the basis for genocide, and it is that which distinguishes crimes of sexual abuse from international crimes that have been perpetrated through acts of sexual abuse.[35] That distinction is crucial when thinking about accountability for peacekeepers who perpetrate sexual abuse, because it then becomes clear why it is impossible to use the ICC, or internationalised courts, or tribunals to

---

[31] W. A. Schabas, *The UN International Criminal Tribunals* (Cambridge: Cambridge University Press 2006).

[32] UN General Assembly, *Rome Statute of the International Criminal Court (last amended 2010)*, 17 July 1998, ISBN No. 92–9227-227–6, www.refworld.org/docid/3ae6b3a84.html (accessed 27 April 2020).

[33] A. Cassesse, P. Gaeta, and J. R. W. D. Jones, *The Rome Statute of the International Criminal Court* (Oxford: Oxford University Press 2002).

[34] Ibid.

[35] For a broad discussion on prosecuting rape as a war crime, see R. J. Goldstone 'Prosecuting Rape as a War Crime' (2002) 34 *Case Western Reserve Journal of International Law* 277.

prosecute those peacekeepers. Although sexual abuse by peacekeepers is widespread, no evidence has been produced to demonstrate that those crimes are committed as part of wider or systematic attempts to repress, subjugate, or destroy local populations,[36] which means that even where those crimes are systemic they do not amount to international crimes.

Even though international courts and tribunals are not appropriate for prosecuting peacekeepers who perpetrate crimes of sexual abuse, there have been proposals for hybrid courts that could prosecute crimes committed within the international arena.[37] Those proposals build upon the hybrid nature of the mechanisms developed for Cambodia, Chad, Iraq, Kosovo, Lebanon, Sierra Leone, and Timor-Leste. Those mechanisms had hybridity in terms of not only composition and applicable law but also the types of crimes they were able to prosecute.[38] The proposals for hybrid courts in Burundi, Central African Republic, Democratic Republic of Congo, Kenya, Liberia, Somalia, South Sudan, and Sudan have all focussed upon prosecuting hybrid rather than international crimes. And while none of those mechanisms have yet been implemented, the discussions around their form, nature, and jurisdiction give a clear indication of the validity and possibility of setting up internationalised hybrid mechanisms able to prosecute criminal acts.

4.3.2 Truth and Reconciliation

During the lengthy period between the Nuremberg Trials and the establishment of the International Criminal Tribunals for Yugoslavia and for Rwanda, a different form of accountability mechanism was widely used across parts of Latin America and later developed and used in many other parts of the world. That mechanism is the truth commission,[39] which is a key form of transitional justice that focusses on restorative rather than retributive models of justice.[40]

---

[36] Despite attempts by some commentators to argue that the ICC is an appropriate mechanism for these crimes. On SEA as an international crime, see M. O'Brien 'Sexual Exploitation and Beyond: Using the Rome Statute of the International Criminal Court to Prosecute UN Peacekeepers for Gender-Based crimes' (2011) 11 (4) *International Criminal Law Review* 803.

[37] See, L. A. Dickinson 'The Promise of Hybrid Courts' (2003) 97 *American Journal of International Law* 295; and P. McAuliffe, 'Hybrid Courts in Retrospect: Of Lost Legacies and Modest Futures' in W. A. Schabas et al. (eds.) *The Ashgate Research Companion to International Criminal Law* (Farnham: Ashgate 2013), 453.

[38] M. P. Scharf 'The Iraqi High Tribunal: A Viable Experiment in International Justice?' (2007) 5 (2) *Journal of International Criminal Justice* 258; and M. Sissons and A. Bassin 'Was the Dujalil Trial Fair?' (2007) 5 (2) *Journal of International Criminal Justice* 272.

[39] Also known as truth and reconciliation commissions.

[40] P. De Greiff, *The Handbook of Reparations* (Oxford: Oxford University Press 2008).

Truth-seeking entities have been used in Latin America, Central and Eastern Europe, and parts of Africa. While the design of those mechanisms has varied, at the heart has been the right to truth and a victim-centred approach. The fundamental principles include truth, transparency, inclusivity, and accountability in the forms of apologies, reparations, or other methods. While a truth-seeking entity is not sufficient on its own to address the problem of peacekeepers who commit sexual abuse, there are many aspects of those mechanisms' methodology and approach that can and should be incorporated into the lens through which UN accountability laws are framed and implemented.

The right to truth is enshrined within international instruments,[41] and it has been focussed upon by the UN Human Rights Council,[42] the Office of the High Commissioner for Human Rights,[43] treaty bodies,[44] and Special Procedures.[45] At the regional level, the Inter-American Commission on Human Rights and the Inter-American Court of Human Rights have been central in developing jurisprudence on the right to truth. That Commission has emphasised the right of societies, as well as individuals, to truth,[46] and has

[41] These include International Covenant on Economic, Social, and Cultural Rights and the International Covenant on Civil and Political Rights; the Geneva Conventions of 12 August 1949 and the Additional Protocols thereto of 8 June 1977; and the International Convention for the Protection of All Persons from Enforced Disappearance, Article 24, para. 2, which sets out the right of victims to know the truth regarding the circumstances of the enforced disappearance, the progress and results of the investigation and the fate of the disappeared person and State party obligations to take appropriate measures in this regard. The Convention's preamble reaffirms the right to freedom to seek, receive, and impart information to that end.

[42] United Nations Human Rights Commission (UNHRC), 'Right to Truth' (1 October 2009) UN Doc. A/HRC/RES/12/12, para. 1; and UNHRC 'Right to Truth' (18 September 2008), UN Doc. A/HRC/RES/9/11, para. 1.

[43] United Nations High Commission for Refugees (UNCHR), 'Study on the Right to the Truth – Report of the Office of the United Nations High Commissioner for Human Rights' (8 February 2006) UN Doc. E/CN.4/2006/91; and UNHRC, 'Right to the Truth, Report of the Office of the High Commissioner for Human Rights' (7 June 2007) UN Doc. A/HRC/5/7.

[44] See, for example, UNCAT, 'Concluding Observations of the Committee Against Torture Colombia' (4 May 2010) UN Doc. CAT/C/COL/CO/4 (2010), para. 27.

[45] UNHRC, 'Report of the Working Group on Enforced or Involuntary Disappearances', (26 January 2011) UN Doc. A/HRC/16/48, para. 39; UNHRC, 'Report of the Special Rapporteur on the Promotion and Protection of Human Rights and Fundamental Freedoms While Countering Terrorism' (1 March 2013) UN Doc. A/HRC/22/52, paras. 23–26, 32–34; UNHRC 'Report of the Special Rapporteur on Torture and Other Cruel, Inhuman or Degrading Treatment or Punishment' (1 October 2007) UN Doc. A/HRC/7/3/Add. 3, para. 82; UNHRC 'Report of the Special Rapporteur on the Promotion and Protection of the Right to Freedom of Opinion and Expression' (20 April 2010) UN Doc. A/HRC/14/23, para. 34.

[46] Inter-American Commission on Human Rights (IACommHR), Annual Report, 1985–86, AS Doc. No. OEA/Ser.L/V/II.68, Doc. 8 rev. 1 (26 September 1986), 193.

4.3 A Victim-Centred Approach to Accountability

framed it as a positive obligation to inform victims and others about what took place in the context of human rights violations.[47] The European Court of Human Rights (ECtHR) also emphasises that the right belongs to victims, their next of kin, and the general public.[48] The African Commission on Human and Peoples' Rights places the right to truth as an aspect of the right to an effective remedy enshrined within the African Charter on Human and Peoples' Rights.[49]

The right to truth entitles the victim, their families, and the general public to seek and obtain all relevant information about an alleged violation.[50] Such information might include the whereabouts of the victim,[51] how the violation was officially authorised,[52] and the facts and context of the violation. The UN Special Rapporteur on Promotion of Truth, Justice, Reparation and Guarantees of Non-Recurrence has emphasised that to fulfil the right to truth institutions, mechanisms, and procedures must be established to enable truth to be revealed, 'which is seen as a process to seek information and facts about what has actually taken place, to contribute to the fight against impunity, to the reinstatement of the rule of law, and ultimately to reconciliation'.[53]

The right to truth necessarily entails a victim-centred approach to justice, which includes meaningful participation in and access to the process. As the Special Rapporteur has emphasised:

'Prosecutions, for their part, can only serve as actual justice measures if the victims and their families are effectively involved in the processes and provided with the necessary information relevant to their participation in proceedings. Local or traditional methods of rendering justice, when

---

[47] Inter-American Court of Human Rights (IACtHR), *Myrna Mack Chang v. Guatemala*, 25 November 2013 (Merits, Reparations and Costs), para. 274.

[48] European Court of Human Rights (ECtHR), *El-Masri v. the former Yugoslav Republic of Macedonia* (n° 39630/09), 13 December 2012, para. 191. The Court emphasises 'the great importance of the present case not only for the applicant and his family, but also for other victims of similar crimes and the general public, who had the right to know what had happened'.

[49] The Principles and Guidelines on the Right to a Fair Trial and Legal Assistance in Africa highlight that the right to an effective remedy includes 'access to the factual information concerning the violations'. Principle C (b) (3).

[50] UNCHR, 'Study on the Right to the Truth – Report of the Office of the United Nations High Commissioner for Human Rights' (n 43) para. 38.

[51] UNHRC (Working Group on Enforced or Involuntary Disappearances), (n 45), 12–17.

[52] General Assembly resolution 60/147, annex, para. 24; see also IACommHR Annual Report, 1985–1986 (n 46 above), 193; IACtHR *Myrna Mack Chang v. Guatemala*, (n 47 above), 274; ECtHR *El-Masri v. the former Yugoslav Republic of Macedonia* (n 48above), para. 192.

[53] UNHRC, 'Report of the Special Rapporteur on the Promotion of Truth, Justice, Reparation, and Guarantees of Non-Recurrence', (30 July 2013) UN Doc. A/HRC/24/42.

compliant with international fair trial guarantees, can reach out to the local population so they recognize them as "justice"'.[54]

Highlighting the role of victims and civil society, the Special Rapporteur takes a holistic approach to justice and to the design and implementation of that process. He also stresses the need for institutional and personnel reform in order to guarantee non-recurrence, which is a crucial aspect of justice. Within the comprehensive approach that he has set out, there is particular emphasis on the centrality of victims not only in relation to participation in criminal justice procedures but also in relation to visibility of victims and recognition of harms caused.[55]

4.3.3 Human Rights

The international human rights law mechanisms have been utilised by the UN to hold accountable state actors through complaints mechanisms within UN treaty bodies, through political methods at the UN Human Rights Council, amongst others. The UN has also set up bodies to examine human rights violations in peacekeeping operations where the mission became the sole sovereign power within a country.[56] But the question of whether a human rights-based approach can be used in relation to the UN is as yet unanswered. Such an approach is based on the UN being bound by fundamental rights to access a court and a remedy to truth and the prohibition against torture.

The right to truth has already been explored in this chapter, but there are other fundamental rights that are also violated by the current laws and practices in relation to accountability and peacekeepers. The right to access a court and an effective remedy is are fundamental rights found within the Universal Declaration of Human Rights, the International Covenant on Civil and Political Rights,[57] the European Convention on Human Rights and, most importantly, Customary Human Rights Law. They are non-derogable rights. They also form part of the general principles found within all legal systems.[58] Whether using the external, internal, or hybrid conception of UN human

---

[54] UNHRC, 'Report of the Special Rapporteur on the Promotion of Truth, Justice, Reparation and Guarantees of Non-Recurrence', (9 August 2012) UN Doc. A/HRC/21/46 para. 54.

[55] Ibid., paras. 54–58.

[56] For example the Human Rights Advisory Panel in Kosovo.

[57] Rios and Flaherty, 'Legal Accountability of International Organization: Challenges and Reforms' (n 9), 445–446.

[58] Statute of the International Court of Justice, annexed to the Charter of the United Nations 1948, Article 38.

4.3 A Victim-Centred Approach to Accountability

rights obligations, discussed in Chapter 3, the UN cannot claim not to be bound by these fundamental rights.

Although the UN 'may be under a duty to provide' access to courts or to seek a remedy for potential claimants, without which '[it] may encounter difficulties in insisting on [its] immunity from suit in national courts',[59] it is clear that the conflict is one between international rules inter se,[60] and many insist that the procedural rules on immunity take priority over the substantive rules on human rights. In order to prioritise human rights (substantive law) over immunities (procedural bars) in the conflict between substantive and procedural rules, we argue that when the UN acts like a state that it should be treated as one, and that includes adopting a human rights-based approach to the interpretation and application of immunity laws. That is not to say that we do not understand the need for immunity in order for the UN to undertake crucial activities but rather that human rights must be upheld and certainly not violated by that immunity: those two areas are not mutually exclusive.

It is clear that the current laws and practices violate that right of victims, either by the vast majority of prosecutions not occurring or taking place in countries where the victims do not have access to those courts or remedies. The prohibition against torture is also violated by the current system of laws and practices. Rape and sexual violence may constitute a human rights abuse in one of three ways: (1) If the rape or sexual violence was committed by a state agent with the explicit or tacit approval of the state (i.e. with impunity); (2) If the rape or sexual violence was committed by a private actor who then had impunity because the state failed to enact or implement effective criminal laws on those crimes; or (3) If state failures to investigate or prosecute amount to a violation of a victim's right to access a court and/or remedy and to truth.[61] When the UN is operating as a pseudo-state, if it is bound by IHRL then it will be liable for human rights abuses resulting from the impunity within which sexual abuse occurs. The prohibition of sexual abuse exists within UN policies and agreements, but the failures to implement those are akin to states failing to implement domestic laws on sexual abuse – thus amounting to torture.

The question that must be addressed, then, is whether the UN is bound by IHRL. The starting point is that other international organisations are viewed as being bound by IHRL. The ECtHR has made clear that it international

---

[59] Reinisch, *International Organizations Before National Courts* (n 8), 291.

[60] Wouters and Schmitt, 'Challenging Acts of Other United Nations' Organs' (n 25), 25.

[61] F. D Gaer 'Rape as a Form of Torture: The Experience of the Committee against Torture' (2012) 15 (2) *CUNY Law Review* 293.

organisations may be bound by IHRL[62] although those cases are not at all concerned with activities related to peacekeeping. Similarly, other international organisations have adopted similar positions to the ECtHR.[63] There clearly is some movement towards international organisations' immunity being restricted for human rights reasons, mainly where there is no alternative or effective dispute settlement mechanism. Some scholars have insisted that this approach 'must be approved' under a right-based approach.[64]

National courts have considered the incompatibility between IHRL and the doctrine of absolute immunity in terms of international organisations[65] and specifically the UN. The first such case, *Manderlier v. Organisation des Nations Unies et l'Etat Belge*,[66] laid foundations for a potential human rights-based challenge to UN immunity. The Appeals Court criticised 'the present state of international institutions [being that] there is no court to which the appellant can submit his dispute with the United Nations' as being a situation that 'does not seem to be in keeping with the principles proclaimed in the Universal Declaration of Human Rights'. Whilst the court ultimately upheld the UN's absolute immunity, the case highlights the tension between absolute immunity and human rights. It is important to note that this case was brought at a time when IHRL was being codified. More than 40 years later, there is greater potential for challenging immunities on the basis of the developed rights.

More recent cases[67] demonstrate that the door is ajar for a human rights-based challenge to the UN immunity laws and frameworks. Each of these cases was decided on its own facts, with the courts finding that there were alternative modes of settlement available to the claimants. The courts, however, did all set out the principle that a human rights-based challenge might be successful if the Organisation's immunity violates an individual's human

---

[62] *Waite and Kennedy v. Germany*, Application No. 26083/94 (2000) 30 EHRR 261; *Beer and Reagan v. Germany*, Application No. 28934/95 (2001) 33 EHRR 54.

[63] *Chadsey v. Universal Postal Union*, ILO Administrative Tribunal, 15 October 1969, Judgement No. 122, UNJYB (1968), at 176; *Teixera v. Secretary-General of the United Nations*, UN Administrative Tribunal, 14 October 1977, Judgement No. 230.

[64] Paust, 'The UN Is Bound By Human Rights (n 5); Wouters and Schmitt, 'Challenging Acts of Other United Nations' Organs' (n 25).

[65] Reinisch 'The Immunity of International Organizations and the Jurisdiction of their Administrative Tribunals' (n 1).

[66] *Manderlier v. Organisation des Nations Unies et l'Etat Belge (Ministre des Affaires Etrangeres)*, Brussels Civil Tribunal, 11 May 1966, (1966) Journal des Tribunaux 721; (1972) 45 ILR 446.

[67] *Urban v. United Nations*, 768 F2d 1497, 1500 (DC Cir 1985); *Mothers of Srebrenica et al. v. State of the Netherlands and the UN*, District Court in The Hague, 10 July 2008, 295247/HA ZA 07-2973; *Mothers of Srebrenica v. Netherlands & United Nations*, Case No. 200.20.151/01, Judgment (Appeal Ct. Hague 30 March 2010).

4.3 A Victim-Centred Approach to Accountability

rights. Wouters and Schmitt assert that the question that arises 'is not so much a conflict between internal and international rules, but rather between international rules *inter se*'.[68] If a national court were to allow the claims to be brought against the UN, it would breach its obligations towards the UN. However, it may be 'permissible justification' if the court were 'to argue that the right' that has been violated 'may be considered as *jus cogens*' (of such a fundamental nature that there can be no limitations of or derogations from these rights). Holding that the rights to access a court or to a remedy are jus cogens[69] would enable a national court to uphold a challenge to the UN's immunity without breaching its own obligations.

Freedman insists that when the UN is acting as a sovereign or hybrid sovereign power, it ought to be treated like a state; therefore, the UN ought to be able to be held accountable if it violates human rights in those circumstances.[70] Hovell takes a different approach, arguing that due process rather than human rights ought to be central to how the UN is treated, but she largely reaches the same conclusions regarding the end result.[71] Indeed, Hovell's thesis is that there is currently insufficient theoretical underpinning to inform the ad hoc practice on UN accountability, and that without the theoretical framework there will be no consistency for victims. That lack of uniformity is all-too-clear when it comes to peacekeeping and accountability.

As discussed in Chapter 3, the UN has taken some steps towards embedding human rights across peacekeeping activities generally. While these are not directly focussed on accountability, they demonstrate UN recognition of the need to foreground human rights in peacekeeping. The Rights Up Front Action Plan emphasises the need to adopt a rights-based approach to all UN activities and requires a focal point within every UN department and agency.[72] Small steps are being taken towards implementing that Action Plan, but it is hampered by current accountability laws that lead to a culture of impunity within which serious harms are caused followed by an ongoing denial of victims' rights. The tension between those incremental steps towards implementing human rights obligations and the current laws on accountability once

---

[68] Wouters and Schmitt, 'Challenging Acts of Other United Nations' Organs' (n 25).

[69] See, for example, A. Bianchi 'Human Rights and the Magic of Jus Cogens' (2008) 19 (3) *European Journal of International Law* 491.

[70] Freedman, 'UN Immunity or Impunity?' (n 28); see also R. Freedman and N. Lemay-Hébert '"Jistis ak Reparasyon pou Tout Viktim Kolera MINUSTAH': The United Nations and the Right to Health in Haiti' (2015) 28 (3) *Leiden Journal of International Law* 507.

[71] D. Hovell 'Due Process in the United Nations' (2016) 110 (1) *American Journal of International Law* 9.

[72] A. Gilmour 'The Future of Human Rights: A View from the United Nations' (2014) 28 (2) *Ethics & International Affairs* 239.

again highlight the need for a new, holistic, victim-centred approach to immunities and jurisdictional bars.

4.3.4 *Political Processes*

Accountability may also occur through political processes that encourage, or even coerce, states to uphold their obligations to investigate and prosecute crimes of sexual abuse. Despite some commentators insisting that political processes cannot be relied upon to ensure accountability,[73] it is clear that such processes have a significant role to play. While politics cannot fulfil the role of law, in the international arena, political processes often are deployed to ensure that states implement international laws. To do so, the political cost of not upholding legal obligations must outweigh any costs to the state of fulfilling their obligations. Of course, political processes are far from sufficient on their own to address the problem. Yet, they play a vital role and must be considered in any discussions about a holistic approach to accountability.

Over recent years, the UN has deployed a range of political processes aimed at encouraging states to investigate and prosecute peacekeepers for crimes of sexual abuse. Steps forward such as 'naming and shaming' states that fail to comply with their obligations as well as repatriating contingents where sexual abuse is rife have contributed to improved investigation and prosecution of sexual crimes. However, there is scope for further efforts in this regard. Political processes could be deployed to ensure that internationally accepted definitions and standards of sexual abuse are agreed within the international arena and then are used for international peacekeepers. Such a move would circumvent the need for a new convention,[74] a proposal that has been mooted but that is unlikely to be accepted by states. Similarly, politics could be used to ensure that other legal gaps and flaws are addressed, for example by not allowing countries to contribute troops or for nationals to apply for UN positions unless or until there are national laws enabling extraterritorial criminal jurisdiction for sexual abuse. Political processes have also been used to encourage the UN to comply with its obligations. Advocacy and lobbying efforts by civil society has placed significant pressure on the UN and member states to address failures within the Organisation. As a result, independent reviews and panels have been appointed that have recommended stronger policies, improved compliance,

[73] See, for example, the Code Blue Campaign: www.codebluecampaign.com/ (accessed April 2020).

[74] Z. Deen-Racsmány 'Towards a Convention on the Criminal Accountability of UN Personnel Including UN Military Experts on Mission and UN Police Officers' (2016) 54 (2) *Military Law and the Law of War* 195.

and greater transparency. That work, in turn, has led to significant improvements in UN compliance with its obligations.

4.4 CONCLUSION

In this chapter, we have set out the laws governing UN immunities, why the UN in its practice of peacekeeping is bound by fundamental human rights, and how those rights are violated by current practices. What becomes clear from the following three case studies is that the current laws and practices on immunities of the UN and its personnel operate in such a way as to undermine individuals' human rights. Given that the UN is bound by IHRL when acting externally, it is bound to implement fundamental rights and to provide remedies where they are violated. Where the UN is in effective control of an area, the denial of individuals' fundamental rights to access a court and a remedy ought not to be able to be justified by pointing to procedural bars. If states are not able to avoid their human rights obligations by using immunities as a shield, then the UN when acting as a sovereign or hybrid-sovereign power ought to be treated in exactly the same manner. Whether this would more effectively and appropriately be operationalised through new international agreements that enshrine human rights or through a human rights-based interpretation of current laws remains to be seen. But it is clear that current practices cannot continue without severely damaging the legitimacy of the UN and its external activities, and without continuing to violate the rights of some of world's most vulnerable individuals.

5

The Cholera Epidemic

Unintended Consequences and Implications

5.1 INTRODUCTION

The UN's involvement in Haiti will long-be remembered by the introduction of cholera by peacekeepers in the aftermath of the 2010 earthquake. To many Haitians and observers, the cholera crisis and UN failures to provide justice for victims is emblematic of the UN presence and legacy within the country. This may of course be unfair when considering the many positives for which the UN and its personnel are responsible, but the scale of the cholera crisis, and the refusal of the UN to clear up its own mess, is arguably one of peacekeeping's starkest wrongs since the military failures to protect humans from genocide in Rwanda and in the Former Republic of Yugoslavia.

There are many facets to this topic. In this chapter, we focus on the Haiti Cholera Claims as the clearest example of how UN immunity can prevent individuals from accessing their fundamental rights to access a court and a remedy. The introduction of cholera into Haiti, failures to contain and eradicate the disease, and denial of access to remedies demonstrates how UN immunity impacts on victims of private law claims. In these circumstances the harms are caused by the UN itself, rather than being attributable to acts of individual personnel, and UN immunity laws violate victims' ability to access a court and a remedy. A decade after cholera was brought into Haiti by UN peacekeepers, the victims are still waiting for justice despite it being promised to them by the former UN Secretary General in 2016. In this chapter we first set out the background to the cholera epidemic in Haiti before turning to how immunity laws and practices in this situation have violated victims' human rights, the fight for justice, and what has, and has not, been done to resolve the situation.

5.2 CHOLERA IN HAITI: AN OVERVIEW

The cholera epidemic broke out in the Artibonite region of Haiti in October 2010, with the first case of severe diarrhoea on 12 October, and the first hospitalisation on 17 October. Prior to that date, there had been no recorded cases of cholera in Haiti for over a century.[1] The population was therefore immunologically naive and highly susceptible to infection.[2] Between October and December 2010, approximately 150,000 people had contracted cholera and 3,500 had died; by the end of 2013, the cholera outbreak had killed more than 8,000 people and infected over 670,000 individuals, making it one of the most deadly cholera outbreaks in recent history.[3] There is no way of knowing how many people have been killed, sickened, or impacted by cholera to date, as all records are acknowledged to be incomplete. It was described by local journalists as the 'Haitian 9-11'.[4] Rumours spread that the Nepalese battalion based in Mirebalais in the Artibonite region was responsible for introducing cholera to Haiti. Associate Press journalists witnessed septic tanks overflowing and the smell of excrement at the Nepalese base on 27 October. A dark liquid apparently flowed out of a broken pipe towards the Meille River,[5] a tributary to the Artibonite River, which is the nation's largest and most important river providing water to 1.5 million people. Other rumours mentioned the possible illegal dumping of waste tank contents next to the river.[6] The Nepalese camp was identified by local inhabitants as the most likely source of the disease, and it is important to note that Nepal suffered cholera outbreaks only weeks before the UN troops' deployment.[7] Within weeks of the first cases, there were reports of crowds

---

[1] D. A. Walton and L. C. Ivers 'Responding to Cholera in Post-Earthquake Haiti' (2011) 364 *New England Journal of Medicine* 3, 4.

[2] Center for Disease Control and Prevention, Cholera Outbreak: Haiti, October 2010, (2010) 59 Morbidity and Mortality Weekly Report 43, 1411

[3] A. Dasgupta et al. 'Evolutionary Perspective on the Origin of Haitian Cholera Outbreak Strain' (2012) 30 (3) *Journal of Biomolecular Structure and Dynamics* 338.

[4] Interview with Daly Valet, Editor-in-Chief, *Le Matin* newspaper in Port-au-Prince, Haiti (1 February 2011).

[5] M. Stobbe and E. Lederer, 'UN Worries Its Troops Caused Cholera in Haiti', *The Associated Press*, 19 November 2010; J. Katz, *The Big Truck That Went By: How the World Came to Save Haiti and Left Behind a Disaster* (New York: St. Martins Press 2013), 228. MINUSTAH officials claimed that the pipe was coming from the kitchen, not the toilets, but as Jonathan Katz put it, 'it doesn't smell like a kitchen'.

[6] F. Tasker and F. Robles, 'Source of Cholera Outbreak May Never Be Known', *Miami Herald*, 20 November 2010. A reporter from the Associated Press witnessed such an occurrence only days after the cholera outbreak. See Katz, *The Big Truck That Went By* (n 5), 229.

[7] L. Maharjan, 'Cholera Outbreaks Looms Over Capital', *The Himalayan Times*, 23 September 2010.

68 *The Cholera Epidemic*

throwing stones at UN peacekeepers' armoured personnel carriers and of repeated clashes between Haitians and the UN forces, many ending in deaths.[8]

A new Nepalese battalion arrived in Haiti in October 2010 and was deployed to the Mirebalais camp in three waves (9 October 2010, 12 October 2010, and 16 October 2010).[9] There is still confusion about whether or not the soldiers were tested prior to their deployment in Haiti, with conflicting reports from different official sources. General Kishore Rana, the Nepalese Army's chief medical officer, stated that 'none of the troops exhibited symptoms of cholera – so no follow-up tests were done'.[10] This statement was contradicted by the Under-Secretary-General for Peacekeeping Operations, Alain Le Roy, who insisted that the soldiers all tested negative for that particular strain.[11] What is clear is that the cholera screening protocols were inadequate to prevent the Haitian epidemic.[12] In general, UN protocol requires that troops pass a basic health screening. Symptomatic individuals undergo laboratory tests for infectious diseases, but the UN does not test individuals who do not exhibit active symptoms. However, many of those shedding viable cholera bacteria remain asymptomatic. Furthermore, the South Asian strain of cholera active in Haiti has been shown to cause greater number of asymptomatic cases, to persist longer in the environment, and to exist in higher concentrations in faeces.[13] However, the problem is not just the lack of appropriate testing. Cholera and diarrhoea are not listed in the *Medical Support Manual for United Nations Peacekeeping Operations* as conditions precluding peacekeeping service,

---

[8] D. Coughlin, 'WikiLeaks Haiti: US Cables Paint Portrait of Brutal, Ineffectual and Polluting UN Force', *The Nation*, 6 October 2011; P. Farmer, *Haiti after the Earthquake* (New York: Public Affairs 2011), 196; N. Lemay-Hébert, 'Resistance in the Time of Cholera: The Limits of Stabilization Through Securitisation in Haiti' (2014) 21 *International Peacekeeping* 2.

[9] Katz, *The Big Truck That Went By* (n 5), 230.

[10] 'Haiti Cholera Outbreak: Nepal Troops Not Tested', *BBC News*, 8 December 2010, www .bbc.co.uk/news/world-south-asia-11949181 (accessed 28 April 2020). This statement is supported by the UN Spokesperson, Vincenzo Pugliese, who mentioned to an Associated Press journalist that none of them tested positive because they had never been tested. Katz, *The Big Truck That Went By* (n 5), 233.

[11] United Nations Department for Public Information, Press Conference by the Under-Secretary -General for Peacekeeping Operations (2010), www.un.org/News/briefings/docs/2010/101215_ Guest.doc.htm; See also: CNN Wire Staff, 'UN Investigates Allegations of Cholera Source in Haiti', CNN, 28 October 2010.

[12] P. S. Keim et al., 'Reply to "South Asia Instead of Nepal may be the Origin of the Haitian Cholera Outbreak Strain"', (2011) 2 *MBio* 6, http://mbio.asm.org/content/2/6/e00245-11.full (accessed 28 April 2020).

[13] Farmer, *Haiti after the Earthquake* (n 8), 195.

and examination only has to take place within three months of deployment, leaving plenty of time for soldiers to contract the disease.[14]

Haiti's inadequate sewage and sanitation systems, exacerbated by the 2010 earthquake, and the deficiencies in the UN sanitation standards, which was already an issue in 2008,[15] have been deemed a 'perfect storm' for the outbreak of a massive epidemic of cholera by a team of researchers from the University of Maryland led by the renowned microbiologist, Rita Colwell. The researchers conclude that the 'assignment of attribution remain[s] controversial'.[16] The 'perfect storm' theory provided a welcome cover for MINUSTAH and the United Nations' legal department, both of which used the theory to claim that responsibility for introducing cholera has not conclusively been attributed to a single source.[17] However, the 'perfect storm' theory has been considered 'a perfect lie' by French epidemiologist Renaud Piarroux, who wrote an initial report on the cholera outbreak in Haiti.[18] For Piarroux and his colleagues, all of the scientific evidence demonstrates that the cholera is attributable to the Nepalese contingent travelling from a country experiencing a cholera epidemic, and that faecal contamination of a local stream draining into the Artibonite River initiated the epidemic.[19] Those scientists rebutted all the claims made by the University of Maryland researchers and clearly demonstrated that their research 'provided no evidence to counter that cholera was brought to Haiti by a contingent of Nepalese United Nations peacekeeping troops'.[20] Despite the

[14] Katz, *The Big Truck That Went By* (n 5), 233. The UN's expert panel mentioned a 10-day free period for Nepalese soldiers to visit their families after medical examination was completed. A. Cravioto et al., Final Report of the Independent Panel of Experts on the Cholera Outbreak in Haiti 12 (2011), www.ijdh.org/2012/08/topics/health/final-report-of-the-independent-panel-of -experts-on-the-cholera-outbreak-in-haiti (accessed 28 April 2020).

[15] Coughlin, 'WikiLeaks Haiti' (n 8).

[16] N. A. Hasan et al. 'Genomic Diversity of 2010 Haitian Cholera Outbreak Strains' (2012) 109 *Proceedings of the National Academy of Sciences of the United States of America* 29, www .pnas.org/content/early/2012/06/12/1207359109.full.pdf+html (accessed 28 April 2020).

[17] Personal interview with MINUSTAH Communications and Public Information Officer, 9 December 2011.

[18] T. Daniel, 'Source of Haiti Cholera Bug Goes Under Microscope', *Associated Press*, 17 July 2012.

[19] R. Piarroux et al. 'Understanding the Cholera Epidemic, Haiti' (2011) 17 *Emerging Infectious Diseases* 1161.

[20] R. R. Frerichs et al. 'Source Attribution of 2010 Cholera Epidemic in Haiti' (2012) 109 *Proceedings of the National Academy of Sciences of the United States of America* 47, www .pnas.org/content/109/47/E3208.full (accessed 28 April 2020). The world-renowned cholera expert, John Mekalanos, was similarly 'shocked' by Hasan et al.'s claims, judging that there was 'compelling evidence' that the cholera strain was inadvertently introduced into Haiti by Nepalese troops. J. J. Mekalanos et al. 'Non-01 Vibrio Cholerae Unlinked to Cholera in Haiti' (2012) 109 *Proceedings of the National Academy of Sciences of the United States of America* 47, www.pnas.org/content/109/47/E3206.full (accessed 28 April 2020).

70 *The Cholera Epidemic*

subtle pressure placed on the scientists not to investigate the cause of the outbreak further,[21] the link with the South Asian strain has been confirmed by numerous field investigations,[22] including the UN's Independent Panel of Experts on the Cholera Outbreak in Haiti.[23] It is now widely accepted that the cholera outbreak is directly attributable to UN peacekeeping troops from Nepal. The UN Special Envoy, Bill Clinton, recognised that UN peacekeepers were the proximate cause of cholera in Haiti.[24]

After the introduction and outbreak, the international aid machinery led by the UN failed to take the necessary steps to contain and eradicate cholera in Haiti in at least two ways. First, the UN's World Health Organization (WHO), amongst other actors, battled against mass vaccination in Haiti, citing cost, logistical challenges and limited vaccine supplies. Vaccination is clearly an option that could have saved lives in the first two years of the outbreak. Instead, the UN adopted a 'wait-and-see' approach. Within weeks, Haiti's Ministry of Public Health and Population (MSPP), the Pan-American Health Organization (PAHO), the Centers for Disease Control and Prevention (CDC), and various UN agencies developed a *National Response Strategy against cholera* to monitor disease trends, detect outbreaks, and characterise the affected population to target relief efforts.[25] At the same time, distrust of some cholera programmes among the population impeded the construction of treatment centres and the delivery of life-saving supplies.[26] Despite this, some non-governmental organisations (NGOs), including *Médecins Sans Frontières* (MSF), and some states, including Cuba, worked effectively in providing fluid resuscitation and dealing with

---

[21] As Martin Enserink reports for the journal Science the passion of cholera experts 'for traditional shoe-leather epidemiology has been tempered by diplomatic and strategic concerns'. M. Enserink 'Despite Sensitivities, Scientists Seek to Solve Haiti's Cholera Riddle' (2011) 28 *Science* 388.

[22] See, for example, R. R. Frerichs et al. 'Nepalese Origin of Cholera Epidemic in Haiti' (2012) 18 *Clinical Microbiology and Infection* 158; R. S. Hendriksen et al. 'Population Genetics of Vibrio Cholera From Nepal in 2010: Evidence on the Origin of the Haitian Outbreak' (2011) 2 *MBio* 4; C. Chin et al. 'The Origin of the Haitian Cholera Outbreak Strain' (2010) 364 (1) *New England Journal of Medicine* 33.

[23] The panel found that 'the strains isolated in Haiti and Nepal during 2009 were a perfect match'. A. Cravioto et al., 'Final Report of the Independent Panel of Experts on the Cholera Outbreak in Haiti' (n 14), 12, 27.

[24] Clinton: UN Soldier Brought Cholera to Haiti, *Al Jazeera*, 8 March 2012.

[25] P. Santa-Olalla et al. 'Implementation of an Alert and Response System In Haiti During the Early Stage of the Response to the Cholera Epidemic' (2013) 89 (4) *American Journal of Tropical Medicine and Hygiene* 688.

[26] D. Sontag, 'In Haiti, Global Failures on a Cholera Epidemic', *The New York Times*, 31 March 2012.

up to 80 per cent of cases.[27] A debate swiftly emerged between public health experts regarding the opportunity for mass vaccination in Haiti. The 'minimalists', including the WHO, favoured investment in health education and massive distribution of chlorine tablets while the 'maximalists' argued that all the tools for preventing its spread should be used, that is including a roll-out of vaccine.[28] With no consensus attained in the first years, the minimalist position was implemented de facto. Two years after the outbreak, the vaccination campaign was finally implemented in the Autumn of 2012.[29]

The second way in which the UN failed Haiti after the cholera outbreak was by not investing in a large-scale improvement of water and sanitation system in Haiti before and immediately after the cholera outbreak despite the peace-keeping mission's mandate to capacity-build and implement national infra-structures. Mark Schuller from New York City University reported that immediately prior to the outbreak, 40.5 per cent of camps did not have water, and 30.3 per cent of camps did not have a single toilet. By January 2011, 37.6 per cent still lacked water and 28.5 per cent remained without a toilet.[30] In the words of an MSF official, 'the inadequate cholera response in Haiti makes for a damning indictment of an international aid system whose architecture has been carefully shaped over the past 15 years'[31] especially the cluster system put into place by the UN's Office of the Coordinator of Humanitarian Affairs. The only hope of eradicating cholera in Haiti would be to couple the vaccination campaign with large scale investments in the water and sanitation system, something that the UN still has not implemented.[32] The UN later agreed on a \$2.2 billion plan to eradicate cholera in Haiti, but again that occurred too late for most observers and remained significantly underfunded.

---

[27] Farmer, *Haiti after the Earthquake* (n 8), 198; Ibid.; J. Biquet 'Haiti: Between Emergency and Reconstruction' (2013) 5 *International Development Policy* 2.

[28] The maximalists included the Deputy UN Special Envoy, Paul Farmer, Economist Jeffrey Sachs, and various medical researchers. See Farmer, *Haiti after the Earthquake* (n 8), 198; D. A. Walton and L. C. Ivers 'Responding to Cholera in Post-Earthquake Haiti' (2011) 364 *New England Journal of Medicine* 3; L. C. Ivers et al. 'Five Complementary Interventions to Slow Cholera: Haiti' (2010) 376 *The Lancet* 2048. The minimalists included the World Health Organization and Pan-American Health Organization.

[29] L. C. Ivers et al. 'Use of Oral Cholera Vaccine in Haiti: A Rural Demonstration Project' (2013) 89 (4) *American Journal of Tropical Medicine and Hygiene* 617.

[30] M. Schuller, *Killing with Kindness: Haiti, International Aid, and NGOs* (New Brunswick: Rutgers University Press 2012), 173.

[31] U. Karunakara, 'Haiti: Where Aid Failed', *The Guardian*, 28 December 2010.

[32] International Crisis Group, 'Towards a Post-MINUSTAH Haiti: Making an Effective Transition', Latin America/Caribbean Report N°44 12, 2 August 2012; P. Adams 'Haiti Prepares for Cholera Vaccination but Concerns Remain' (2012) 379 *The Lancet* 16.

5.3 UN-ACCOUNTABLE: THE FIGHT FOR JUSTICE

Not only did the UN fail to protect Haitians from the introduction of cholera into the country and to prevent the spread and continued existence of the disease, it also failed to provide a remedy to individuals affected by the outbreak of cholera. As explained in Chapter 4, the UN has immunity from the jurisdiction of national courts. As a counterbalance to that immunity, as discussed, the UN must set up alternative dispute resolution mechanisms to enable victims to access a court and a remedy. In Haiti, the UN failed to set up such mechanisms for the cholera victims.

After the outbreak of cholera, the UN refused to take responsibility for introducing cholera into Haiti. According to a senior UN official with signifi-cant field experience in Haiti, the decision not to accept responsibility was based on the context within the country at that time: 'Haiti was hanging by a thread at that time, particularly in terms of civil disobedience, and with no functioning police or jails after the earthquake. If the UN had admitted liability it would have been unable to help with all of the other issues going on at that time, so instead the UN said that it was waiting for scientific reports and evidence on cholera'.[33] He also claimed that 'many different factors contributed to the difficulty in dealing with the outbreak. First and foremost, the perception of UN being involved led to difficulty in helping possible victims, with staff being stoned and attacked by local populations. The per-ception of UN involvement meant that many internationals, including those not working for the UN, were kept behind closed doors for their own safety, which meant that supplies did not get through to the people who needed them'.[34]

Amongst the first responders to the cholera victims were staff members from *Bureaux des Avocats Internationaux* (BAI) and the Institute for Justice and Democracy in Haiti (IJDH).[35] Those linked organisations, based in Port au Prince and Boston, respectively, are public interest lawyers who work in Haiti to implement human rights and rule of law, alongside their political objective of restoring Aristide as President. When it became clear that the UN was refusing to take responsibility for the outbreak and was not taking sufficient steps to contain and eradicate the disease, BAI and IJDH began to collect testimonies and stories from cholera victims, their families, and their

---

[33] Interview with senior UN official from the Executive Office of the Secretary General, UN Headquarters, New York, 15 June 2015.

[34] Ibid.

[35] www.ijdh.org/2010/01/topics/law-justice/institute-for-justice-democracy-in-haiti-home-67/?cat=1849 (accessed 28 April 2020).

communities.[36] According to Beatrice Lindstrom, an IJDH lawyer working in Haiti at that time, 'we were all waiting for the UN to investigate and respond to cholera; especially when evidence emerged so quickly that the UN was responsible. But nothing happened'.[37] She explained that the Haitians with whom they worked 'knew immediately that the UN would not respond justly' and that 'connections were being made between cholera and past grievances against the UN. It was part of the same narrative that instances of abuse were not being responded to in a just way'.[38] Despite that, IJDH and BAI decided 'to just wait, because the evidence was so clear that we believed that the UN had to respond'.[39] However, by late October, the Haitian grassroots and diaspora were asking BAI and IJDH to help with cholera. They initially went to one village for a town hall meeting: 'We were expecting 15 people to show up, but 300 people had come from all over to tell their stories about cholera and its impact. No-one had come to talk to them from the government or the UN or the NGOs. We were the first ones even to show up.'[40]

Lindstrom and the team from BAI recorded information from everyone who came to that first town hall meeting, as they 'realised from a humanitarian and accountability perspective that this information needed to be recorded'.[41] It soon became apparent to them 'that the healing process could not occur without accountability and without people's voices being heard. We were not thinking about legal action, but simply about connecting with communities and giving voice to survivors'.[42] However, in January 2011, the UN Secretary General appointed a panel of experts, and the turning point for IJDH and BAI was when they saw the final report[43] and 'realised that the UN would not accept responsibility or be honest about the evidence. We realised that we needed to do something, to find a strategy for getting accountability from the UN'.[44]

The decision to attempt to sue the UN represented a last-gasp attempt to influence the organisation to provide remedies or dispute resolution to Haiti's cholera victims. Almost every legal expert acknowledged that the procedural

---

[36] IJDH, 'Cholera Litigation: Frequently Asked Questions', available at www.ijdh.org/cholera-litigation-frequently-asked-questions/ (accessed 28 April 2020).

[37] Interview with Beatrice Lindstrom, lawyer for IJDH, New York, 17 June 2015.

[38] Ibid.

[39] Ibid.

[40] Ibid.

[41] Ibid.

[42] Ibid.

[43] A. Cravioto et al., 'Final Report of the Independent Panel of Experts on the Cholera Outbreak in Haiti' (n 14).

[44] Interview with Beatrice Lindstrom, lawyer for IJDH, New York, 17 June 2015.

bars preventing the UN being brought before a national court would not be overturned or circumvented. However, the lawsuit itself brought such strong and sustained publicity that it became pivotal as a piece of strategic litigation that achieved its aims outside of the courtroom. Before turning to the lawsuit as part of the overall advocacy strategy, it is important to understand why the very idea of suing the UN was both radical and unlikely ever to succeed.

As any good lawyer will acknowledge, the courtroom ought to be the last resort in any dispute. After BAI and IJDH had gathered stories and testimonies from cholera-affected communities, they first sought alternative dispute resolution from the UN in line with section 29 of the CPIUN. The UN, first at MINUSTAH in Haiti and later at headquarters in New York, blocked attempts by BAI and IJDH to access alternative dispute resolution mechanisms on behalf of cholera victims.[45] They were first told that no claims commission had been established for MINUSTAH, and eventually the UN Office of Legal Affairs informed them that claims could be filed directly with MINUSTAH but did not provide any information about how to do so.[46] In August 2011, after months of research, IJDH found a UN General Assembly Resolution with a claims form attached in the annex. Using that form, 5,000 victims filed claims in November 2011, petitioning for remedies in the form of eradicating cholera, compensation, and a public acknowledgement of wrongdoing.[47] Although the Office of Legal Affairs acknowledged receipt of the claim form, there was no response from the UN to the cholera victims or their representatives.[48] The UN's Office of Legal Affairs, according to a senior UN official, is staffed with attorneys who 'act as though the UN is their client'.[49] Once the claims were filed, UN staff were told not to discuss it on the record, and all political efforts to resolve the claims ceased 'because everything freezes while the UN was waiting for case to be resolved'.[50]

It took until February 2013 for the UN to respond, which it did by stating that the claims were 'not receivable pursuant to Section 29 [of the CPIUN]' because the 'consideration of these claims would necessarily include a review of political and policy matters'.[51] The claimants asked for clarification of the grounds for the UN not receiving the claims, and sought alternative dispute resolution, all of

---

[45] IJDH, 'Cholera Litigation' (n 36).
[46] Ibid.
[47] Interview with Beatrice Lindstrom, lawyer for IJDH, New York, 17 June 2015.
[48] IJDH, 'Cholera Litigation' (n 36).
[49] Interview with senior UN official from the Executive Office of the Secretary-General, UN Headquarters, New York, 15 June 2015.
[50] Ibid.
[51] UN Secretary General's statements and messages, 'Haiti Cholera Victims' Compensation Claims 'Not Receivable' under Immunities and Privileges Convention, United Nations Tells

5.3 Un-Accountable: the Fight for Justice

which were refused. In October 2013, the case of *Georges v. United Nations* was filed in the United States District Court for the Southern District of New York.[52] Those claims were filed against the UN, MINUSTAH, the UN Secretary General, and the former head of MINUSTAH. The claims were filed in New York because the UN is headquartered in that city, and because major decisions about cholera in Haiti were made in those headquarters.[53] The court case was a class action suit filed on behalf of thousands of victims, something that could not occur in the Haitian court system.[54] Although it was filed in 2013, the UN did not formally respond to the claims. Had it done so, that response would have been used to demonstrate that the UN did not hold absolute immunity from being brought before a national court. Instead, the UN asked the US Government, as the UN's host nation, to seek dismissal of the case. In March 2014, the US attorney submitted a Statement of Interest, which insisted that the UN has absolute immunity in US courts,[55] a position upheld by Judge Oetken in dismissing the case on 9 January 2015.[56] A notice of appeal was filed on 12 February 2015, the oral arguments were heard on 1 March 2016, and on 18 August 2016 the Court upheld the UN's immunity from claims.

5.3.1 *The Legal Argument*

It is important to understand those claims and the different arguments presented by the lawyers before turning to how the dispute was resolved using politics and human rights. The claims filed in a New York District Court and later to the Appeals Court on behalf of 5,000 individuals affected by cholera in Haiti[57] alleged negligence, gross negligence and/or recklessness by the UN and MINUSTAH. The lawsuit filed against the UN stated that the Organisation's actions and failures to act are

the direct and proximate cause of the cholera related deaths and serious illnesses in Haiti to date, and of those certain to come. The U.N. did not

---

Their Representatives', 21 February 2013, UN Doc. SG/SM/14828, available at www.un.org/press/en/2013/sgsm14828.doc.htm (accessed 28 April 2020).

52 Class Action Complaint, *Georges v. United Nations*, Docket # 1:13-cv-07146-JPO 65, ¶ 2 (S.D. N.Y. filed 9 October 2013).

53 IJDH, 'Cholera Litigation:' (n 36)

54 Ibid.

55 United States Government Statement of Interest, *Georges v. United Nations*, No. 1:13-cv-07146-JPO (S.D.N.Y. filed 7 March 2014).

56 *Georges v. United Nations*, 84 F. Supp.3d 246, 2015 WL 129657, at *4 (S.D.N.Y. 2015)

57 For analysis on the lawsuit and the human-rights based challenge to UN absolute immunity, see R. Freedman 'UN Immunity or Impunity? A Human Rights Based Challenge' (2014) 25 (1) *European Journal of International Law* 239.

adequately screen and treat personnel coming to Haiti from cholera stricken regions. It did not adequately maintain its sanitation facilities or safely manage waste disposal. It did not properly conduct water quality testing or maintain testing equipment. It did not take immediate corrective action in response to the cholera outbreak.[58]

In February 2013, the UN responded to the Haitian claims by detailing the financial aid and other resources it has provided to prevent and reduce the spread of cholera. As has already been discussed, the UN's efforts in leading the international aid community's response to the cholera outbreak have been inadequate, at best, in terms of responding to and eradicating cholera in Haiti. The UN has failed to address the substance of the claims – that it was responsible for the cholera and therefore liable to the victims. Instead, the UN insists that the claims were 'not receivable' by the Organisation.[59] The UN's position is that the claims involve review of political and policy matters[60] and therefore are not private law claims. This essentially bars the claims being heard by the UN's dispute resolution mechanisms. In July 2013, the UN refused a request for compensation filed on behalf of the cholera victims, again citing its immunity from jurisdiction.[61]

The claims filed on behalf of the cholera victims focus on compensation for private law claims. They key issue for the courts was whether to place greater emphasis on the principles of the UN holding absolute immunity from jurisdiction of national courts or on the fundamental human rights to access a court and to access a remedy. At both stages, the courts dealt with this issue as a procedural matter and were concerned with whether the absolute immunity of the UN resulted in the claims not being able to be heard. Despite sympathetic judgments from the court of first instance and the appeals court, at both stages it was ruled that the procedural bar created by the UN's absolute immunity prevented the courts from hearing the claims.

The lawsuit was concerned with private law claims and therefore does not address whether the UN is bound by international human rights law and whether it has violated any human rights in respect of the cholera outbreak.

---

[58] 'Petition for Relief', 3 November 2011, para. 57 available at www.ijdh.org/wp-content/uploads/2011/11/englishpetitionREDACTED.pdf (accessed 28 April 2020)

[59] UN Department of Public Information (New York), Haiti Cholera Victims' Compensation Claims 'Not Receivable' under Immunities and Privileges Convention, United Nations Tells Their Representatives, UN Doc. SG/SM/14828 (21 February 2013).

[60] Ibid.

[61] Letter from Ban Ki-moon, UN Secretary-General, to Maxine Waters, US Representative for California's 43rd congressional district (5 July 2013) www.ijdh.org/wp-content/uploads/2013/07/UNSG-Letter-to-Rep.-Maxine-Waters.pdf (accessed 28 April 2020).

That question goes to the heart of whether and in what circumstances the UN may be bound by international human rights law, as discussed in Chapter 3. Those arguments complement the claims being brought against the UN by demonstrating that the organisation is bound not only to prevent future violations but also to remedy those that have already occurred. And those arguments were at the heart of the broader political strategies deployed for resolving the dispute. In many ways the legal case was strategic litigation, taken forward as a method for gaining attention to the situation which in turn strengthened the ongoing political efforts to resolve the dispute.

5.4 HOW THE DISPUTE WAS (NOT) RESOLVED BY POLITICS

Holding accountable the UN is not a simple matter, or one that can occur quickly or easily, and it relies as much – if not more – on politics than on law. It requires many stakeholders coming together and pursuing separate and inter-linked avenues. A key obstacle to finding a political resolution in the early years was that once the initial court case had been filed, the UN and its member states, under instructions from the UN Office for Legal Affairs, refused to discuss a political settlement for fear that it may prejudice or jeopardise the UN's position that it held absolute immunity from the jurisdiction of national courts.[62] By the time that the appeal was filed in 2016, the landscape had changed significantly, with many member states recognising that there was almost no chance that UN immunity would not be upheld, and with many stakeholders inside and outside of the UN calling for justice for the victims. It is crucial to understand the role of the activities that took place in parallel to the court cases, and to understand the timing of those activities. Most significantly, the UN Secretary General finished his term in December 2016, and pressure was placed on him to address the stain on his legacy of the failure to provide justice to the cholera victims. Second, from 2016, the UN Security Council was engaged in ending the UN stabilisation presence in Haiti, and transforming its presence to a rule of law, demilitarised operation. Third, it was clear that if the appeal was not successful that IJDH was unlikely to seek appeal to the US Supreme Court.

Key to resolving the cholera claims were the many different pressure points placed on the UN, including through law, politics, advocacy, and public pressure. In parallel to the strategic litigation there were significant efforts by many stakeholders – some public and some private – to encourage the UN to

---

[62] Interview with senior UN official from the Executive Office of the Secretary General, UN Headquarters, New York, 15 June 2015.

resolve the dispute. Key among those were the activities of UN human rights bodies and independent experts, in particular Philip Alston, academics including those involved with the Birmingham Initiative, and member states particularly the Elected Members of the Security Council and the Group of Friends of Haiti. At the heart of that work was the desire to ensure justice for the survivors, and in parallel to all of that work was public advocacy undertaken by all actors and entities involved with the fight for justice for cholera victims and survivors.

The head of IJDH, Brian Concanon, emphasised that 'the case also enables bringing in a huge network of people including academics, scientists, civil society organisations, and others to become actors and advocates on cholera. The IJDH vision of the case is that no one is independent; everyone is part of a broader connected network and everyone informs the advocacy'.[63] The diplomatic, political, and advocacy strategies were undertaken by different actors and stakeholders, with varying levels of formal or informal coordination with the one another and with the lawyers representing the cholera victims. Key actors included UN independent experts on human rights who placed private and public pressure on the UN Secretary General, the former UN Office of Legal Affairs staff members who advised IJDH and BAI, academics who wrote amici briefs and academic work on the topic, physicians and public health experts, journalists who provided media coverage, and the victims who engaged with the UN and member states. Many of the activities of those broad networks are on the public record, including the letters[64] and reports written by UN independent experts, and the coverage by individual journalists such as Colum Lynch for *Foreign Policy* and Somini Sengupta for *The New York Times*. Other activities remain off the record, particularly where they involved senior members of the UN working for the Organisation at that time.

5.4.1 *Public Awareness*

One pressure point on the UN was raising awareness, within the UN and member states and amongst the wider public, of the cholera outbreak, the UN's role, and the failure to provide justice to the victims. Initially little attention was paid to the issue by international media. However, in the two

---

[63] Interview with Brian Concanon, head of IJDH, New York, 16 June 2015.

[64] P. Alston, Extracting Accountability: Special Rapporteurs and the United Nations' Responsibility for Cholera in Haiti: *UN Report – unpublished Alston, P. (n.d.). Extracting Accountability: Special Rapporteurs and the United Nations' Responsibility for Cholera in Haiti* (February 2018) NYU School of Law, Public Law Research Paper No. 18-10. Available at SSRN: https://papers.ssrn.com/sol3/papers.cfm?abstract_id=3125084 (accessed 28 April 2020).

5.4 How the Dispute Was (Not) Resolved by Politics

years after the outbreak scientific analyses,[65] academic articles,[66] and policy reports[67] were published that provided key material for advocacy efforts. After the court cases were filed, media interest increased, as did the interest of civil society groups outside of the core organisations working in Haiti or within its diaspora populations. Initially coverage was limited to areas such as Miami where large Haitian diaspora live, Boston where IJDH is based, as well as some articles in New York where the claims were filed and in Washington where there was interest in the United States defending the court case. By 2015, media coverage included regular articles in international media such as *Foreign Policy*, *The Guardian*, and *The New York Times*, as well as news channels such as *Al-Jazeera*, *Channel 4 News*, and *France 24*.[68] Academics, former UN staff members, former diplomats, and civil society groups regularly wrote and spoke out about Haiti and cholera, ensuring greater awareness and sustained attention on the fight for justice. The strategic litigation clearly was key to securing this level of public awareness, as the court cases provided a hook for stakeholder to understand and explore the key issues. Off the record, more than five interviewees within the UN spoke of the pressure placed on the Secretary General by each major news story, in particular, those that appeared in *The New York Times*. Awareness was also raised and pressure exerted by victims telling their stories to the media, to the UN, and to member states. One instrumental example was the letter-writing campaigns organised by IJDH and aimed at the UN and at its member states' missions to UN headquarters,[69] which many of the states we later met with referenced in their knowledge and understanding of the cholera claims.

5.4.2 UN Independent Experts on Human Rights

United Nations independent experts on human rights are appointed specific thematic or country mandates for a fixed term. They are unpaid, and conduct their duties part-time with some logistical and research support from the Office of the High Commissioner for Human Rights. Appointed by the

---

[65] For example, R. Piarroux et al. 'Understanding the Cholera Epidemic, Haiti' (2011) 17 (7) *Emerging Infectious Diseases* 1161.

[66] For example, F. Megret 'La Responsabilité Des Nations Unies Aux Temps Du Choléra' (2013) 46 (1) *Revue Belge de Droit International* 161.

[67] For example, Centre for Economic and Policy Research, 'MINUSTAH by the Numbers', 8 December 2011, www.cepr.net/minustah-by-the-numbers (accessed 28 April 2020).

[68] For a representative list of media coverage, see: www.ijdh.org/choleraaccountability/cholera-resources/ (accessed 28 April 2020).

[69] IJDH, 'Cholera Victims' Letters and Translations', 2015, www.ijdh.org/2015/12/topics/health/cholera-victims-letters-and-translations/ (accessed 28 April 2020).

Human Rights Council, those experts report to that body and to the General Assembly, and the system of 'Special Procedures'[70] – the term for all of the mandate holders – is considered the 'crown jewel' of the UN human rights system. Given their expertise and their status within the UN, key mandate holders were able to use their positions to place considerable pressure on the UN, and to raise awareness in UN human rights bodies in Geneva.

On 25 September 2014, four mandate holders with particular interests in the cholera claims wrote to the UN Secretary General to express concern about the way in which the UN was handling the claims. Those mandate-holders were responsible for (1) housing (Leilani Farha), (2) Haiti (Gustavo Gallón), (3) health (Dainius Pūras), and (4) water and sanitation (Catarina de Albuquerque).[71] The UN response was sent by Assistant Secretary General Pedro Medrano, Senior Coordinator for Cholera, in which he set out the UN's legal arguments for not receiving the claims.[72] That letter was significantly more detailed than any response given by the UN to the cholera victims or their lawyers either prior to or during the litigation.

On 23 October 2015, the four original mandates (three being the same individuals, and the fourth on water and sanitation now being held by Leo Heller), joined by the Special Rapporteur on extreme poverty and human rights (Philip Alston) again wrote to the UN Secretary General. They expressed concern about victims being denied an effective remedy, and suggested that the UN hold informal consultations.[73] The UN Deputy Secretary General Jan Eliasson responded on 25 February 2016, after the appeal had been filed, welcoming the mandate holders' offer 'to engage further on this matter and discuss what further steps the United Nations could take, in keeping with its mandates, to assist the victims of cholera and their communities'.[74] According to Alston, prior to that letter and to the appeal being filed, on 15 January 2016 'the Secretary-General met at UN Headquarters with the Special Rapporteur on extreme poverty. Two issues were discussed, one of which was the importance of UN engagement in response to the cholera communication'.[75]

The impact of the pressure from the UN independent experts cannot be underestimated, and continued after the Security Council meeting in

---

[70] See A. Nolan, R. Freedman, and T. Murphy (eds.), *The United Nations Special Procedures 'System'* (Leiden: Brill-Nijhoff 2017).
[71] Alston, Extracting Accountability (n 64 above), 7-14
[72] Ibid., 15–48.
[73] Ibid., 49–52.
[74] Ibid., 53–64.
[75] Ibid.

5.4 *How the Dispute Was (Not) Resolved by Politics* 81

March 2016 at which many member states for the first time in that body spoke out about the need for the UN to address cholera in Haiti. While we will go into that in detail in Section 4, it is crucial to understand that the continued public and private pressure from Philip Alston, Special Rapporteur on extreme poverty, was instrumental in ensuring that the cholera claims were resolved. He had further meetings with the other mandate holders and with the Secretary General, in April[76] and June[77] respectively, and wrote a report for the UN General Assembly that was sent to the Secretary General on 8 August 2016[78] prior to the appeal court ruling, and that was officially published on 26 August 2016[79] after the appeal ruling upheld UN immunity. However, the blow to the victims of that appeal court ruling was somewhat softened by a front page story on that same day – 18 August 2016 – in The New York Times setting out 'key details of the draft report and quoted a spokesman for the Secretary-General as saying in response that "over the past year, the UN has become convinced that it needs to do much more regarding its own involvement in the initial outbreak and the suffering of those affected by cholera", and announcing that a "new response will be presented"'.[80] The efforts of Alston and other mandate holders had a clear impact and were crucial aspects of the activities parallel to the strategic litigation and that resulted in resolution of the dispute.

5.4.3 *Birmingham Initiative*

The Birmingham Initiative was another parallel activity that occurred as part of the global efforts seeking justice for the cholera victims. In 2013, two academics at the University of Birmingham – Rosa Freedman and Nicolas Lemay-Hébert – were approached by IJDH and asked to provide research on a human rights-based challenge to UN immunity from the jurisdiction of national courts.[81] Together they fused their knowledge of Haiti, peacekeeping, unintended consequences of interventions, the UN, and human rights, to contribute to the activities seeking justice for the cholera victims. They also continued to work with IJDH including writing an amici brief for the court,

---

[76] Ibid., 65–69.

[77] Ibid.

[78] Ibid.

[79] UN General Assembly, 'Extreme Poverty and Human Rights', 26 August 2016, UN Doc. A/ 71/367.

[80] Alston, Extracting Accountability (n 64 above) citing Jonathan M. Katz, 'U.N. Admits Role in Cholera Epidemic in Haiti,' *New York Times*, 18 August 2016, available at www.nytimes.com /2016/08/18/world/americas/united-nations-haiti-cholera.html?_r=0.

[81] That report formed the basis for Freedman, 'UN Immunity or Impunity?' (n 57).

publishing and presenting academic work,[82] writing media articles,[83] and raising awareness in the public sphere.[84] In August 2015, before the Appeals were filed, it was agreed with IJDH that the University would convene an independent expert workshop in Birmingham that would focus on parallel processes to take place while the appeals were filed and heard. Although supported by IJDH, the Birmingham workshop was convened and held independently of that organisation.

The timing of the workshop was key because there was a need to provide an alternative political solution for dispute resolution that could be table when the appeals were filed. All actors and stakeholders were aware that if the appeals were not successful, which was likely given the procedural bar of UN immunity, there was a short period of time in which to place pressure on the UN Secretary General before his term came to an end. Attendees included current and former senior UN officials, UN independent experts on human rights, and experts on epidemiology, water and sanitation, humanitarian responses, and transitional justice. Attendees came from all regions of the world, and included individuals from Haiti and from regional allies in neighbouring countries. The workshop aimed to produce a broad resolution framework that might be acceptable to and accepted by all parties, that would take into account the local context, and that might serve as a starting point for political and diplomatic discussions in parallel to the legal processes going through the New York court system. The workshop, held in December 2015, produced a draft resolution framework (Appendix I) and an executive summary (Appendix II). Broadly, the three parts of that resolution framework were: (1) an apology and an acknowledgement that the UN caused harm, (2) reparations or remedies for the victims, and (3) elimination of cholera in Haiti.

In March 2016, soon after the oral arguments were heard by the Appeals Court, a small representative delegation from the Birmingham Initiative visited New York to undertake bilateral diplomatic meetings with states seized with the Haiti cholera situation, and with key UN personnel. The purpose of those meetings was to present the draft resolution framework as a potential starting point for the basis of diplomatic negotiations. That framework

---

[82] For example, R. Freedman and N. Lemay-Hébert, 'Human Rights and UN Immunities' in T. Ruys et al. (ed.) *Handbook on Immunities in International Law* (Cambridge University Press 2018); R. Freedman and N. Lemay-Hébert, '"Jistis ak reparasyon pou tout viktim kolera MINUSTAH": The United Nations and the Right to Health in Haiti' Leiden Journal of International Law (2015), 507–527; R. Freedman and N. Lemay-Hébert 'Towards an Alternative Interpretation of UN Immunity: A Human Rights-Based Approach to the Haiti Cholera Case' (2015) 19 *QIL-Questions of International Law*, 5–18.

[83] Including for *The Conversation*, CNN, *Georgetown Journal*, *MUNPlanet*, amongst others.

[84] Including interviews for *Al-Jazeera*, *France 24*, *Sky News*, amongst others.

5.4 *How the Dispute Was (Not) Resolved by Politics*

represented only the expertise of individuals at the Birmingham workshop and was used to move the conversations beyond the usual phrasing that 'something ought to be done' and towards a discussion of what that something might look like in practice. The timing of the visit was a few weeks before the UN Security Council mid-year review of MINUSTAH, with the aim of ensuring that justice for cholera victims was discussed at that Council session. In all, the delegation met with 8 members of the UN Security Council and another 7 countries with strong links to Haiti. As a result of those meetings and of other parallel activities, 11 of the 15 Council members raised the issue of cholera during that Council session, and many of those states became central to the efforts to secure justice for the victims.

5.4.4 *The Security Council*

One of the sources of power of the permanent members of the Security Council is their ability to chair 'informal sessions', where the 'real work of the Council takes place'.[85] These sessions do not need to be open to elected members, as they are not official meetings, and the work done in these informal meetings structures the official meetings, making them a 'proforma affair, scripted in these advance informal consultations'.[86] This is particularly true in the case of Haiti, with dynamics within the Security Council regarding Haiti illustrating the dominance of its five permanent members, and the importance of the United States within that group.[87] According to former Canadian Ambassador to the UN, David Malone, 'non-permanent members influence the course of events, often by participating in Groups of Friends, but theirs are not the key voices'.[88] The key voices tend to be the P3 – the United States, the United Kingdom, and France as a grouping of three of the five permanent members of the UN Security Council – and especially the United States in the case of Haiti. However, in a rather unusual configuration, none of the Permanent Members were willing to take the lead on the cholera issue in 2016. In bilateral meetings with France, the United Kingdom, and the United States, different reasons were set out for each country neither supporting nor blocking resolution of the Haiti Cholera Claims. This allowed space for the

---

[85] I. Hurd 'Legitimacy, Power, and the Symbolic Life of the UN Security Council' (2002) 8 (1) *Global Governance* 43.

[86] Ibid.

[87] D. Malone 'Haiti and the International Community: A Case Study' (1997) 39 *Survival* 126. The role of the United States as 'penholders' has been recognised by other P3 countries in private interviews.

[88] Ibid., 138.

Elected Members to take the lead in calling for a political resolution and for justice without being blocked by the Permanent Members or losing political capital with those states.

The United States remained largely silent on this issue because, as the host nation to the UN headquarters, it was tasked with defending UN immunity from the jurisdiction of its New York courts. Hence, the main focus of the American delegation was on the court cases, and on the potential precedents any recognition of liability could create for other cases of 'unintended consequences' of peacekeeping operations. The reticence of the American delegation, usually in the leading seat regarding Haitian issues, was clearly the crucial factor in opening up political space for other actors – first and foremost, the elected members of the Security Council and other member states – to play a role in the settlement of the cholera issue. France, with its history in Haiti, was unwilling to speak out on behalf of the need for compensations of victims of cholera – which may have led to entangle the issue with the slave-reparations to the country. This happened in a context of the first formal visit of a French President in Haiti, in May 2015, which put the 'independence debt' of Haiti back in the news.[89] Finally, the United Kingdom has little, if any, interest in Haiti as a former-Francophone colony halfway across the world. The United Kingdom was also similarly worried about the legal liability of the organisation, as well as the potential precedent this would set. Russia and China paid little interest to Haiti or to the cholera victims, with both countries opposed to human rights being brought into the body's work, and with their attention focussed firmly on ensuring that resolutions on Syria were blocked or even not tabled during those years.

When the 'powerful states' do not use the Security Council to either pass or block Resolutions, it 'creates an opening for weaker agents to appropriate and manipulate the meaning of the symbols'.[90] The elected members can then act as agents of 'discursive power', understood as the ability to promote and impose concepts as the basis of preferred policies. As Langmore and Farrall argue, 'the litmus test of effectiveness for elected members is whether and how they are able to adapt to the constraints and make the most of their limited opportunities to promote their desired outcomes'.[91] Elected members of the Security Council clearly past the test in our test case, seizing the opportunity offered by the P3 silence, hence demonstrating that strategic and innovative

---

[89] See for instance: www.theguardian.com/world/2015/may/13/hollande-haiti-visit-france-former-colony

[90] Hurd, 'Legitimacy, Power, and the Symbolic Life of the UN Security Council' (n 85), 36.

[91] J. Langmore and J. Farral 'Can Elected Members Make a Difference in the UN Security Council? Australia's Experience in 2013–2014' (2016) 22 *Global Governance* 59, 63.

5.4 How the Dispute Was (Not) Resolved by Politics

non-members can contribute to and influence UN Security Council outcomes in a variety of ways.[92]

Outside of the Security Council membership, other states took a keen interest in the initiative and used their political capital to encourage elected members to champion the cause. This is especially true for the Group of Friends of the UN Secretary General for Haiti (hereafter referred to as The Group of Friends), a particularly dynamic group influencing governance in the Security Council. Already in 1995, Boutros-Boutros Ghali explained that 'a new concept, that of "Friends of the Secretary-General" ... means that, while the UN peacekeepers are on the ground, intense diplomatic efforts continue with many parties to a conflict in order to reach a political settlement'.[93] After the military coup that ousted Jean-Bertrand Aristide in 1991, the Group of Friends was established approximately in January 1993,[94] with four states with long-standing economic and other ties with Haiti as members: France, Canada, and the United States, along with Venezuela.[95] These four countries were to form a loose alliance in support of democracy in Haiti. When the United Nations reengaged in Haiti in 2004, a larger core group – including many troop-contributing countries from Latin America – was formed even as the Friends of Haiti drove the decision-making in the Security Council.[96] The Group of Friends of Haiti has steered the Haiti issue in the UN Security Council (UNSC) since 1993.[97]

At the March 2016, UN Security Council mid-year review of MINUSTAH, the cholera issue, and even the issue of the source of the epidemic and the need for a new approach, was distinctly raised. The meeting, as is the case for all review meetings of peace operations, was meant to provide a contact point

---

[92] J. Farrall and J. Prantl 'Leveraging Diplomatic Power and Influence on the UN Security Council: The Case of Australia' (2016) 70 *Australian Journal of International Relations* 601, 602.

[93] United Nations, 'SG's Statement at Institute of International Affairs, New Zealand, DPI Press Release' (1995) U.N. Doc. SG/SM/5624, 1 May. For an overview of the influence of informal groups of states, see: J. Prantl 'Informal Groups of States and the UN Security Council' (2005) 59 *International Organization* 559; J. Prantl, *The UN Security Council and Informal Groups of States: Complementing or Competing for Governance?* (Oxford: Oxford University Press 2006).

[94] J. Prantl and J. E. Krasno, 'Informal Groups of Member States' in J. E. Krasno, (ed.) *The United Nations: Confronting the Challenges of a Global Society* (London: Lynne Rienner 2004), 342.

[95] Malone 'Haiti and the International Community' (n 87), 127.

[96] T. Whitfield, *Working with Groups of Friends* (Washington: US Institute of Peace Press 2010), 43. The Group of Friends now includes Argentina, Brazil, Canada, Chile, Colombia, France, Guatemala, Peru, the United States, Uruguay, and Venezuela.

[97] Malone 'Haiti and the International Community' (n 87), 140. Confirmed by Deputy Permanent Representative of France at the UN, Alexis Lamek in a personal interview, 29 February 2016, New York.

86 *The Cholera Epidemic*

between the Secretary General and his representative in Haiti, and Council members over the performance of the mission and challenges faced on the ground. The most important issue raised by all parties was the stalled electoral process at the time, but mentions of cholera did not go unnoticed. Most Council members raised the issue along the traditional line of the humanitarian challenge posed by cholera, which is how cholera has been discussed at the UN Security Council in previous meetings, but some elected members did raise the cholera issue as a human rights issue. This was a pivotal moment in relation to Haiti and cholera, as it represented the first time that states had publicly called for the UN to ensure justice for the victims. Rather than this issue being raised by stakeholders outside of the UN or by the UN's independent human rights experts, its member states were breaking the years of silence on cholera, and sending a clear message to the Secretary General and his team. The need for a new approach was carried loud and clear by specific elected members, as permanent members decided to frame the cholera issue as a humanitarian issue.

Interestingly enough, the *Security Council Report* published ahead of the March meeting,[98] considered by a former diplomat who operated at the Security Council as a 'highly valuable reservoir of virtual institutional memory on which the E10 diplomats (and probably those from the P5) repeatedly draw',[99] did not forecast any discussion on a new approach to deal with the cholera issue in its briefing, or on compensations and reparations to victims, with only a brief mention in the reports of the humanitarian challenge posed by the illness. The Special Representative of the Secretary General, Ms Sandra Honoré, opened up the March meeting with her briefing of the situation of the country, in which there was not a single mention of the cholera issue. She also presented, as it is the tradition, the Secretary General Report on Haiti, which only included references to cholera as a humanitarian issue – looking at prevention and containment of the illness, but without mentioning the political issue of reparation and compensations to victims. The framing of cholera as a humanitarian issue was also shared by P-5 states at the meeting. The representative of the United Kingdom mentioned 'that terrible disease is a scar on Haitian citizens. After all that they have been through, they cannot afford to fact that further assault

---

[98] Security Council Report 'Haiti' March 2016 Monthly Forecast www.securitycouncilreport.org /monthly-forecast/2016-03/haiti_9.php (accessed 28 April 2020); see also: What's in Blue, Council Debate on Haiti 16 march 2016 www.whatsinblue.org/2016/03/council-debate-on-haiti.php (accessed 28 April 2020).

[99] Langmore and Farral, 'Can Elected Members Make a Difference in the UN Security Council? (n 91), 70.

5.4 How the Dispute Was (Not) Resolved by Politics

on their lives and livelihoods'.[100] The framing of cholera as humanitarian issue also shared by the French delegation, mentioning that 'we must do more as an international community to eradicate cholera in Haiti once and for all'.[101] The representative of the Russian Federation also mentioned his concern for 'the unstable situation that has resulted from cholera',[102] without getting into specifics, and the American and Chinese representatives did not raise the cholera issue. The framing of cholera as a humanitarian issue was also shared by certain non-permanent members and other invited states in their formal statements, including Brazil, Chile, Colombia, Egypt, Guatemala, Haiti, Mexico, Peru (on behalf of the Group of Friends), Saint Vincent and the Grenadines (on behalf of Caribbean Community, CARICOM), Ukraine, and Uruguay.

However, other non-permanent members raised the issue of cholera through a human rights lens and the need for a new approach from the UN. In the formal statements, the clearest message came from the representative of Malaysia, who said that 'we would encourage greater engagement by the Secretariat with those [cholera] victims, particularly on the issue of possible remedies and compensations, where appropriate. It is important for the continuing credibility of and respect for the United Nations as a whole that the Secretary-General exercise and demonstrate leadership on this issue, including by responding to the letter of allegations from the Human Rights Council special procedures'.[103] The representative of New Zealand also mentioned that 'the United Nations must continue to support those affected in Haiti and take appropriate action to help close that chapter and ensure that the new Government is not left alone to address the ongoing consequences and political legacy of the outbreak'.[104] The representative of Venezuela further mentioned that 'the grave human impact of the emergence and spread of cholera since 2010 cannot be ignored'.[105]

Soon after the Security Council session, a delegation from the Organisation of Americas States visited Haiti, and cholera was high on their list of discussion points, and many of those countries continued to be seized of the issue of how to provide justice for cholera victims. Alongside those efforts, many states raised the issue at the UN Human Rights Council during the March 2016 session, partly in response to the report of the Independent Expert on Haiti who repeated

---

[100] United Nations Security Council, The Question Concerning Haiti, UN. Doc. S/PV.7651, 17 March 2016, 11/29.

[101] Ibid., 14/29.

[102] Ibid., 11/29.

[103] Ibid., 16/29.

[104] Ibid., 6/29.

[105] Ibid., 9/29.

88 *The Cholera Epidemic*

his recommendations on resolving the cholera claims,[106] but also because they had been briefed by their missions in New York. After the Secretary General introduced his new approach to cholera in Haiti, most importantly underlining the political question behind the issue, the next semi-annual review of MINUSTAH at the Security Council saw a number of representations discussing the political nature of the issue. As the representative of Uruguay mentioned, 'we welcomed with great satisfaction the new United Nations approach to cholera, and in our capacity as Chair of the Group of Friends of Haiti, we coordinated the efforts towards the adoption of General Assembly resolution 71/161, which welcomed that new approach. Today, we also welcome the references to cholera contained in the report of the Secretary-General, in particular the reference to the certain political role for the new mission, in complement to the efforts of the United Nations country team'.[107]

5.5 CONCLUSION

The use of political processes to complement legal ones, and relying on the UN to use its own institutions, ensured that some positive steps were taken but did not result in effective remedies for all cholera victims in Haiti. That being said, it was clear that the legal route would not succeed, and ultimately was a vehicle for ensuring public attention to ensure that the situation was not altogether ignored and pushed under the carpet. Despite the UN Secretary General appointing a task force on cholera in September 2016, and his apology to cholera victims at the end of that year, to date the UN has not provided remedies to the victims, and it has not contained cholera in Haiti. The UN agreed on a $2.2 billion plan to eradicate cholera, but this occurred too late and remains significantly underfunded. There are many factors underpinning these failures, ranging from lack of funding from member states, a retreat from multilateralism by the United States, a new Secretary General who is not seized of this matter, and ongoing instability and development needs in Haiti. Regardless of those factors, the fact remains that nearly eight years after cholera first broke out in Haiti, victims are still waiting for justice. As one cholera victim told us in 2017: 'I am not asking for much, all I want is some money to replace the goats I had to sell to take my sick child to hospital. Without those goats I cannot afford to educate that child. Apologies do not cure diseases'.

---

[106] UN General Assembly, 'Extreme Poverty and Human Rights' (n 79).
[107] United Nations Security Council, The Question Concerning Haiti, UN. Doc. S/PV.7920, 11 April 2017, 4/30-5/30.

6

Sexual Exploitation and Abuse

Who Guards the Guardians?

6.1 INTRODUCTION

Peacekeepers have been implicated in sex scandals since the early 1990s when cases were reported in Bosnia-Herzegovina, Cambodia, the DRC, East Timor, Eritrea, Haiti, Kosovo, Liberia, South Sudan, and West Africa. This issue continues today, as has most recently been exposed in relation to peacekeepers in the Central African Republic. As peacekeeping operations have evolved and grown, there have been greater numbers of victims of sexual exploitation and abuse (SEA). Since 2001 the United Nation (UN) has sought to implement reforms and policies to address, prevent, and remedy the perpetration of those harms, with varying degrees of success.

The catalyst for UN focus on sexual exploitation and abuse by peacekeepers was the report by consultants from Save the Children UK and the UN Refugee Agency (UNHCR) of widespread child abuse by humanitarian workers and peacekeepers in West Africa. Responding to those allegations, the UN conducted an investigation in Guinea, Liberia, and Sierra Leone. The UN investigation did not find evidence to support all of the allegations and some of its findings contradicted the earlier reports. However, the Secretary-General's subsequent 2002 report based on those findings prompted the UN to address the causes and consequences of sexual exploitation and abuse. In particular, the definitions of sexual exploitation and abuse provided the basis for the UN's zero tolerance policy contained in the Secretary General's 2003 Bulletin that has become known as the 'Zero Tolerance' policy.[1] Key recommendations included identifying areas where policies, procedures, and practices should be put in place to prevent sexual exploitation and abuse.

---

[1] UN Secretary-General (UNSG), *Secretary-General's Bulletin: Special Measures for Protection from Sexual Exploitation and Sexual Abuse*, 9 October 2003, ST/SGB/2003/13, www .refworld.org/docid/451bb6764.html (accessed 29 April 2020).

After those reports on sexual exploitation and abuse of children were published, scholars and practitioners focused significant attention on the causes and consequences of sexual harms being perpetrated in such a widespread manner. Proposals for reforms and improvements were set out, with particular emphasis on laws, gender, human rights, cultural understandings, training, accountability, justice, and remedies. Those areas are reflected in UN proposals and reforms aimed at tackling sexual exploitation and abuse over the past fifteen years, although many have occurred *ad hoc* or in piecemeal ways. Moreover, those proposals and reforms have been aimed at different actors and entities, and have been implemented to different degrees of success in different parts of UN peacekeeping operations.

With each new revelation of systematic abuse and systemic failures, to deal with such abuse there has been another round of attempts by the UN to reform the laws and governing practices around the edges of the problem. But, as we shall see, none of those reform proposals provides holistic and robust methods for tackling sexual exploitation and abuse by all actors within all peacekeeping entities. Understanding these reform attempts and why they have not fully been successful is crucial when turning to the case study of UN peacekeeping in Haiti and identifying areas of good practice and of weakness.

6.2 SEXUAL EXPLOITATION AND ABUSE IN PEACEKEEPING

Since 1996, when the first UN report connecting sexual abuse and peacekeeping was published,[2] there have been some key developments aimed at addressing the problem. However, following allegations of sexual exploitation and abuse by peacekeepers in West Africa, reform efforts began in earnest. The UN General Assembly adopted resolution 57/306,[3] which in turn led to a Secretary–General's Bulletin on 'Special measures for protection from sexual exploitation and sexual abuse' in October 2003.[4] The 'Zero Tolerance Policy',[5] as it has become known, provides extensive guidance regarding sexual

---

[2]   G. Machel, 'Impact of Armed Conflict on Children' (United Nations Office of the Special Representative of the Secretary-General for Children and Armed Conflict 1996), 98.

[3]   UN General Assembly, Investigation into sexual exploitation of refugees by aid workers in West Africa: Resolution adopted by the General Assembly 22 May 2003, www.refworld.org/docid/3f45e4f4o.html (accessed 29 April 2020).

[4]   UN Secretary-General, *Secretary-General's Bulletin: Special Measures for Protection from Sexual Exploitation and Sexual Abuse*, 9 October 2003, ST/SGB/2003/13.

[5]   For further discussion see: N. Dahrendorf, *Sexual Exploitation and Abuse: Lessons Learned Study, Addressing Sexual Exploitation and Abuse in MONUC* (UNDPKO, Best Practices Unit, March 2006); S. Mendelson, *Barracks and Brothels: Peacekeeping and Human Trafficking in the Balkans* (Washington: Centre for Strategic and International Studies, February 2005).

conduct by UN staff and peacekeepers. It includes a prohibition on sexual relations with members of the local community, given the 'inherently unequal power dynamics'; sexual activity with children, 'regardless of the age of majority or age of consent locally', and engaging in prostitution in general.[6] The Bulletin also mandates that the Secretary–General publishes an annual report with data on allegations and information on measures being taken to strengthen prevention, enforcement, and remedial action.

In 2005, after further scandals, the UN published 'A Comprehensive Strategy to Eliminate Future Sexual Exploitation and Abuse in United Nations Peacekeeping Operations'.[7] The 'Zeid Report', as it has become known, noted the *ad hoc* development of an 'extensive mosaic of provisions' dealing with sexual abuse,[8] and the differences in rules for different categories of personnel. The report emphasized the different problems in relation to rules pertaining to troops and to civilians. Recommendations from that report ranged from incremental and softer approaches to radical reform proposals. Those proposals were aimed at the full range of actors and entities involved in peacekeeping operations, with different ones directed to states, Troop-Contributing Countries (TCCs), UN entities, and the UN itself. Some proposals have been adopted by some actors – albeit not in a uniform or consistent manner – such as troop-contributing countries holding more *in-situ* courts martial to make it easier for victims and witnesses to testify.

The report also focused on formal legal agreements, proposing amendments to the model Memoranda of Understanding and Security Council resolutions that would strengthen how sexual abuse was dealt with by troop-contributing countries, including requirements on reporting and on definitions of sexual abuse. It was noted, however, that the rules on state sovereignty preclude the UN from being able to obligate troop-contributing countries to prosecute their nationals. That issue, coupled with the problems in terms of civilian staff who commit sexual abuse in countries with inadequate or no functioning legal systems, led to a more radical reform proposal that has not been enacted, even though it still has not formally been rejected at the time of

---

[6] *Secretary-General's Bulletin: Special Measures for Protection from Sexual Exploitation and Sexual Abuse*, ST/SGB/2003/13 (n 4 above), 3.2.

[7] *A comprehensive strategy to eliminate future sexual exploitation and abuse in United Nations peacekeeping operations*, (Zeid Report) UN General Assembly Resolution A/59/710, 24 March 2005. See also General Assembly Resolution 59/300 on Comprehensive Review of a Strategy to Eliminate Future Sexual Exploitation and Abuse in United Nations Peacekeeping Operations, A/RES/59/300, 22 June 2005.

[8] Zeid Report 2005 (n 7), 22.

writing. That proposal was the development of an international convention that would subject UN personnel to the jurisdiction of host states of peace-keeping operations. Initially the proposed convention was aimed at all peace-keepers, although in subsequent discussions it has only been discussed in relation to civilians and experts on mission. The alternative, somewhat softer, suggested solution was 'to try to get agreement with the host state when negotiating the status-of-forces agreement for the UN to provide assistance to the host state to ensure that criminal proceedings against United Nations personnel satisfied international human rights standards'.

The UN has also focused on ensuring that all types of personnel are required to have adequate standards of training on international laws and standards, such as on what constitutes a child, definitions of sexual abuse and exploitation, and codes of conducts. Training on its own is not suffi-cient to tackle the problem but is one key component to prevent sexual abuse by peacekeepers. It now asks countries to certify that troops have been trained prior to deployment and also provides in-theatre training itself following deployment. There has been concerted efforts at the UN Security Council, especially within resolutions about women, peace and security that include requests for 'the Secretary-General to continue and strengthen efforts to implement the policy of zero tolerance on sexual exploitation and abuse by UN personnel and urges concerned Member States to ensure full accountability, including prosecutions, in cases of such conduct involving their nationals'.[9] These efforts, combined with reports and investigations by the UN and independent experts, have been criticised by some observers as not going far enough to effect meaningful change.[10] Others, however, have pointed to the downward trend in allega-tions and the potentially positive impact of UN reforms and initiatives in preventing abuse,[11] although of course fewer reports of allegations in any organisation are one indicator that there may be failings or weaknesses in the reporting systems. Moreover, using reports as an indicator does not take into account that many allegations relating to sexual exploitation and

---

[9]   UN Security Council Resolution S/RES/2106 of 24 June 2013.

[10]   For example, 'Seminal reports by experts have been commissioned and revised memoran-dums that afford the UN much stronger powers of oversight have been signed, yet years after a series of comprehensive strategies were recommended in 2006, little appears to have changed: accountability remains the exception to the rule, new abuses continue to be reported, and the business of sexual exploitation and abuse in peacekeeping continues' – C. Ferstman, *Criminalizing Sexual Exploitation and Abuse by Peacekeepers*, Special Report 335 (Washington: USIP 2013), 2.

[11]   J. Stern, *Reducing Sexual Exploitation and Abuse in UN Peacekeeping: Ten Years after the Zeid Report* (Washington: Stimson Centre, February 2015).

abuse related to acts from years in the past. Certainly, the greater transparency since 2003 has had an impact in terms of sharing and disseminating information on the problem and how it is being dealt with by the UN and member states, which in turns strengthens all stakeholders engaged with tackling the issue.

Other incremental and softer approaches have taken place. Since 2015, when grave allegations of SEA perpetrated by French troops in Central African Republic became public,[12] the UN began 'naming and shaming' countries whose soldiers or police were alleged to have committed sexual abuse. It started with a report from the arms-length OIOS in May 2015, which published a list of countries whose soldiers were accused from 2010–2013. The Secretary–General's annual report in 2016 included data of the country of nationality of each allegation.[13] The UN's 2016 report on tackling sexual abuse acknowledged the need for 'a holistic response' from the UN system and member states, 'which considers accountability for acts of misconduct, including sexual exploitation and abuse, as well as programmatic action to address underlying political, security and socio-economic factors'.[14] The adoption of Security Council resolution 2272 provides three new contributions to consequences for TCCs, the accountability chain, and new political impetus for tackling sexual exploitation and abuse. The 2017 appointment of a Victim's Rights Advocate to lead efforts to focus on and respond to victim's needs is also a crucial development, as is Security Council Resolution 2467 (2019) which includes provisions of reparations for survivors and livelihood support to enable them to rebuild their lives and support their families.[15]

In order to understand the strengths and weaknesses in terms of implementation of those laws and policies in Haiti, we draw upon data gathered through desk research, interviews, and observational research. The empirical research was conducted in 2017 and 2018, with interviews of senior UN officials and civilian personnel, senior staff from TCCs and PCCs, civil society organisations working in Haiti as UN implementing partners or as community-based organisations, and former personnel now based at UN Headquarters or in other peacekeeping missions.

---

[12]   See, for example, S. Laville, 'UN Aid Worker Suspended for Leaking Report on Child Abuse by French Troops', *The Guardian*, 29 April 2015, www.theguardian.com/world/2015/apr/29/un-aid-worker-suspended-leaking-report-child-abuse-french-troops-car (accessed 29 April 2020).

[13]   U.N. Secretary-General, *Special Measures for Protection from Sexual Exploitation and Sexual Abuse*, UN Doc. A/70/729 (16 February 2016).

[14]   Ibid.

[15]   Security Council Resolution 2467 UN Doc. S/RES/2467 (23 April 2019).

6.3 LAWS AND FRAMEWORKS

The *ad hoc* evolution of peacekeeping operations, combined with the *ad hoc* nature of laws and policies governing such activities and personnel, has contributed to a crisis of accountability for harms caused by peacekeepers. The weak laws combined with international organisations assuming the functions of states while navigating who is in command and control has resulted in the current state of crisis. Because peacekeeping was not conceived of by the UN's founders, no one specific legal framework was created to cover peacekeeping personnel. Instead, what has occurred is the use of more general frameworks for some personnel and the development of bilateral and multilateral agreements for others. As indicated in Chapter 4, there are two main categories of peacekeeping personnel: civilian and military.[16] Different laws apply to each category, leading to a complex system that contains a myriad of problems and weaknesses in terms of the laws, their implementation and responsibility for ensuring that obligations are upheld. However, it is not just the laws that are the problem, but also the practices in relation to how those laws operate and are implemented on the ground. This section sets out the laws and frameworks governing UN peacekeepers, and in Section 4 we consider the practices that occur after an allegation is brought to the relevant authorities.

6.3.1 *Immunities and Jurisdictional Bars*

The immunities and jurisdictional bars afforded to peacekeeping personnel seek to protect them from frivolous or pernicious interference by the host state, thus enabling personnel to undertake their functions and duties while on missions. The basic premise is sound and has its roots in diplomatic immunities.[17] In order for nationals of one country to operate in other states, frequently where such operations might be viewed with hostility, those personnel require protection from local interference. The counterbalance for these protective laws in relation to diplomats and states is that there is a series of bilateral relations and agreements between those countries that have diplomatic relations with one another. Therefore, if one country refuses to waive immunity or to prosecute its national personnel who commit crimes when

---

[16] Police deployed on peacekeeping operations may fall under the category of troops, civilians, or experts on mission, therefore this article does not deal with police as a separate category of peacekeepers.

[17] For a detailed discussion of the law on diplomatic immunity see E. Denza, *Commentary on the Vienna Convention on Diplomatic Relations* (Oxford: Oxford University Press 2016).

abroad then there are two options open to the other country: first, to declare the individual *persona non grata*, revoke his/her diplomatic credentials, and force the diplomat to leave the country, or second, to break diplomatic ties and relations with that state altogether. That counterbalance has been used effectively to leverage compliance with national criminal laws, and there have been some very public examples of states severing diplomatic relations for these very reasons.[18] Where it comes to the UN, however, such a counterbalance does not exist. Host countries do not have the ability to exert such leverage against the UN; thus, a system results where the UN holds all of the power despite its personnel operating on the sovereign territory of the host state.

That power imbalance is key to understanding why peacekeeping personnel are able to 'get away' with crimes with such alarming frequency. As we shall see, in theory the immunities or jurisdictional bars will not protect UN personnel who commit crimes from being brought to justice. The system is designed in such a way that only frivolous or pernicious interference is blocked by the multilateral or bilateral agreements. Crucially, however, in practice the current legal frameworks have created a culture of impunity owing to the difficulties or unwillingness to prosecute personnel who do commit crimes during peacekeeping operations. In order to understand the problem, it is important first to understand the separate regimes governing different types of personnel before then turning to what happens in practice and the impact on justice and accountability.

6.3.2 *Civilian Staff*

Civilian peacekeeping personnel are international civil servants with immunity from jurisdiction of any national court. UN officials are granted immunities under provisions in Article V of the Convention on the Privileges and Immunities of the United Nations (CPIUN).[19] Immunity provides an individual with protection from all aspects of legal processes, and there are two types of immunity in relation to UN civilian staff: personal or functional. Personal immunity protects an individual from all legal processes at any time and is given to the highest level UN staff, such as the Secretary–General, heads of offices and agencies, and the heads of peacekeeping operations, among others. All other civilian staff are given functional immunity, which protects them from legal processes in relation to any act that falls within their official functions.

---

[18] See, for example, R. Higgins 'The Abuse of Diplomatic Privileges and Immunities: Recent United Kingdom Experience' (1985) 79 (3) *The American Journal of International Law* 641.

[19] UN General Assembly Resolution 22(1), 'Convention on the Privileges and Immunities of the United Nations', 13 February1946.

Officially, the UN agrees with the idea that immunity of most civilian personnel is functional as opposed to absolute, thus that no immunity will operate in respect to actions that are not part of a person's official functions. Whether the crime committed was part of official functions is not about whether the person was 'on duty' at that time, but rather whether the act being carried out that led to a crime was part of that person conducting his/her job. It is clear then, that some crimes such as driving while drunk or unlawful killing may in some contexts be covered by functional immunity, whereas others such as rape will never fall within that sphere.[20] Where there is a question as to whether functional immunity applies, the UN must make such a determination based on internal investigations not into whether the crime was *committed* but rather *the context within which it occurred*. No such determination needs to be made in relation to those crimes or contexts that do not fall within an individual's official functions.

The theory, then, is sound, but the problems exist in relation to how they are implemented in practice. There are two problematic areas in this respect: first, the UN investigations into whether functional immunity applies, and second, the host states' lack of counterbalance to the UN's power in this regard. In relation to investigations, despite the clear lack of mandate to do so, the UN conducts its own internal investigations into all allegations of crimes irrespective of whether the crime committed is able to form part of an individual's official functions and of whether the context in which the crime was part of a person's official duties. Moreover, those investigations typically go beyond whether functional immunity applies, and instead focus on whether there is sufficient evidence to cooperate with local authorities.[21] This, clearly, is deeply problematic and undermines the very foundations of functional immunity, providing a cloak for perpetrators rather than a shield against pernicious allegations. The result is that the current system of immunities operates as absolute despite clearly only being intended to be functional. In relation to the host states' lack of counterbalance, there is the related problem that after conducting such investigations the UN then must provide explicit or tacit waiver of immunity.[22] The waiver must be explicit where the crime formed part of official functions, but there is a tacit waiver in other

---

[20] See, for example, A. J. Miller 'Legal Aspects of Stopping Sexual Exploitation and Abuse in UN Peacekeeping Operations' (2006) 39 *Cornell International Law Journal* 71, 92

[21] This has been exposed most recently in terms of UN investigations into allegations against personnel in Haiti and Central African Republic, as evidenced in UN Office of Internal Oversight Services reports (e.g. 2015).

[22] 'Convention on the Privileges and Immunities of the United Nations', General Assembly Resolution 22(1), 13 February 1946, (United Nations 1 *Treaty Series* 15), Article V Section 20 and Article VI, Section 23.

circumstances given that the UN has taken upon itself the ability to determine whether functional immunity applies despite it being an objective rather than subjective test. As already noted, where a diplomat commits a crime that does fall within official functions and is covered by functional immunity and the sending state fails to waive that immunity, the host state has two options to counterbalance that decision. However, there is no clause allowing host states to declare UN staff *persona non grata*, thus meaning that there is no recourse for the host state if a crime is committed and the UN fails to waive immunity or to comply with local investigative authorities.

6.3.3 *Experts on Mission*

Similar provisions (Article VI CPIUN) and practices govern UN experts on missions as occur in relation to civilian staff.[23] Those experts on mission have functional immunity in relation to acts committed while on mission. However, in addition those individuals are deemed to be inviolable while on mission. Inviolability goes beyond immunity from legal processes in relation to an act and provides a protection of the person from any interference with their integrity while on mission. Inviolability attaches directly to the person and prevents an individual from being arrested or detained until after their mission finishes. Therefore, even if an act falls outside of their official functions nothing can be done while the expert remains on mission. This is an important additional aspect to understand given that many police deployed on peacekeeping missions are experts on mission, and therefore hold both functional immunity and are considered inviolable.

6.3.4 *Military Personnel*

Military personnel are not afforded the same immunities as their civilian counterparts.[24] Soldiers are not directly employed by the UN; they remain under the control of their home country, which in turn has a contract with the UN. Those individuals are covered by bilateral agreements[25] between their

---

[23] A. J. Miller 'United Nations Experts on Mission and their Privileges and Immunities' (2007) 4 *International Organisations Law Review* 11.

[24] For an in-depth discussion, see Z. Deen-Racsmány 'Exclusive Criminal Jurisdiction over UN Peacekeepers and the UN Project (s) on Criminal Accountability: A Self-Fulfilling Prophecy' (2013) 53 *Military Law & Law of War Review* 247.

[25] These are based on the model memorandum of understanding between the United Nations and [participating State] contributing resources to [the United Nations Peacekeeping Operation] in 'Manual on Policies and Procedures Concerning the Reimbursement and

sending state (the TCC) and the UN, and it is that document which sets out jurisdiction over such personnel if they commit crimes while on peacekeeping operations.[26] Military personnel operate under a system where the host state is barred from exercising jurisdiction in relation to crimes committed by those individuals. That is not an immunity *per se* as the TCC retains exclusive jurisdiction over its own soldiers and commits to exercise that jurisdiction to prosecute troops who commit criminal offences while on missions.[27] However, it does operate as an absolute immunity from the jurisdiction of the host state. The jurisdictional bars prevent host countries from investigating or prosecuting any crimes, regardless of whether they were committed as part of official functions. The TCC is obligated to investigate and prosecute such crimes, with the UN being limited to administrative investigations and even then only if the TCC fails to undertake its own investigations within ten days of an allegation being handed over to its authorities. Prosecutions may occur by the host state if a soldier is court-martialled *in situ* and handed over to local authorities, or if that soldier is taken to military courts or national courts in their home state. The decision as to how to proceed, therefore, belongs exclusively to the TCC.[28]

There are two main problems with this system. First, troops frequently are not held accountable by their own countries, for legal and political reasons. As will be explored later, not all TCCs are able to exercise extraterritorial jurisdiction over acts committed by their soldiers while on peacekeeping operations. Even where they are able to do so, the reality is that such states rarely if ever prosecute their soldiers. Often, that is because there is insufficient evidence gathered to do so – a problem attributable to investigate crimes committed abroad and in fragile states or conflict zones. Or it may be because of the national political implications of doing so, and the likelihood that such prosecutions would undermine national support for contributing troops to UN peacekeeping operations. Second, the removal of host state jurisdiction results in a lack of access to justice for victims, something that highlights the problem with the legal frameworks centring on perpetrators and state sovereignty rather than on victims and human rights.

Control of Contingent-Owned Equipment of Troop/Police Contributors Participating in Peacekeeping Missions', UN Doc. A/C.5/66/8, 27 October 2011.

[26] The bilateral agreements between the UN and the host states (UN Model SOFA, 'Report of the SG, Model Status-of-Forces Agreement for Peace-Keeping Operations', UN Doc A/45/594, 9 October 1990), further underscore that jurisdiction over military personnel belongs exclusively to the troop-contributing countries.

[27] UN General Assembly, 'Model Status-of-Forces-Agreement for Peacekeeping Operations,' Report of the Secretary General, A/45/594, 9 October 1990.

[28] On these matters, see R. Burke, *Sexual Exploitation and Abuse by UN Military Contingents: Moving Beyond the Current Status Quo and Responsibility under International Law* (Brill/Martinus Nijhoff 2014).

6.4 Investigations and Prosecutions

What becomes clear from these laws is that the system has been designed in such a way that peacekeepers are able and ought to be prosecuted for serious crimes whilst being protected from unwarranted interference. In practice, however, the record of immunities and jurisdictional bars has been deeply problematic. Currently, civilian personnel frequently operate with impunity owing to the UN failing to ensure that immunity is waived where crimes have been committed, and soldiers almost always are returned to their country and the matter is quietly dropped.[29] Ultimately, then, the country where the crime or abuses occurred is prevented from holding the perpetrators accountable because of the jurisdictional bars and immunities; and in relation to soldiers, at least, the country that does have jurisdiction (and potentially custody) is the one that will not exercise its jurisdiction.

6.4 INVESTIGATIONS AND PROSECUTIONS

The problem of sexual abuse by, and lack of accountability of, peacekeepers has its roots not only in flawed laws and frameworks governing immunities and jurisdictional bars but also in the practices that occur once an allegation is made. The most problematic issue in relation to such practices is that the institutions employing those peacekeepers are tasked with, or assume responsibility for, investigating allegations. As with the laws themselves, different regimes cover civilian and military peacekeepers, with deep flaws throughout the rules and practices of those investigatory regimes. It is important to understand the problems with both regimes because this is an issue that cuts across all categories of peacekeeping personnel.[30]

6.4.1 UN Internal Investigations

In theory, under the laws governing functional immunity when an allegation is made against a UN civilian staff member, the UN's sole investigatory role is to determine whether functional immunity applies. Such a determination would require a two part test: Objectively, is the act one that may form part of official functions? And, if so, subjectively, did that individual commit the act as

---

[29] See, for example, K. Grady 'Sex, Statistics, Peacekeepers and Power' (2016) 79 (6) *Modern Law Review* 931.

[30] Indeed, a detailed breakdown of the UN's figures show that, contrary to commonly held perceptions, around half of the total number of complaints of sexual abuse over the last decade have been made against police and civilian UN staff, rather than its peacekeeping soldiers, despite soldiers vastly outnumbering police and civilians in most peacekeeping missions. See the UN's SEA database at http://cdu.unlb.org/.

part of his or her official functions? Of course, in many circumstances, the UN must conduct some form of administrative investigation into its personnel to determine whether functional immunity applies. Those powers are intended only to enable the UN to determine whether its personnel holds immunity in relation to the allegation, and, if so, to make a decision as to whether to waive that immunity. In practice, however, the UN uses those investigatory powers to examine evidence of an allegation, and by doing so, the Organisation acts *ultra vires*. This is a fundamental issue that frequently is overlooked in scholarship and in practitioner reports.

There are two points to note here. First, the UN holds the same powers as all employers to conduct internal investigations regarding its personnel in relation to whether an act committed is in violation of contractual obligations. Second, some peacekeeping operations take place where there are no functioning rule of law institutions able to conduct investigations or prosecutions. While these factors must be borne in mind, they are ones that ought to be addressed after establishing the frameworks governing UN investigations rather than being used as a *carte blanche* method for the UN overreaching its investigatory powers when an allegation is received.

As it stands, UN investigations into serious misconduct could be carried out by at least four different bodies. While there are links between the works carried out by those bodies, they serve very different functions and are governed by different rules. Their overlap can, and frequently does, lead to situations where no particular body takes responsibility for an investigation, which in turn results in allegations being mishandled at best.[31]

The Conduct and Discipline Unit (CDU) was originally created at UN Headquarters in 2005 following recommendations by the Zeid Report.[32] It is one of the few recommendations that was enacted almost immediately after the report was published[33]and was fully operational by April 2006.[34] Its two

---

[31]   The problems with overlap and duplication can be seen in relation to how allegations were handled in relation to the Central African Republic in 2015, where Anders Kompass blew the whistle on the UN's failure to hand over allegations of abuse by French peacekeepers during a France-run peacekeeping operation: R. Freedman, 'French Peacekeeper Abuse Scandal Fits an Old Pattern of Impunity' *The Conversation*, 29 April 2015 available at https://theconversation.com/french-peacekeeper-abuse-scandal-fits-an-old-pattern-of-impunity-40991 (accessed 29 April 2020). For further discussion on the broader issues, see Grady, 'Sex, Statistics, Peacekeepers and Power' (n 29).

[32]   UN General Assembly, 'Comprehensive Review of the Whole Question of Peacekeeping Operations in All their Aspects', 24 March 2005, UN Doc A/59/710, para. 42.

[33]   It was enacted in November 2005.

[34]   UN General Assembly, 'Report of the Office of Internal Oversight Services on its Investigation into Allegations of Sexual Exploitation and Abuse in the Ituri Region (Bunia) in the United

6.4 Investigations and Prosecutions

main functions are: 'to advise personnel and mission leadership alike on all matters of conduct and discipline; [and to] ensure the coherence of administrative and disciplinary procedures'.[35] Alongside the main CDU at headquarters, conduct and discipline units also form part of all peacekeeping missions. Those in-country units have specific functions including receiving all allegations of misconduct, making recommendations on investigations including forwarding to the Office of Internal Oversight Services (OIOS),[36] and reporting all serious misconduct to mission heads.[37] They also report allegations to relevant investigative bodies and report back to victims and local populations about investigation results, as well as liaise with UN gender and children teams.[38]

All allegations of sexual abuse received by CDU must be reported to the OIOS, which contrasts with all other allegations of serious misconduct and reflects the pernicious and widespread incidents of sexual abuse perpetrated by peacekeepers. OIOS then records and evaluates all allegations before prioritising those to be investigated and about which it will conduct preliminary investigations[39] or dismissing those it deems to have insufficient evidence for investigation. OIOS was established in 1994 to carry out audit, investigation, inspection, and evaluation services including establishing 'facts related to reports of possible misconduct to guide the Secretary General on jurisdictional or disciplinary action to be taken'. It also partly replicates the work of the UN Ethics Office, which was established in 2006 after the World Summit conference of the previous year, to ensure 'that all staff members perform their functions consistent with the highest standards of integrity as required by the Charter of the United Nations'.

There are other mechanisms involved with allegations against civilian staff. In 2009, a UN Dispute Tribunal (UNDT) was established as a civil tribunal to

---

Nations Organization Mission in the Democratic Republic of the Congo', 5 April 2007, UN Doc A/61/841, para. 32.

[35] W. Durch, K. Andres, and M. England, *Improving Criminal Accountability in United Nations Peace Operations* (Washington: Stimson Center, Report No 65, June 2009), 12.

[36] United Nations, Comprehensive report of conduct and discipline including full justification of all posts, Report of the Secretary-General, A/62/758, 20 March 2008, paras. 23–28.

[37] UN General Assembly, 'Comprehensive Report Prepared Pursuant to General Assembly Resolution 59/296 on Sexual Exploitation and Sexual Abuse, Including Policy Development, Implementation and Full Justification of Proposed Capacity on Personnel Conduct Issues', 24 May 2006, UN Doc A/60/862, paras. 38-53.

[38] Durch, Andres, and England, *Improving Criminal Accountability in United Nations Peace Operations* (n 35), 13.

[39] UN Doc A/60/862, (n 37), para. 7; UNGA, 'Implementation of the Recommendations of the Special Committee on Peacekeeping Operations, Report of the Secretary-General, Addendum', 22 December 2006, UN Doc A/61/668/Add.1, para. 8.

102   *Sexual Exploitation and Abuse: Who Guards the Guardians?*

hear and decide cases filed by, or on behalf of, current and former staff members. Many peacekeeping missions also have police components, which may be tasked with carrying out internal investigations into alleged criminal wrongdoing by the UN peacekeeping personnel. In addition, there is a Digital Forensics Unit for forensic recovery and analysis of digital information,[40] as well as integrated teams in some countries.[41] The overlap among these various investigatory and adjudicative bodies, however, can hinder effective investigations and make it difficult for victims of sexual exploitation and abuse to know how to lodge and track complaints. Crucially, none of those bodies has the power to undertake criminal investigations into acts that fall outside of official functions.

It is important to note that the UN will not hand over a civilian staff member to local authorities in situations where there are issues with the rule of law, human rights, or institutions within the host state (and in the case of fair trial or other fundamental human rights, the UN *cannot*). This is an exception to the rule on how the UN ought to deal with crimes that do not fall within official functions. In those cases, however, civilians could be prosecuted by their home states, but it would only occur if their home country has legislation that asserts extraterritorial criminal jurisdiction for these particular actions and sufficient evidence for a successful prosecution can be gathered, which is not always the case.

6.4.2 *Troop-Contributing Countries' Investigations*

The UN creates bilateral Status of Forces Agreements (SOFAs) with host countries. Those agreements contain the jurisdictional bars that preclude the host state from using legal processes in relation to soldiers who commit crimes whilst on mission. Of course, that absolute immunity can be waived by the TCC, although that rarely happens. Instead, TCCs prefer – in word, at least, if not in deed – to investigate and prosecute their troops if they commit crimes.

TCCs are bound by legal obligations to investigate and, where appropriate, punish soldiers who commit sexual abuse whilst operating under the UN umbrella. The bilateral agreements that those countries make with the UN – Memoranda of Understanding (MOU)[42] – set out that TCCs have ten days to start an investigation from the time they receive information from the

---

[40]   Activities of the Office of Internal Oversight Services on peacekeeping operations for the period 1 January to 31 December 2012, UN Doc A/67/297 (Part II) 13 March 2012 [7].

[41]   E.g. Central African Republic.

[42]   *Draft Model Memorandum of Understanding* Annex to Report of the Special Committee on Peacekeeping Operations and its Working Group, A/61/19 (Part III), New York, 12 June 2007.

6.4 Investigations and Prosecutions

UN regarding allegations of misconduct by its troops. If a TCC fails to do so, the UN may initiate its own administrative investigation. In practice, however, those obligations frequently have been ignored both by states[43] and by the UN. Many TCCs do not send national investigating officers with the troops that are deployed, which undermines their ability to conduct prompt investigations into allegations. And even where such investigations do occur, the UN has little power – and seemingly little desire – to compel the countries to report on the findings.

A key problem with accountability of troops goes beyond investigations and revolves around TCCs frequently being unwilling or even unable to prosecute crimes committed by troops when operating abroad.[44] First, and as mentioned, many countries do not have the legal authority to prosecute domestic crimes extraterritorially.[45] National laws frequently only cover crimes committed on national territory, and while some militaries do have extraterritorial reach in terms of laws governing soldiers, this is not always the case. Other countries only have such extraterritorial powers if the acts are deemed criminal in both the country where they occurred and the country of nationality of the perpetrator,[46] which is problematic when it comes to definitions of sexual abuse. Soldiers may be held accountable through their military justice systems, but again that is not the case for all TCCs. And even where such prosecutions are able to take place, TCCs have to balance domestic pressures not to prosecute troops with UN efforts to encourage them to do so.[47]

It is important to understand the economics and politics of contributing troops to UN peacekeeping operations. Many of the countries that contribute the most troops do so for the status and power that it gives them within the UN,

---

[43] Z. Deen-Racsmány 'The Amended UN Model Memorandum of Understanding: A New Incentive for States to Discipline and Prosecute Military Members of National Peacekeeping Contingents?' (2011) 16 (2) *Journal of Conflict and Security Law* 321.

[44] See, generally, S. Wills 'Continuing Impunity of Peacekeepers: The Need for a Convention' (2013) 4 (1) *Journal of International Humanitarian Legal Studies* 47.

[45] UN General Assembly, 'Report of the Secretary-General, Criminal Accountability of United Nations Officials and Experts on Mission', 11 August 2008, UN Doc A/63/260.

[46] UN General Assembly, 'Ensuring the Accountability of United Nations Staff and Experts on Mission with Respect to Criminal Acts Committed in Peacekeeping Operations' UN Doc A/60/980.

[47] See, for example, UN General Assembly 'Investigation by the Office of Internal Oversight Services into Allegations of Sexual Exploitation and Abuse in the United Nations Organization Mission in the Democratic Republic of the Congo', 5 January 2005 UN Doc A/59/66, especially paragraphs 46 and 38; and the comments on this topic by the Congolese delegates to the Sixth Committee in 2009 and 2011: UN Summary Records of the Sixth Committee, UN Doc A/C.6/64/SR.7 (10 November 2009) and UN Doc A/C.6/66/SR.9, (7 October 2011).

and because the financial rewards of doing so can be significant. The UN gives countries a standard fee for troops, which in some states far exceeds the salaries that those troops are paid. Those countries, then, have significant interests in remaining contributors to UN peacekeeping operations, and are reluctant to invoke any domestic pressures to reduce those contributions.

As a result of TCCs taking little action in relation to allegations of sexual abuse perpetrated by their soldiers, a range of political measures have been recommended or implemented over recent years. In March 2016, the Security Council voted to give the Secretary–General the right to repatriate entire units if the TCC fails to prosecute alleged perpetrators of sexual misconduct within six months.[48] The Council requested that the Secretary–General ensure that the replacement of personnel from troop- or police-contributing countries be a process that upheld standards of conduct and discipline, and appropriately addressed allegations or confirmed acts of sexual exploitation and abuse by their personnel. This was heralded by United States Ambassador to the UN, Samantha Power, as the UN 'finally doing something about the cancer in the United Nations system',[49] despite it being a discretionary and political tool. A similar method for dealing with this issue is 'naming and shaming' countries that do not investigate, prosecute, and report allegations of sexual abuse. It will take some time to know whether such measures are effective, particularly in relation to the larger and more powerful TCCs.

6.5 PEACEKEEPER SEXUAL EXPLOITATION AND ABUSE IN HAITI

In Haiti since the creation of MINUSTAH and until the transition to MINUJUSTH there have been many allegations and reports of sexual exploitation and abuse by peacekeeping personnel.[50] Those allegations and reports broadly fall into four categories: (i) sexual exploitation and abuse of children, (ii) transactional sex, (iii) 'consensual' relations, and (iv) paternity claims. Although there are common themes and links across those categories, we will address each in turn, using empirical data combined with multidisciplinary theories before analysing the strengths and weaknesses of the current systems and what might be done to provide more robust and holistic solutions.

---

[48] UN Security Council Resolution 2272, 11 March 2016 UN Doc. S/RES/2272 (2016).

[49] *UN News Centre*, 'Security Council Asks Secretary-General to Replace Contingents from Countries Failing to Hold Sexual Predators Accountable', 11 March 2016, www.un.org/press/en/2016/sc12277.doc.htm (accessed 29 April 2020).

[50] See the annexes to the UN Secretary-General's annual reports on special measures for protection from sexual exploitation and abuse.

6.5 Peacekeeper Sexual Exploitation and Abuse in Haiti

Sexual exploitation and abuse of women and children in Haiti is perpetrated by international and national actors, and the laws and structures governing them differs according to whom they are and by which frameworks they are governed. A victim-centred approach to sexual exploitation and abuse requires an understanding of those laws and frameworks, but with the central focus on how the victim views, understands, and can access those laws and systems. In this section we will first explore different types of sexual exploitation and abuse, some main ways they have been perpetrated in Haiti, and what infrastructure and practices exist for victims and survivors, before turning in the next section to the gaps that remain and how they may be addressed.

The UN defines sexual exploitation as, 'any actual or attempted abuse of a position of vulnerability, differential power, or trust, for sexual purposes, including, but not limited to, profiting monetarily, socially or politically from the sexual exploitation of another'.[51] Sexual abuse is defined as 'the actual or threatened physical intrusion of a sexual nature, whether by force or under unequal or coercive conditions'.[52] Sexual exploitation is defined by the UN as, 'any actual or attempted abuse of a position of vulnerability, differential power, or trust, for sexual purposes, including, but not limited to, profiting monetarily, socially or politically from the sexual exploitation of another'.[53] Those early definitions, from the Secretary General's 2003 Bulletin on special measures for protection from sexual exploitation and sexual abuse 2003 were a direct response to the decade of repeated exposures of widespread SEA starting in Cambodia in 1993 (the UNTAC mission), where the numbers of prostitutes rose from 6,000 to 25,000,[54] and again in 1995 in Bosnia and Herzegovina, where women and girls were sex trafficked by UN personnel,[55] and reports of widespread SEA against children in Guinea, Liberia, and Sierra Leone in 2001.[56] As previously discussed, this led to the Secretary–General issuing the Zero Tolerance policy.[57]

---

[51] UN Secretary–General, 'Secretary-General's Bulletin: Special Measures for Protection from Sexual Exploitation and Sexual Abuse ST/SGB/2003/13', 2003, p. 1.

[52] Ibid.

[53] Ibid.

[54] S. Whitworth, *Men, Militarism, and UN Peacekeeping* (Boulder, CO: Lynne Rienner 2004), 67, 68.

[55] O. Simic, *Regulation of Sexual Conduct in UN Peacekeeping Operations* (New York: Springer 2012), 42.

[56] United Nations High Commission for Refugees (UNHCR) and Save the Children UK. 2002. 'Sexual Violence & Exploitation: The Experience of Refugee Children in Guinea, Liberia and Sierra Leone, Initial Findings and Recommendations from Assessment Mission 22 October to 30 November 2001'. www.savethechildren.org.uk/content/dam/global/reports/health-and-nutrition/sexual_violence_and_exploitation_1.pdf (accessed 29 April 2020).

[57] UN Secretary-General, *Secretary-General's Bulletin: Special Measures for Protection from Sexual Exploitation and Sexual Abuse* (n 386 above).

Sexual Exploitation and Abuse: Who Guards the Guardians?

A key problem is the lack of universally-accepted definitions of sexual exploitation and abuse, and of understanding how they manifest and by whom in conflict and crisis zones. Without such understanding, top-down policies are too vague to be implemented effectively, and are not able to be context-specific for different countries and environments. Sexual abuse typically is understood to refer to crimes of a sexual nature, whereas exploitation are acts perpetrated that are an abuse power but may not be of a criminal nature. For example sex being demanded for goods or services may be exploitative and, while it likely might not amount to a criminal offence, it can be made a disciplinary matter in terms of employment policies. Indeed the UN Zero Tolerance bulletin outlaws all such acts and treats exploitation as a breach of employment codes of conduct. Similarly, many TCCs adopt a similar approach, for example in relation to transactional sex even where it is lawful within the host country.[58] But the lack of clear definitions, and the lack of knowledge about what constitutes sexual abuse in different countries, is an obstacle to effective prevention, protection, and remedies.

Westendorf and Searle identify different ways in which sexual exploitation and abuse manifest and are perpetrated in crisis and conflict zones. Their categories include: (i) opportunistic abuse, (ii) sadistic or planned sexual abuse, (iii) transactional sex, and (iv) networked sexual exploitation and abuse.[59] Within each of these categories, the authors point to environments, cultures and contexts, asserting that conditions are at the heart of facilitating sexual exploitation and abuse. Those categories are important for understanding how and why those acts are perpetrated, and for thinking about how best to prevent perpetrators. However, while those categories provide a method for exploring different types of harms perpetrated, they do not interrogate specific types of sexual exploitation and abuse, the impact upon survivors, or potential solutions that may prevent, protect, mitigate harm, or provide remedies. The focus, then, remains on the perpetrator – their motives and actions – rather than taking a victim-centred perspective and approach.[60]

---

[58] See, for example, Uruguay whose military rules state that soldiers may not have transactional sex at home or abroad, whether on or off duty.

[59] J. K. Westendorf and L. Searle 'Sexual Exploitation and Abuse in Peace Operations: Trends, Policy Responses and Future Directions' (2017) 93 (2) *International Affairs* 368.

[60] There is a wealth of literature on victim-centred approaches. On the UN recognition of the need for a victim-centred approach see UN General Assembly 'Comprehensive Strategy on Assistance and Support to Victims of Sexual Exploitation and Abuse by United Nations Staff and Related Personnel', UN Doc. A/RES/62/214, 8 March 2008; UN General Assembly, 'Report of the Group of Legal Experts', UN Doc. A/60/980, paras. 27, 44; and see also resources and reports at the website of the UN Victims' Rights Advocates, available here: www.un.org/preventing-sexual-exploitation-and -abuse/content/victims-rights-advocate (accessed 29 April 2020).

6.5 Peacekeeper Sexual Exploitation and Abuse in Haiti

Our research in Haiti focused on different ways of categorising of sexual exploitation and abuse that, like Westendorf and Searle's, each demonstrate environmental and contextual factors within which the harms occur, but also seeks to foreground the impact, steps taken to tackle them, and gaps that must be addressed. Those four categories are: (i) abuse of children, (ii) transactional sex, (iii) 'consensual' relationships, and (iv) children fathered by peacekeepers. Although our focus is on a victim-centred approach, when exploring how each of these categories has manifested, the impact it has had, and the systems that do or should exist to address them, the enabling environments set out by Westendorf and Searle clearly play an important role in understanding the SEA perpetrated.

6.5.1 Children

Sexual exploitation and abuse of children within crisis and conflict zones is not a newly discovered issue. As discussed earlier, instances are frequently uncovered about peacekeepers and humanitarians sexually exploiting and abusing children. In Haiti, a string of sexual scandals afflicting the military components of MINUSTAH fuelled the anti-UN sentiment. In 2007, 111 Sri Lankan soldiers were repatriated after allegations of sexual exploitation and abuse of children.[61] In January 2011, Pakistani troops were accused of the rape of a boy in Gonaïves and of sexually abusing children in the capital; three of them were later found guilty of sexual exploitation and abuse and were condemned to a one-year jail sentence.[62] In July 2011, Uruguayan troops were accused of sexually assaulting a young man in the southern town of Port-Salut (while only being charged with coercion offences when brought before their home domestic courts). As Lemay-Hébert points out, an 'amplification factor' was at work, with each scandal building on the narrative of occupation in Haiti and feeding latent hostility towards international troops in certain segments of the society (especially in highly-politicised student circles in Port-au-Prince).[63] More recently, there have been reports of cover-ups of

[61] Bri Kouri Nouvèl Gaye et al., 'Haiti's Renewal of MINUSTAH's Mandate in Violation of the Human Rights of the Haitian People', 24 March 2011, submission to the UN Universal Periodic Review (UPR), Twelfth Session of the Working Group on the UPR Human Rights Council, October 2011.

[62] Ibid.

[63] Interview with Daly Valet, Editor-in-chief, *Le Matin newspaper*, 1 February 2011, Port-au-Prince, cited in N. Lemay-Hébert 'Resistance in the Time of Cholera: The Limits of Stabilization through Securitization in Haiti' (2014) 21 *International Peacekeeping* 198.

senior Oxfam officials sexually exploiting and abusing young women in the country, and these are known to be just the tip of the iceberg.[64]

Many of the allegations of sexual exploitation and abuse of children appear to be opportunistic abuse, compounded by the low rates of birth registration in Haiti which results in difficulties knowing who is a child – that is, under the age of 18, according to the definition in the Convention of the Rights of the Child.[65] However, there have been clear cases of sadistic and networked sexual abuse of children, the most prominently egregious of which was the paedophile ring created by Sri Lankan troops.[66] It took many years for those allegations to come to the fore, despite local populations openly discussing and seeking to expose the rape and abuse of those children. 'We petitioned MINUSTAH but were not answered and could not access LogBase'.[67] Instead, Sri Lanka repatriated all of its peacekeepers, and allowed those alleged to have perpetrated those crimes to be redeployed in other peacekeeping missions.[68]

Even when allegations of child abuse are exposed swiftly and with robust evidence, frequently little is done to address them. Local NGOs in Haiti pointed to the case of Jean-Jean, a boy who allegedly was abused by Uruguayan soldiers,[69] pointing to the public protests and the lack of follow-up from the Troop-Contributing Country. Although Uruguay prosecuted the soldiers involved for private violence, many interviewees insisted that 'justice has not been done'[70] and that 'the UN and Haiti's government have shown that they do not care about our children being raped'.[71] Interviewees from the Uruguayan armed forces insisted that 'not all the facts are

---

[64] See, for example, D. Gayle, 'Timeline: Oxfam Sexual Exploitation Scandal in Haiti', *The Guardian*, 15 June 2018, www.theguardian.com/world/2018/jun/15/timeline-oxfam-sexual-exploitation-scandal-in-haiti (accessed 29 April 2020); S. Merope-Synge, 'The Oxfam Sex Abuse Scandal Demonstrates the Urgent Need for Legal Accountability in the Humanitarian Aid Sector', *Al Jazzera*, February 2018, www.ijdh.org/2018/02/topics/womens-issues/the-oxfam-sex-abuse-scandal-demonstrates-the-urgent-need-for-legal-accountability-in-the-humanitarian-aid-sector/ (accessed 29 April 2020).

[65] Article 1, *Convention on the Rights of the Child*, UN General Assembly, 20 November 1989 (United Nations 1577 *Treaty Series* 3).

[66] See A. R. Kolbe 'It's Not a Gift When It Comes with Price': A Qualitative Study of Transactional Sex between UN Peacekeepers and Haitian Citizens' (2015) 4 (1) *Stability: International Journal of Security & Development* 44.

[67] Interview with Haitian woman victim on the basis of anonymity, Port au Prince, 8 June 2017.

[68] Redress, *Litigating Peacekeeper Child Sexual Abuse* January 2020, 33–35 https://redress.org/wp-content/uploads/2020/01/LitigatingPeacekeeperChildSexualAbuseReport.pdf (accessed 29 April 2020).

[69] Ibid., 24–26.

[70] Interview with Defensurs Plus, Port au Prince, 7 June 2017.

[71] Interview with Le Réseau National de Défense des Droits Humains (RNDDH) Port au Prince, 7 June 2017.

known'[72] and that 'the boy [Jean-Jean] was told to make these allegations for money'.[73] However, even in this most prominent and publicised case, the systems were too weak for accountability or justice for the alleged victim or perpetrator. As one lawyer in Haiti stated: 'There has only been one case where they compensated the victim, but it was not a lot of money. In the case of Jean-Jean the soldiers were sent home. This is no sanction, and it is a form of impunity. In that case there was a procedure but they held the court case there and not here in Haiti. This is not justice, it is a small sanction'.[74]

6.5.2 Transactional Sex

The UN adopts a Zero Tolerance policy towards sexual contact between its personnel and local populations, which includes prostitution or transactional sex even where it is lawful in a country. To be clear, there is no such thing as 'child prostitution' because all sexual contact with a person under the age of eighteen is child sexual abuse according to international standards and definitions. Therefore, when discussing transactional sex we focus only on individuals over the age of eighteen in line with those standards and definitions, despite the difficulties that arise in a country with low levels of birth registration. There is a wealth of literature and discussion about the terminology used about the provision of goods, services, or money for sex with an adult, the gendered power dynamics involved, and the impact of peacekeeping on this area.[75] These are not issues that we will explore, but they are important to understand when focusing on transactional sex involving peacekeepers and local populations. Transactional sex is defined as the exchange of sex for goods, services, or money.[76] In Haiti a distinction is drawn in local

---

[72] Interviews with senior Uruguay military officials on the basis of anonymity, 6 June 2017.

[73] Ibid.

[74] Interview with Defenseurs Plus, Port au Prince, 7 June 2017.

[75] See for instance: C. Lutz, M. Gutmann, and K. Brown (2009) 'Conduct and Discipline in UN Peacekeeping Operations: Culture, Political Economy and Gender' Watson Institute Report submitted to the Conduct and Discipline Unit, Department of Peacekeeping Operations, United Nations; J. K. Westendorf, 'WPS and SEA in Peacekeeping Operations' in S. Davies and J. True (eds.) *The Oxford Handbook of Women, Peace and Security* (Oxford: Oxford University Press 2019); J. Stern, *Reducing Sexual Exploitation and Abuse in UN Peacekeeping: Ten Years After the Zeid Report* (Washington: Stimson Center, Policy Brief No. 1 2015); Y. Chilmeran and J. True, 'The Political Economy of Gender and Peacebuilding' in N. Lemay-Hébert (ed) *Edward Elgar Handbook on Intervention and Statebuilding* (Cheltenham: Edward Elgar 2019).

[76] B. Beber et al. 'Peacekeeping, Compliance with International Norms, and Transactional Sex in Monrovia, Liberia' (2017) 71 (1) *International Organization* 1.

understandings, even if not in law, between sex workers in the streets, bars, hotels, or brothels, and those engaging with ongoing transactional sex with the same people on an ongoing basis. Indeed, it is common for women to refer to international personnel as their 'boyfriends' when they provide money for school fees, medicines, food, or other goods in exchange for sex. There is also the added complexity, identified by Kolbe amongst others,[77] of the gendered power dynamics within Haitian society, whereby there is an expectation that any man who has a sexual relationship with a woman will provide financial and other support for her as part of that reciprocal relationship.[78] We will consider that type of sexual exploitation in the following sub-section.

In Haiti prostitution is illegal, but enforcement of those laws is lacking, and there is widespread prostitution particularly in areas where international intervenors live and work.[79] This is not surprising given that Haiti is one of the poorest countries in the world, and given the levels of international interventions in the country, leading to an environment of power and financial disparity in which prostitution is likely to thrive.[80] Indeed studies in Cambodia, Liberia, and other countries with similar factors to Haiti in this regard demonstrate that the combination of crisis and poverty lead to a significant increase in prostitution when international interventions take place.[81] A leaked 2015 UN report clearly linked transactional sex to the context of poverty, highlighting that for some women it is the only opportunity to obtain food or money.[82] The lack of domestic law enforcement regarding prostitution results in international intervenors being able to engage in transactional sex with impunity, unless those individuals fall under the UN

---

[77] Kolbe, 'It's Not a Gift When It Comes with Price' (n 66), 3–4.

[78] Ibid.

[79] Ibid. See also S. Lee and S. Bartels '"They Put a Few Coins in Your Hand to Drop a Baby in You": A Study of Peacekeeper-fathered Children in Haiti' (2020) 27 (2) *International Peacekeeping* 177.

[80] On the increase of transactional sex UN peacekeepers and international humanitarian workers are present see, for example, K. M. Jennings 'Service, Sex, and Security: Gendered Peacekeeping Economies in Liberiaand the Democratic Republic of the Congo' (2014) 45 (4) *Security Dialogue* 313.

[81] See, K. Jennings and V. Nikolić-Ristanović, *UN Peacekeeping Economies and Local Sex Industries: Connections and Implications* (Brighton: Micron, Research Working Paper 17, 2009); and K. Jennings 'Unintended Consequences of Intimacy: Political Economies of Peacekeeping and Sex Tourism' (2010) 17 (2) *International Peacekeeping* 229.

[82] T. Awori, C. Lutz, and P. J. Thapa, 'Final Report: Expert Mission to Evaluate Risks to SEA Prevention Efforts in MINUSTAH, UNMIL, MONUSCO, and UNMISS', 3 November 2013, https://static1.squarespace.com/static/514a0127e4b04d7440e8045d/t/599da7f7f5e2310b13539b6b/150 3504383454/2013+Expert+Team+Report+FINAL.pdf (accessed 29 April 2020).

umbrella. This has recently been brought to the fore of global public attention in relation to allegations that Oxfam staff in Haiti paid for sex with prostitutes,[83] that those allegations were covered up by the NGO, and that there is little or no infrastructure for holding those individuals accountable in Haiti's legal systems.

In relation to the UN, there are SEA hotlines and methods of reporting that cover UN personnel procuring transactional sex. Interviewees from the armed forces clearly understood the Code of Conduct's prohibition on sex with prostitutes emphasising that 'prostitution is wrong to use; during the UN contract we cannot use prostitutes'. However, many interviewees were unclear about transactional sex, indicating that in some circumstances they viewed these as consensual and legitimate relationships. This directly contradicts the Code of Conduct, and goes against the 'No Excuses' cards handed out by the Conduct and Discipline Team to all armed forces personnel upon arrival in the mission in Haiti. Moreover, as a member of the Force Command pointed out, 'different militaries and police forces have different approaches; some are ashamed and do nothing, others place all the blame on the commander, and most will not go looking for it even if they are told that their troops are using prostitutes'.[84] UN agencies in Haiti were clearer about the requirement not to have any sexual contact with locals, and the disciplinary steps that could be taken, particularly in relation to transactional sex, although interviewees emphasised that 'unless a woman reports the sex and what she was given for it, we cannot do anything about it'.[85]

6.5.3 'Consensual'/Survival Relationships

The UN prohibits sexual contact between personnel and locals, but as one senior military staff member emphasised 'It is not a criminal offence to have sex with a local. The military can make it a military crime; but policemen in a union cannot be criminalised for that sex'.[86] There is ongoing debate as to whether, given the significant power imbalance, there can be truly consensual relationships between international intervenors and local members of the population. Of course, even those debates deny agency to locals, particularly those who are educated, middle-class, and indeed work for or with international

---

[83] Staff & Agencies in Port-au-Prince, 'Haiti Shuts Down Oxfam GB over Prostitution Scandal', *The Guardian*, 14 June 2018, www.theguardian.com/world/2018/jun/14/haiti-shuts-down-oxfam-gb-over-prostitution-scandal (accessed 29 April 2020).

[84] Interview with senior Uruguay military officials on the basis of anonymity, 6 June 2017.

[85] Interview with UN Women, 8 June 2017.

[86] Interview with senior Canadian military official on the basis of anonymity, 7 June 2017.

entities. While those may be the rare exception rather than the rule, it is important to acknowledge that there is no clear answer as to whether all relationships between international and locals are exploitative, particularly when they live, work, and fraternise in the same places. The blanket rule for UN personnel, therefore, of no sexual contact, provides protection for all involved. Problems therefore arise when those rules are not understood, followed, or when they do not apply to other international intervenors.

The vast majority of 'consensual' relationships between peacekeepers and locals in Haiti were ones of 'survival' sex. As noted above, there is a blurred boundary between transactional sex (in exchange for money, goods, or services) and survival sex, with many women reporting[87] that they referred to the men as their boyfriends and sometimes sought out those relationships in order to ensure financial support for the families.[88] Sexual exploitation in the Zero Tolerance bulletin covers adult prostitution and survival sex.[89] There are some feminist critiques of this provision, focusing on the failure to acknowledge women's agency throughout the policy.[90] Others have gone further arguing that the policy fails to consider the legitimacy of transactional sex.[91] As Mudgway explains, 'such arguments can overestimate the ability of some local women to negotiate terms of an exchange or exercise true agency'.[92] The assumption that women are exercising a choice to consent to sex in such contexts 'oversimplifies the reality of such relationships. It is not about agency, it is about survival'.[93]

Survival sex encompasses a spectrum ranging from sex being exchanged for aid or assistance already owed to the population[94] to regular sexual relations in

---

[87] Kolbe, 'It's Not a Gift When It Comes with Price' (n 66); See also Lee and Bartels, 'They Put a Few Coins in Your Hand to Drop a Baby in You' (n 79).

[88] Kolbe, 'It's Not a Gift When It Comes with Price' (n 66).

[89] In the bulletin 'sexual exploitation' is defined as 'actual or attempted abuse of a position of vulnerability, deferential power or trust for sexual purposes including, but not limited to, profiting from monetarily, socially, or politically from the sexual exploitation of another'.

[90] See, for example, C. Harrington, *Politicisation of Sexual Violence: From Abolitionism to Peacekeeping* (Surrey: Ashgate 2010); Jennings, 'Service, Sex, and Security' (n 80); Jennings and Nikolic-Ristanovic, *UN Peacekeeping Economies and Local Sex Industries* (n 81); Kolbe, 'It's Not a Gift When It Comes with Price' (n 66).

[91] See D. Otto, 'Making Sense of Zero-Tolerance Policies in Peacekeeping Sexual Economies' in V. Munro and C. Stychin (eds.) *Sexuality and the Law: Feminist Engagements* (Abingdon and New York: Routledge 2014), 259; and J. McGill 'Survival Sex in Peacekeeping Economies: Re-reading the Zero Tolerance Approach to Sexual Exploitation and Sexual Abuse in United Nations Peace Support Operations' (2014) 18 *Journal of International Peacekeeping* 1.

[92] C. Mudgway 'Sexual Exploitation by UN Peacekeepers: The "Survival Sex" Gap in International Human Rights Law' (2017) 21 (9) *The International Journal of Human Rights* 1453, 1456.

[93] Ibid., 1457.

[94] Ibid., 1457.

6.5 Peacekeeper Sexual Exploitation and Abuse in Haiti

return for ongoing provision of financial support.[95] Studies in Haiti show that survival sex with peacekeepers was significantly prevalent in rural whereas in urban areas there was far more likelihood of transactional sex: in the former the provision of support usually was for food, clothes, medicines, and other necessities, whereas in urban areas it was more likely to be in the form of support for education and gifts of non-necessities such as cell phones, electronic devices, and jewellery.[96]

The gendered context in Haiti is one that gives rise to traditional gender roles being reinforced within families and communities. Despite legal advances on rape laws over the past twenty-five years, rape in marriage is still not prosecuted in the Haitian court system.[97] Women are expected to care for the home and family,[98] while men are expected to provide financial support, which leads to women having the perception that they are obligated to have sex with their husbands or boyfriends even when they do not want to do so.[99] As a result, many women did not view survival sex with peacekeepers as exploitative because it was not seen as outside the realms of 'normal' sexual relationships and power dynamics within Haitian society.[100] Therefore, very few instances of sexual exploitation were reported to the UN during its presence in Haiti, with the exception being where paternity claims were being pursued.

6.5.4 Children Fathered by Peacekeepers

Over the past twenty years there has been a much-needed focus on children born of war,[101] but insufficient attention paid to children fathered by peacekeepers and international humanitarians. In Haiti there are significant

---

95 Kolbe, 'It's Not a Gift When It Comes with Price' (n 66).

96 Ibid; See also Lee and Bartels, 'They Put a Few Coins in Your Hand to Drop a Baby in You' (n 79).

97 Kolbe, 'It's Not a Gift When It Comes with Price' (n 66), 4.

98 C. Fox 'Violent Sex: How Gender-Based Violence Is Structured in Haiti, Healthcare & HIV/ AIDS' (2013) 2 (1) *Indiana Journal of Law and Social Equality* 10.

99 M. Joshi et al. 'Language of Sexual Violence in Haiti: Perceptions of Victims, Community-level Workers, and Health Care Providers' (2014) 25 (4) *Journal of Health Care for the Poor and Underserved* 1623; and M. J. Small et al. 'Intimate Partner and Nonpartner Violence against Pregnant Women in Rural Haiti' (2008) 102 (3) *International Journal of Gynecology & Obstetrics* 226.

100 See empirical date in Kolbe, 'It's Not a Gift When It Comes with Price' (n 66). See also Lee and Bartels, 'They Put a Few Coins in Your Hand to Drop a Baby in You' (n 79).

101 See, for example, J. Neenan, *Closing The Protection Gap For Children Born of War* (LSE Women, Peace and Security Centre, 2018), www.lse.ac.uk/women-peace-security/assets/docu ments/2018/LSE-WPS-Children-Born-of-War.pdf (accessed 29 April 2020).

numbers of children fathered by UN personnel, with recent studies demonstrating that these children have been born to women across the country, and that there is a name in Creole for such children.[102] Haitian women are reported as saying that they wanted to conceive a child fathered by peacekeepers for a variety of reasons, including child maintenance, social hierarchies of having a lighter-skinned child, and the belief that the peacekeeper would take them and the child to their country of origin when repatriated.[103]

Attempts have recently started to be made by the UN and by NGOs to ensure access to paternity claims for those children. At the UN level the Victims' Rights Advocate has made paternity claims and support for children fathered by peacekeepers as one of the key priorities of her mandate, and has prioritised meeting with mothers to determine what best support they require,[104] as well as prioritising this issue with TCCs. Her work builds on steps taken at the UN level over the past fifteen years. In 2007 the UN General Assembly adopted a resolution on victim support[105] that, amongst other matters, acknowledge that children conceived in relationships between peacekeepers and local women are among those directly affected by SEA. The Comprehensive Strategy sets out that children 'who are found by a competent national authority to have been born as a result of acts of SEA by UN staff or related personnel' are entitled to support. Since 2013 the UN Secretary–General's reports on SEA have included country-specific data on children born of conflict-related sexual violence as well as calls for action. A victim-centred approach to children born of SEA has been extended in UN Security Council Resolution 2467, which calls for a more holistic understanding of accountability and justice and includes reparations as part of the measures for survivors.

Data gathered in Haiti demonstrate the difficulties of securing access to justice for children fathered by peacekeepers. During interviews with UN staff it became clear that to obtain paternity test children needed to be brought to UN mission headquarters, which presented logistical challenges particularly for rural-based women and children, in addition to the ongoing challenges faced by all claimants of gaining access to UN premises owing to security checks and requirements.

---

[102] Kolbe, 'It's Not a Gift When It Comes with Price' (n 66). See also Lee and Bartels, 'They Put a Few Coins in Your Hand to Drop a Baby in You' (n 79).

[103] Kolbe, 'It's Not a Gift When It Comes with Price' (n 66).

[104] www.ijdh.org/2018/04/topics/law-justice/the-bai-welcomes-the-uns-victims-rights-advocate-meeting-with-victims-of-sexual-exploitation-and-abuse-in-haiti/ (accessed 29 April 2020).

[105] General Assembly Resolution 62/214, 'Comprehensive Strategy on Assistance and Support to Victims of Sexual Exploitation and Abuse by United Nations Personnel and Related Personnel' UN Doc. A/RES/62/214, 7 March 2008.

In January 2018 BAI brought claims to Haitian courts in Port-au-Prince and Jacmel on behalf of ten Haitian women for child support and to establish custody against peacekeeper fathers.[106] To date those claims have not been resolved. The TCCs have not complied with the justice system, and under their agreements with the UN the Organisation has no power to compel them to do so. As a result, these test cases remain unlikely to succeed, thus leaving the children fathered by peacekeepers with no access to justice through the courts. The UN Victims' Rights Advocate has continued to take actions to provide justice for those children through the UN, political, and other avenues.[107]

6.6 CONCLUSION

The UN legacy in Haiti includes many acts of sexual exploitation and abuse that have not been addressed, with many victims and survivors having been denied access to their rights to truth, to a court and a remedy. This is a key issue across UN activities, both within peacekeeping and beyond, and remains a stain on the reputation of the Organisation and its personnel. Concerted efforts are being made within and across the UN to foreground and address sexual exploitation and abuse, and those efforts are being supported by member states, civil society, and independent experts. In order to move forwards changes need to be made across the UN, including to the laws governing the Organisation and its personnel, the internal rules and processes, and the practice at headquarters and on the ground. This is a multifaceted problem that requires a range of solutions to be designed and implemented in order to uphold the fundamental rights of the women and children affected by sexual exploitation and abuse perpetrated by all types of personnel working for or acting on behalf of the UN.

---

[106] www.ijdh.org/wp-content/uploads/2018/07/Press-Release_child-support-claims-filed-in-Haiti-against-UN_121117.pdf (accessed 29 April 2020).

[107] See for example, A. S. G Jane Connors, 'UN Supporting Abandoned Haiti Mothers and Children, Urging Others to Come Forward', 13 March 2020, https://news.un.org/en/audio/2020/03/1059351 (accessed 29 April 2020).

7

UN Peacekeepers' Use of Deadly Force to Maintain Law and Order

7.1 INTRODUCTION

This chapter examines the use of deadly force by UN peacekeepers mandated under Chapter VII of the UN Charter but operating outside the context of hostilities. Such actions may occur, for example when peacekeepers are deployed to a country where there is no armed conflict or when they are conducting operations against persons or groups who do not belong to the armed forces of a party to an armed conflict. The chapter will draw on the practice of the UN Stabilization Mission in Haiti (MINUSTAH), deployed from June 2004 to October 2017, during which time there was no armed conflict as defined in international law[1] in Haiti.

The majority of current peacekeeping missions are mandated by the Security Council acting under Charter VII of the UN Charter. Most of the Chapter VII peacekeeping mandates use 'all necessary means' or 'all necessary measures' formula to explicitly authorize the mission to use force,[2] although this is not essential.[3] Security Council resolutions authorizing a mission to use

---

[1] *Final Report on the Meaning of Armed Conflict in International Law*, International Law Association Committee on Use of Force, Hague Conference, 2010.

[2] 'All necessary means' or 'all necessary measures' are euphemisms routinely used by the Security Council to authorize force: Y. Dinstein 'The Right to Humanitarian Assistance' (2000) 53 (4) *Naval War College Review* 78, 87; N. Blokker, 'Ch. 9 Outsourcing the Use of Force: Towards More Security Council Control of Authorized Operations?' in M. Weller (ed.) *The Oxford Handbook of the Use of Force in International Law* (Oxford: Oxford University Press 2015), 210.

[3] Resolution 1509, establishing the UN Mission in Liberia in 2003, did not include the phrase 'all necessary means/measures' or any similar equivalent, but the Office of Legal Affairs of the UN Secretariat advised that 'the absence of the phrase was not critical, since an authorization to use force depends upon the interpretation of the resolution, specifically, on the ordinary and natural meaning which is to be given to its terms when they are read in the context of the resolution as a whole and in the light of its object and purpose, and against the background of the discussions leading to, and the circumstances of, its adoption, in particular the report that

7.1 Introduction

force – whether explicitly or not – deal only with use of force in the ius ad bellum context. This does not automatically remove any applicable use of force restrictions derived from international humanitarian law (IHL) and international human rights law (IHRL). The core elements of the IHRL and IHL rules on using deadly force constitute customary law, and are widely regarded as constituting peremptory norms that bind both the Security Council and troop contributing states.[4]

Under IHL intentional use of deadly force against the armed forces of a party to an armed conflict is lawful. IHL also permits foreseeable deaths and injuries to non-combatants provided that the victims were not directly targeted and provided that the 'expected ... incidental loss of civilian life, injury to civilians, damage to civilian objects, or a combination thereof' was not 'excessive in relation to the concrete and direct military advantage anticipated'.[5] But IHL rules on use of force apply only during armed conflict.

IHRL sets the standards for use of force outside of hostilities in armed conflict, and is clear that use of force that is likely to result in deaths is only permitted where it is 'strictly unavoidable in order to protect life'.[6] Exceptional circumstances, such as internal political instability or any other public emergency, may not be invoked to justify any departure from this principle.[7] These rules were adopted by the General Assembly in 1990[8] and are widely regarded as a codification of customary law.[9]

Since 1999 UN peacekeepers have been required to comply with at least the fundamental rules and principles of IHL when actively engaged as combatants

---

the Secretary-General submitted pursuant to resolution 1497 (2003)'. Note to the Under-Secretary-General of the Department of Peacekeeping Operations, *United Nations Juridical Yearbook 2003* (United Nations, Legal Publications of the Codification Division of the Office of Legal Affairs 2003), 538–539.

4   L. Hanikainen, *Peremptory Norms (Jus Cogens) in International Law: Historical Development, Criteria, Present Status* (Helsinki: Finnish Lawyers' Publishing Company 1988) 516–517; K. M. Larsen, *The Human Rights Treaty Obligations of Peacekeepers* (Cambridge: Cambridge University Press 2012), 323–333; A. Orakhelashvili 'The Impact of Peremptory Norms on the Interpretation and Application of United Nations Security Council Resolutions' 16 (1) *European Journal of International Law* 58; J. Paust 'The UN is Bound by Human Rights: Understanding the Full Reach of Human Rights, Remedies and Nonimmunity' (2010) 51

5   Protocol I additional to the Geneva Conventions, 8 June 1977, Article 51 (1)(b).

6   *Basic Principles on the Use of Force and Firearms by Law Enforcement Officials*, Adopted by the Eighth United Nations Congress on the Prevention of Crime and the Treatment of Offenders, Cuba, 1990, para. 9.

7   Ibid., para. 8.

8   Ibid.

9   Ibid., para. 8.

in an armed conflict.[10] But the UN has not published any formal statement as to the legal framework governing peacekeepers' use of force when they are not engaged in that way. UN peacekeeping missions frequently engage in operations designed to curb violent activity by people that are not party to an armed conflict and therefore are not legitimate military targets under IHL. This is particularly true of missions mandated to support 'the restoration and extension of State authority', which according to the UN's peacekeeping website is one of the activities in which 'UN peacekeepers are often mandated to play a catalytic role'.[11] Commonly this role includes the use of 'military means to stabilize a country, sometimes with all necessary means to neutralize potential "spoilers."'[12]

The Capstone Doctrine, which sets out the principles and guidelines that govern peacekeeping operations, explains that peacekeepers are often deployed into situations often 'characterized by the presence of militias, criminal gangs, and other spoilers' and that:

> In such situations, the Security Council has given United Nations peacekeeping operations "robust" mandates authorizing them to "use all necessary means" to deter forceful attempts to disrupt the political process, protect civilians under imminent threat of physical attack, and/ or assist the national authorities in maintaining law and order.[13]

The UN Department of Peacekeeping (DPKO)'s *Draft Concept Note on Robust Peacekeeping* asserts that the use of force by peacekeeping operations is pursued on a case-by-case basis only and 'in full compliance with the applicable humanitarian, human rights and refugee law'.[14]

Neither IHL nor IHRL permit the use of deadly force against spoilers or criminals that are not parties to an armed conflict or against civilians directly participating in such a conflict, yet two of the three examples given in the Capstone Doctrine focus on such scenarios.[15] The UN has not produced

---

[10] UN Secretary General, *Bulletin on Observance by United Nations Forces of International Humanitarian Law*, 12 August 1999, UN Doc ST/SGB/1999/13.

[11] United Nations Security Council Field Missions Mandate Table, 30 June 2019 www.un.org /securitycouncil/file/122688 (accessed 25 April 2020).

[12] J. Karlsrud 'The UN at War: Examining the Consequences of Peace-enforcement Mandates for the UN Peacekeeping Operations in the CAR, the DRC and Mali' (2015) 36 (1) *Third World Quarterly* 42.

[13] United Nations, *Peacekeeping Operations Principles and Guidelines* (United Nations, 2008), 34.

[14] *Draft DPKO/DFS Concept Note on Robust Peacekeeping?* (New York: United Nations 2010), section 3. The concept note is still draft ten years on, an indication perhaps of tensions on the topic even within the UN, but this paragraph is uncontroversial.

[15] In order to 'deter forceful attempts to disrupt the political process' or to 'assist the national authorities in maintaining law and order' at page 34 of *Peacekeeping Operations Principles and Guidelines* (United Nations, 2008).

guidance on how troops should interpret 'all necessary means' in these circumstances, nor is there any guidance on the applicable legal framework. DPKO's guidelines for peacekeeping missions make no reference to the protected status of civilian spoilers, nor indeed to IHRL, and make no distinction between operations conducted against the armed forces of a party to an armed conflict and law enforcement operations aimed at curbing crime and controlling political unrest.[16] Similarly, such matters are not addressed in mission-specific Rules of Engagement (ROE).

7.2 STABILIZATION AND USE OF FORCE AGAINST 'SPOILERS'

The International Committee of the Red Cross (ICRC)'s 2015 guidance on *Violence and the Use of Force* states that in a peace support operation 'as in any other, the legal nature of the situation in which the force is deployed determines the legal framework and rules to be respected' and that the mandate, ROE, and status of force agreements 'are only indicative'.[17] It goes on to state that when peacekeepers use force the 'same rules then apply as for other operations depending on the situation's legal categorization'.[18] Although the circumstances in which a peace support operation may use force is subject to the terms of its mandate, this does not affect the applicable legal framework which will be the determined in the same way as for other military operations.[19]

The year 1999 saw a major development in that for the first time the UN formally accepted that IHL rules apply to peacekeeping operations in certain circumstances[20] – that is, when peacekeepers are 'actively engaged as combatants' in a situation of 'armed conflict'.[21] In all other circumstances peacekeepers have the same right to protection from attack as non-combatants, and therefore IHL does not apply to their operations.[22] The key issue, then, is

---

[16] UN Guidelines for the Development of Rules of Engagement and Sample ROE for UN Peacekeeping Operations, Jean-Marie Guehenno, 1 December 2000.

[17] ICRC, *Violence and the Use of Force*, 1 January 2015, 37 www.icrc.org/en/publication/0943-violence-and-use-force (accessed 29 April 2020).

[18] Ibid., 45.

[19] D. Murray et al., *Practitioner's Guide to Human Rights Law in Armed Conflict* (Oxford: Chatham House Royal Institute of International Affairs and Oxford University Press 2016), 260.

[20] UN Secretary General, *Bulletin on Observance by United Nations Forces of International Humanitarian Law*, UN Doc ST/SGB/1999/13, 12 August 1999.

[21] Ibid.

[22] This is in order to ensure that both the obligations and privileges of IHL apply to all combatants regardless of whom they fight for: Adam Roberts notes that if this principle were to be undermined 'all respect for the 1949 Geneva Conventions may be destroyed'. A. Roberts

whether there is an armed conflict to which the peacekeepers are actively engaged as combatants.

Although a Chapter VII peacekeeping mandate indicates that the Security Council has determined that there is a threat to international peace and security, this is not in-and-of-itself determinative of whether an armed conflict exists.[23] The International Criminal Tribunal for the former Yugoslavia Appeals Chamber has ruled that 'an armed conflict exists whenever there is a resort to armed force between States or protracted armed violence between governmental authorities and organized armed groups or between such groups within a state'.[24] Under customary international law, for a situation of armed violence to meet the legal criteria for armed conflict it must at the very least involve organised armed groups capable of conducting hostilities even if they do not have the same capabilities or means as state armed forces.[25] The International Law Association insists that armed conflict must distinguished from riots, banditry, short-lived insurrections, terrorist activities, and civil unrest[26] because in an armed conflict 'states have expanded rights to kill without warning, detain without trial, and suspend or derogate from treaties and other obligations'.[27] Moreover, 'United Nations forces engaged in armed conflict will have rights and duties not applicable in operations outside of armed conflict'.[28]

Even if the situation is one of armed conflict, IHL will only apply if the peacekeepers are engaged as combatants in an operation directed against members of the armed forces of a party to the conflict or against civilians directly participating in the conflict. This is because lawful use of armed force against people that are not directly participating in an armed conflict – for

---

and R. Guelff, *Documents on the Laws of War*, 3rd ed. (Oxford: Oxford University Press 2000), 625.

[23] Murray et al., *Practitioner's Guide to Human Rights Law in Armed Conflict* (n 19), 261.

[24] International Tribunal for the former Yugoslavia, *Prosecutor v. Tadić*, IT-94-1-AR72, Appeals Chamber, Decision on the Defence Motion for Interlocutory Appeal on Jurisdiction, 2 October 1995, para. 70.

[25] N. Melzer, *Interpretive Guidance on the Notion of Direct Participation in Hostilities in International Humanitarian Law* (Geneva: ICRC 2009), 32; How is the Term 'Armed Conflict' Defined in International Humanitarian Law? International Committee of the Red Cross (ICRC) Opinion Paper, March 2008, www.icrc.org/eng/assets/files/other/opinion-paper -armed-conflict.pdf (accessed 29 April 2020); *Protocol Additional to the Geneva Conventions of 12 August 1949 and relating to the Protection of Victims of Non-International Armed Conflicts*, (Geneva 1977) para. 1 (2).

[26] *Final Report on the Meaning of Armed Conflict in International Law*, ILA Committee on Use of Force, Hague Conference, 2010, 28.

[27] Ibid., page 4.

[28] Ibid., page 1.

example, criminals, rioters, civilian perpetrators of war crimes – is 'a matter of law enforcement or defence of self or others' and not governed by IHL.[29] According to the ICRC, in order for an act by a civilian to qualify as direct participation in hostilities the act must specifically be designed to directly cause the required threshold of harm in support of a party to the conflict and to the detriment of another.[30] In the view of the ICRC even perpetration of war crimes or violations of IHL do not necessarily constitute direct participation in hostilities.[31] Such conduct may give rise to lawful use of armed force as a matter of law enforcement or defence of self or others, but '[l]oss of protection against direct attack within the meaning of IHL is not a sanction for criminal behavior'.[32]

Therefore, unless the peacekeeping mission is a party to an armed conflict any use of force actions will be governed by IHRL.[33] The Leuven Manual states that 'the use of lethal force in Peace Operations is informed in particular by the right to life' which is recognised as customary law, and so applies to international organizations conducting Peace Operations.[34] Whilst the rules relating to the conduct of hostilities 'will apply when force is used by one party against another party to that conflict or against civilians who directly participate in hostilities' use of force outside the conduct of hostilities 'will generally have to comply with the more restrictive rules relating to law enforcement'.[35]

The UN has not yet formally adopted a resolution or bulletin setting out the circumstances in which IHRL applies to UN forces but nevertheless appears to have accepted that IHRL obligations, including those governing use of deadly force, apply to peacekeeping operations. Despite ongoing controversy regarding the extent to which the UN is bound by IHRL owing to it not being a state, DPKO's *Guidelines on Use of Force* specify that when peacekeepers use force

---

[29] Melzer, *Interpretive Guidance on the Notion of Direct Participation in Hostilities under International Humanitarian Law* (n 25), 62.

[30] The act must be likely to adversely affect the military operations or military capacity of a party to an armed conflict or, alternatively, to inflict death, injury, or destruction on persons or objects protected against direct attack and there must be a direct causal link between the act and the harm likely to result either from that act, or from a coordinated military operation of which that act constitutes an integral part and the act must be specifically designed to directly cause the required threshold of harm in support of a party to the conflict and to the detriment of another: Melzer, *Interpretive Guidance on the Notion of Direct Participation in Hostilities under International Humanitarian Law* (n 25), 16.

[31] Ibid., 62.

[32] Ibid.

[33] Melzer, *Interpretive Guidance on the Notion of Direct Participation in Hostilities under International Humanitarian Law* (n 25), 261.

[34] *Leuven Manual on the International Law Applicable to Peace Operations* eds. T. Gill et al., (Cambridge: Cambridge University Press 2017) 150, 152.

[35] Ibid.

they must comply with 'human rights norms, principles and standards' as well as any 'applicable international humanitarian law'.[36] IHL is applicable only during armed conflict; therefore outside of armed conflict the obligation on peacekeepers to comply with 'human rights norms, principles and standards' is not subject to potential modification by IHL.

There are states – including some permanent members of the Security Council – that reject the position that IHRL applies extraterritorially except in very limited circumstances. Nevertheless, guidance issued to UN police peacekeeping units routinely requires them to comply with IHRL.[37] The IHRL obligations that apply to military personnel when carrying out law enforcement operations are the same as those that apply to police: this is equally true of UN peacekeepers as of national police and military forces: yet the UN only requires UN police to comply with IHRL.[38] The Specialized Training Materials for UN Police on *Human Rights Standards in the Use of Force* sets out that 'UN Police must comply with both treaty based and customary international human rights'[39] and recommend that trainees read the Basic Principles on the Use of Force and Firearms by Law Enforcement Officials and the Code of Conduct for Law Enforcement Officials for further guidance[40] and that they ought to be required reading for instructors.[41] Similarly DPKO's 2017 Guidelines on The Role of United Nations Police in Protection of Civilians states that '[i]n all instances, members of the police component must respect international human rights and criminal justice standards, notably as laid down in the United Nations Basic Principles on the Use of Force and Firearms by Law Enforcement Officials'.[42]

---

[36] *Use of Force by Military Components in United Nations Peacekeeping Operations*, United Nations Department of Peacekeeping Operations/ Department of Field Support Ref: 2016.24, approved by Hervé Ladsous, USG DPKO; Atul Khare, USG DFS Effective date: 1 February 2017.

[37] See, for example, *The UN Manual on Mission-based Police Planning in Peace Operations* Reference 2017.13 (UNHQ, New York, 2017), which states at paragraph 2.5.4.1 page 13, that use of force is regulated by the *Basic Principles on the Use of Force and Firearms by Law Enforcement Officials, the Code of Conduct for Law Enforcement Officials* and mission specific *Directives on the Use of Force.*

[38] *Basic Principles on the Use of Force and Firearms by Law Enforcement Officials* (n 37); Interview with Philip Alston Special Rapporteur on Extrajudicial, Summary or Arbitrary Executions, New York, November 2016.

[39] Specialised Training Materials for UN Police, Human Rights Standards in the Use of Force, United Nations Peacekeeping Resource Hub, 7, https://research.un.org/c.php?g=636989& p=4462845 (accessed 29 April 2020).

[40] Ibid., page 8.

[41] Ibid., page 3.

[42] UNDPKO, Department of Field Support, *Guidelines: The role of United Nations police in protection of civilians* Ref. 2017.12, 1 August 2017, https://police.un.org/sites/default/files/protec tion-of-civilians-unpol_guidelines_2017.pdf (accessed 29 April 2020).

7.3 Right to Life Obligations of UN Peacekeeping Troops

Clearly the UN does not have a problem *per se* with requiring its peace-keeping personnel to comply with IHRL, including obligations restricting the use of deadly force, and there is no evidence that member states have objected, notwithstanding the views of some regarding the extra-territorial scope of IHRL. To the extent that controversy exists about the applicability of IHRL to UN peacekeeping, this appears in practice to be focused on its potential applicability to military operations rather than to legal disputes as to the extraterritorial reach of IHRL or the fact that the UN is not party to any IHRL treaties.

7.3 RIGHT TO LIFE OBLIGATIONS OF UN PEACEKEEPING TROOPS

In his 2014 report as Special Rapporteur on Extrajudicial, Summary or Arbitrary Executions, Christof Heyns reviewed the international law on the right to life relevant to use of force and concluded that, under generally applicable international law, even when police or troops are acting in response to a public emergency (except when they are using force 'in the conduct of hostilities in armed conflict')[43] 'the only objective that can be legitimate when lethal force is used is to save the life of a person or to protect a person from serious injury'.[44] In Heyns' view, the obligation on law enforcement officers to comply with international law standards on the right to life also applies to United Nations peacekeeping troops.[45] Philip Alston, Heyns' predecessor as Special Rapporteur, shares that view.[46] Such a view has been underscored by practitioners who assert that outside of hostilities in armed conflict the only justification for resort to deadly force by armed forces, including peacekeeping forces, 'must be a real and imme-diate danger to life or limb'.[47] The UN training materials for UN Police are fully in line with these views, stating that '[i]ntentional lethal use of force and firearms shall be permitted only when strictly unavoidable in order to protect human life'.[48]

---

[43] *Report of the Special Rapporteur on extrajudicial, summary or arbitrary executions, Christof Heyns*, UN Doc. A/HRC/26/36, 1 April 2014, para. 38.

[44] Ibid., para. 58.

[45] Ibid., paras. 74 and 145.

[46] Report of Philip Alston, Special Rapporteur on Extrajudicial, summary or arbitrary execu-tions, UN Doc. E/CN.4/2006/53/Add.1, 27 March 2006, 323; Interview with Philip Alston at New York University Law School, November 2016.

[47] Ibid., 125.

[48] Specialised Training Materials for UN Police, Human Rights Standards in the Use of Force (n 39),12.

General Maqsood Ahmed, Military Adviser for Peacekeeping Operations of the United Nations from 2013 to 2016, has emphasized that IHRL obligations protecting the right to life apply not only to UN police but also to the military contingents of UN peacekeeping missions.[49] He states that, with the rare exception of missions that are explicitly mandated to neutralize combatants,[50] UN peacekeepers' obligation to respect the right to life 'includes the perpetrator of violence ... To use pre-emptive force against perpetrators of violence we would need substantial evidence that they were about to attack civilians'.[51] He added that because of the UN's obligations under IHRL:

> We do not carry out robust operations in populated neighbourhoods. We are very careful not to use force in situations where civilians may be killed or injured. The only circumstances in which we would use heavy force in the presence of civilians is if civilians are being held hostage, and their lives are at risk.[52]

In contrast to the detailed guidance on compliance with IHRL in the UN's materials for police, the ROE for the military contingents of UN peacekeeping missions make no reference to IHRL.[53] They also make no distinction between ROE for use in hostilities and ROE for use in law enforcement despite the Basic Principles on the Use of Force and Firearms by Law Enforcement Officials applying to all officials carrying out a law enforcement role, and despite DPKO's guidance that all UN peacekeepers must comply with human rights norms, principles, and standards.[54]

General Maqsood's view on the IHRL obligations constraining peacekeepers' use of deadly force was not shared by everyone working in DPKO and the UN Office of Legal Affairs. A legal advisor with many years service in the UN Office of Legal Affairs stated that, under the UN's current approach, the mandate is the key factor that determines the circumstances in which peacekeepers can use deadly force and therefore:

---

[49] General Maqsood Ahmed, interview with Siobhán Wills, June 22 2016, UN Headquarters, New York.

[50] Such as the Intervention Brigade (part of the UN Stabilisation Mission in the DRC, MONUSCO) mandated under Security Council Resolution 2098, UN Doc. S/RES/2098 (28 March 2013) to carry out targeted offensive operations to neutralize armed groups.

[51] General Maqsood Ahmed, interview with Siobhán Wills, June 22 2016, UN Headquarters, New York.

[52] Ibid.

[53] United Nations' Guidelines for the Development of Rules of Engagement (ROE) for United Nations Peacekeeping Operations, Rule 1.5, U.N. Doc. MD/FGS/0220.0001 (2002).

[54] *Use of Force by Military Components in United Nations Peacekeeping Operations*, United Nations Department of Peacekeeping Operations/ Department of Field Support Ref: 2016.24

7.3 Right to Life Obligations of UN Peacekeeping Troops

A person that would not be a military target under traditional IHL may become an authorized military target of a UN peacekeeping operation (and therefore killed) provided that: the peacekeepers' use of force is pursuant to an authorization in a Chapter VII mandate and is provided for in the mission's rule of engagement; that the use of force is proportionate to achieving the authorized objective; that minimum force is used; and that force is used only as a last resort. This framework applies across the board to all UN peacekeeping missions, regardless of whether the situation is one of armed conflict or not.[55]

In a separate interview, another senior advisor in the UN Office of Legal Affairs explained the UN's doctrine in very similar terms.[56] Both legal officers added that the customary principles of both IHL and IHRL are 'nonetheless integral to the conduct of the mission including its military component'.[57] But in the context of use of force it is difficult to see how customary IHRL obligations regarding the right to life can be properly applied and upheld if the UN does not explicitly affirm that peacekeepers must adhere to IHRL standards on the right to life in all law enforcement operations,[58] and does not require missions to distinguish between use of deadly force against combatants and use of deadly force against criminals, rioters and other 'spoilers'.

One problem that arises from a failure to distinguish between armed conflict and non-armed conflict situations concerns the meaning of proportionality. All guidance on use of deadly force by peacekeepers states that it must be proportionate, but the 'proportionate to what?' element differs. The Chatham House Practitioners' Guide to Human Rights Law in Armed Conflict states that when carrying out law enforcement operations any use of deadly force by armed forces including peacekeepers, 'must be proportionate to the aim of protecting life'.[59] This contrasts with the UN formulation of proportionality provided on the UN's website:

> A UN peacekeeping operation should only use force as a measure of last resort. It should always be calibrated in a precise, proportional and appropriate manner,

---

[55] Senior Officer, with the UN Office of Legal Affairs, Interview with Siobhán Wills, UNHQ, United Nations, New York, June 2016.

[56] Senior Officer, UN Office of the Legal Counsel, Interview with Siobhán Wills, UNHQ, United Nations, New York, June 2016.

[57] Ibid.

[58] Murray et al., *Practitioner's Guide to Human Rights Law in Armed Conflict* (n 19), at page 91, uses the term 'security operations' to denote activities 'which are largely of the nature of law enforcement' but conducted during an armed conflict. However, law enforcement is the term used by both the International Committee of the Red Cross and the International Law Association.

[59] Murray et al., *Practitioner's Guide to Human Rights Law in Armed Conflict* (n 19), 136.

within the principle of the minimum force necessary to achieve the desired effect, while sustaining consent for the mission and its mandate.[60]

An obligation to use the minimum force necessary to 'achieve the desired effect' is open to broad interpretation and the qualification while 'sustaining consent for the mission and its mandate' implies a political rather than legal constraint. The definition of proportionality set out in the *UN Guidelines for the Development of Rules of Engagement*, which are used in training and as a template for drafting mission specific ROE is as follows:

> Any force used must be limited, in its intensity and duration, to that which is necessary to achieve the authorized objective. In some circumstances, operational urgency may dictate that immediate use of deadly force may be necessary for this purpose.
>
> The use of force must be commensurate with the level of the threat. However, the level of force that is used may have to be higher than the level of the threat in order to avoid or minimise UN or civilian casualties, or, in the case of offensive action, to ensure that the authorized objective is achieved.[61]

This is loose guidance compared with peacekeepers' legal obligation under IHRL to ensure that any use of deadly force is 'proportionate to the aim of protecting life'.[62] Given that peacekeeping mandates routinely authorise the use of 'all necessary means' to carry out a wide variety of tasks, including law enforcement, this is a critical difference that has significant implications for host state communities living in the vicinity of UN operations.

7.4 'COLLATERAL DAMAGE' CAUSED BY MINUSTAH IN CITÉ SOLEIL THE YEARS 2004–2007

The UN Stabilisation Mission in Haiti (MINUSTAH) was deployed in the aftermath of the departure of former President Aristide in February 2004. The armed violence associated with the coup against Aristide lasted just three weeks and involved no more than three hundred armed men.[63] The

---

[60] United Nations website, 'Principles of UN Peacekeeping' https://peacekeeping.un.org/en/pr inciples-of-peacekeeping (accessed 29 April 2020).

[61] United Nations, *Guidelines for the development of ROE for UNPKO*, UN document MD/ FGS/0220.0001, May 2002 authorized by Major Tim Ford, Military Advisor, Department of Peacekeeping Operations 2000–2002; The *UN Guidelines for the Development of Rules of Engagement and Sample ROE for UN Peacekeeping Operations*, authorized by Jean-Marie Guehenno, 1 December 2000.

[62] Murray et al., *Practitioner's Guide to Human Rights Law in Armed Conflict* (n 19), 136.

[63] C. Call and G. Sorensen, *U.N. Operations and State-building: A Case Study of Haiti* (New York: Center on International Cooperation, 3 March 2009), 5 https://reliefweb.int/site

International Crisis Group has concluded that throughout the entire period of violence in Haiti in the twenty-first century there were no 'clearly identified parties to a conflict' and the situation 'never escalated into an internal armed conflict'.[64] Several ICRC reports reflect a similar view.[65] The Center on International Cooperation, in a case study cited by the UN Department of Peacekeeping in its own reports, also concludes that there was no armed conflict in Haiti.[66]

According to DPO the 'core of the problem' in Haiti has been 'policing'.[67] General Augusto Heleno Ribeiro Pereira, MINUSTAH's force commander from June 2004 to August 2005, said that Haiti 'was facing what was at root a police problem – criminal gangs had sunk their roots deep into a society beset by poverty'.[68] For Lt-General Peixoto Vieira Neto, who headed MINUSTAH's operations section under General Heleno, and was later force commander, the situation in Haiti could not be characterised as 'similar to a "war among the people"' but 'a number of threats were spread among Haitian society, the real centre of gravity of the whole peace operation'.[69] Siman and Santos note that there was no civil war and no parties to an armed

---

s/reliefweb.int/files/resources/5BE236AD3CB233CA49257591000A778B-Full_Report.pdf (accessed 29 April 2020); J. Cockayne 'Winning Haiti's Protection Competition: Organized Crime and Peace Operations Past, Present and Future' (2008) 16 (1) *International Peacekeeping* 77, 82.

[64] 'Towards a Post-MINUSTAH Haiti: Making an Effective Transition: Latin America/ Caribbean Report N°44', International Crisis Group, 2 August 2012, 16; M. Schuberth 'A Transformation from Political to Criminal Violence? Politics, Organised Crime and the Shifting Functions of Haiti's Urban Armed Groups' (2015) 15 (2) *Conflict, Security & Development* 169, 176.

[65] A. Serafin, 'Urban Violence: War by Any Other Name' (2010), 1. The Magazine of the International Red Cross and Red Crescent Movement, www.redcross.int/EN/mag/magazine2010_1/20-23.html (accessed 29 April 2020); ICRC, Haiti bulletin, 26 February 2004, www.icrc.org/en/doc/resources/documents/update/5wjlkb.htm (accessed 29 April 2020).

[66] Call and Sorensen, *U.N. Operations and State-building* (n 63), 5. Call and Sorenson conducted interviews in Haiti and at UN headquarters with various units at DPKO, DPA, UNDOCO and UNDP, which suggests that this view reflects a degree of consensus at the UN. The study is cited in *Second Generation Disarmament, Demobilization, and Reintegration Practices in UN Peacekeeping Operations* (UN DPKO, Office of Rule of Law and Security Institutions 2010), 67, https://peacekeeping.un.org/sites/default/files/2gddr_eng_with_cover.pdf (accessed 29 April 2020).

[67] A. Sotomayor, *The Myth of the Democratic Peacekeeper: Civil-Military Relations and the United Nations* (Baltimore: John Hopkins University Press 2014), 139.

[68] E. Aldunate, *Backpacks Full of Hope: The UN Mission in Haiti* (Waterloo: Wilfrid Laurier University Press 2010), 47.

[69] F. Peixoto Vieria Neto 'The Brazilian military experience in Haiti' in *Brazil's participation in MINUSTAH (2004–2017): perceptions, lessons and practices for future missions*, (Rio de Janeiro: Igarapé Institute 2017), 16, 19, https://igarape.org.br/wp-content/uploads/2018/03/Brazils-Participation-in-MINUSTAH-2004-2017.pdf (accessed 29 April 2020).

conflict in Haiti, and therefore the focus of MINUSTAH's military activities 'easily came to include offensive actions against criminal gangs'.[70]

Part of the mandate for the UN Stabilization Mission in Haiti was adopted under Chapter VII. Resolution 1542 mandating the mission did not refer to 'all necessary means' but the authority to use force to carry out certain of the mission's tasks was determined from the text of the resolution and associated UN documents.[71] The mandate did not refer to armed conflict but noted 'the existence of challenges to the political, social and economic stability of Haiti'.[72] The Secretary–General's report published the same month as S/RES 1542 was adopted, stated that 'the greatest threat to security' in Haiti came from 'community-organized armed groups' that were 'highly fragmented, located primarily in impoverished urban areas' and relied on 'banditry and other criminal activities in order to sustain themselves' as well as politically motivated intimidation which 'now mainly targets Fanmi Lavalas supporters'.[73]

MINUSTAH is credited with successfully reducing the 'banditry and other criminal activities' of armed groups based in marginalized communities bordering Port-au-Prince.[74] But numerous reports suggest that the death toll as result of MINUSTAH's raids was high.[75] The largest operations took place between 2005 and 2007 in Cité Soleil, a densely populated city of less than eight square miles with a population, at the time, of between 200,000 and 300,000.[76] Exact figures of casualties are impossible to obtain since the UN did not conduct any post-operation investigations in the city to ascertain the number of people killed and injured. However, several independent investigations by human rights groups, and by Harvard and Miami law schools, as

---

[70] M. Siman and V. Santos 'Interrogating the Security-Development Nexus in Brazil's Domestic and Foreign Pacification Engagements' (2018) 18 (1) *Conflict, Security and Development* 61, 69.

[71] Security Council resolution 1542 UN Doc. S/RES 1542 30 April 2004.

[72] Ibid.

[73] Report of the Secretary-General on Haiti UN Doc. S/2004/300, 16 April 2004 para. 23. Fanmi Lavalas is the political party founded by Aristide.

[74] M. Dziedzic and R. M. Perito, *Haiti Confronting the Gangs of Port-au-Prince* (Washington: USIP, September 2008) www.usip.org/sites/default/files/sr208.pdf (accessed 29 April 2020); M. Berdal and D. Ucko 'The Use of Force in UN Peacekeeping Operations: Problems and Prospects' (2015) 160 (1) *RUSI Journal* 6, 8.

[75] Sotomayor, *The Myth of the Democratic Peacekeeper* (n 67), 141; Dziedzic and Perito, *Haiti Confronting the Gangs of Port-au-Prince* (n 74), 5; G. Hammond, *Saving Port-au-Prince: United Nations Efforts to Protect Civilians in Haiti in 2006–2007* (Washington: Stimson Centre, June 2012), 33, 47.

[76] D. Revol, 'Hoping for change in Haiti's Cité-Soleil', *International Red Cross and Red Crescent Movement*, 2006 www.redcross.int/EN/mag/magazine2006_2/10-11.html (accessed 29 April 2020).

7.4 'Collateral Damage' Caused by Minustah in Cité Soleil

well reports by the United States Institute for Peace and the Stimson Center, indicate that scores of people were killed, and many more injured, as a direct result of UN fire.[77] Archive film footage taken by local reporters, memos sent by the US Embassy in Haiti,[78] and a 2018 documentary *It Stays With You: Use of Force by UN Peacekeepers in Haiti* also indicate high levels of casualties.[79]

Walter Dorn, who worked in intelligence for MINUSTAH, describes how in conducting operations against the gangs in Bois Neuf and other marginalized communities in Cité Soleil, MINUSTAH 'deliberately sought to draw fire from the gangs ... knowing that the gangsters' pride would force them to retaliate, thus allowing the United Nations to return fire from relatively safe positions.'[80] Deliberately drawing fire in densely populated neighbourhoods creates a high risk of casualties, particularly because MINUSTAH blockaded Cité Soleil's exits for at least twenty-four hours after each of its operations ended.

Dorn also states that from December 2006 to March 2007 MINUSTAH's operations were 'guided by the principle of overwhelming force for psychological

---

[77] T. M. Griffin and I. P. Stotsky, *Haiti Human Rights Investigation* (Miami: Center for the Study of Human Rights, University of Miami 2004); *Keeping the Peace in Haiti? An Assessment of the United Nations Stabilization Mission in Haiti Using Compliance with its Prescribed Mandate as a Barometer for Success* (Cambridge and Rio de Janeiro: Harvard Law Student Advocates for Human Rights, & Centro de Justiça Global, 2005); S. Donnelly, 'Eyewitnesses Describe Massacre by UN Troops in Haitian Slum', *Democracy Now*, 11 July 2005, www.democracynow.org/2005/7/11/eyewitnesses_describe_massacre_by_un_troops (accessed 30 April 2020); S. Donnelly, *A Summary of Findings of the US Labor and Human Rights Delegation to Haiti* (San Francisco: San Francisco Labor Council and margueritelaurent.com 2005) www.margueritelaurent.com/campaigns/campaignone/human_rights_reports/unmassacre.html (accessed 30 April 2020); T. Griffin, *UN in Haiti*, Report for Lamp for Haiti, April 2007; 'UN in Haiti accused of second massacre' (2007) News HaitiAction.net http://haitiaction.net/News/HIP/1_21_7/1_21_7.html (accessed 30 April 2020); M. L. Mendonça, *UN Troops Accused of Human Rights Violations in Haiti* (Washington: Americas Program, Center for International Policy 2008) www.worldpress.org/Americas/3056.cfm (accessed 30 April 2020); Dziedzic and Perito, *Haiti Confronting the Gangs of Port-au-Prince* (n 74); Hammond, *Saving Port-au-Prince: United Nations Efforts to Protect Civilians in Haiti in 2006–2007* (n 75), 33, 47.

[78] Cable from US Embassy estimating about 20 women and children killed on 6 July 2005: 'Haiti Post-Dread Wilme' Cable Number 'Port au Prince 001829' from US embassy Port au Prince to State Department Headquarters 12 July 2005. Freedom of Information Act release to K Yearman http://haitiinformationproject.blogspot.com/2016/07/eleventh-anniversary-of-cite-soleil.html (accessed 30 April 2020); K. Pina (director) *Haiti: We Must Kill the Bandits* (90 minutes 2007), www.cinemapolitica.org/film/haiti-we-must-kill-bandits (accessed 30 April 2020).

[79] C. McLaughlin and S. Wills (directors) *It Stays With You: Use of Force by UN Peacekeepers in Haiti* (52 minutes, 2018), www.itstayswithyou.com/film

[80] W. Dorn 'Intelligence-led Peacekeeping: The United Nations Stabilization Mission in Haiti (MINUSTAH), 2006–07' (2009) 24 (6) *Intelligence and National Security* 805, 814.

advantage'.[81] Use of 'overwhelming force for psychological advantage' is difficult to square with the core principles of UN peacekeeping and is impossible to square with peacekeepers' legal obligations under IHRL, particularly when the operations are conducted in urban neighbourhoods where people live in fragile homes that can be easily penetrated by bullets.

Many of the wounds inflicted during MINUSTAH's operations were too severe to have been caused by the kind of weapons owned by Haitians and could only have been caused by fire from MINUSTAH. Survivors say that several children and a pregnant woman were killed in their beds by bullets coming through the roofs.[82] The bullet holes have been repaired but are still clearly visible today.[83] John Carroll, a US based doctor who works with Médecins Sans Frontières, said he spoke with the family who 'said the helicopter fired down on Cité Soleil for 3 hours. I saw the holes in the roof and the holes in the people'. He also said 'I went to St. Catherine's Hospital in Cite Soleil . . . I examined the patients myself and their stories seemed to correspond with their injuries'.[84] Cité Soleil's only public hospital was 'blasted by a bullet from a 20-millimeter cannon, a weapon that is mounted on the Jordanian tanks but is not used by the local armed groups'.[85] The only entity in Haiti that possessed helicopters and armoured vehicles was the UN peacekeeping mission. The outcry over the casualties caused by MINUSTAH led to an inquiry by the Brazilian Bar Association, which sent a team to Haiti to investigate. Their report to Brazil's Congress in December 2004 strongly criticized General Heleno,[86] who explained that MINUSTAH was 'under extreme pressure' from the United States, Canada, and France 'to use violence' in Cité Soleil.[87]

Six months later, in Operation Iron Fist, undertaken on July 6 2005 to arrest gang leader Dread Wilme, MINUSTAH reported that it fired 22,700 bullets,

---

[81] Ibid.

[82] Survivors' testimonies in McLaughlin and Wills (directors) *It Stays With You* (n 79); Donnelly, 'Eyewitnesses Describe Massacre by UN Troops in Haitian Slum' (n 77); Donnelly, *A Summary of Findings of the US Labor and Human Rights Delegation to Haiti* (n 77); T. Griffin, *UN in Haiti*, (Cité Soleil Lamp for Haiti 2007).

[83] Seen by Siobhán Wills on visits to Bois Neuf, Cité Soleil in 2016 – 2018.

[84] A. Buncombe, 'Civilians Caught in Crossfire During Port-au-Prince Raids', *Independent*, 2 February 2007, www.independent.co.uk/news/world/americas/civilians-caught-in-crossfire-during-port-au-prince-raids-434723.html (accessed 30 April 2020).

[85] L. Reed, *Peace Despite the Peacekeepers in Haiti* (New York: North American Congress on Latin America, 25 September 2007) https://nacla.org/article/peace-despite-peacekeepers-haiti (accessed 30 April 2020).

[86] A. Bussinger Carvalho, Member of the Human Rights Commission of the Federal Organization of Advocates in Brazil and Official representative on their Human Rights Missions in Haiti in 2005 and 2007, Interview with Siobhán Wills, 27 November 2019.

[87] 'Peacekeeping in Haiti: Operation Deep Pockets' (2004) 373 *The Economist* 846, 47

7.4 'Collateral Damage' Caused by Minustah in Cité Soleil   131

78 grenades, and 5 mortars, over a period of approximately seven hours.[88] Reports by the United States Embassy in Haiti suggest that more than twenty women and children were killed.[89] Seth Donnelly, who visited Bois Neuf twenty-four hours after Operation Iron Fist as part of a human rights delegation from the United States, reported that a number of dead were still lying in their homes, including a mother and child, and:

> We found homes, which when we say homes, we are talking basically shacks of wood and tin, in many cases, riddled with machine gun blasts as well as tank fire. The holes in a lot of these homes were too large just to be bullets. They must have been tank-type shells penetrating the homes. We saw a church and a school completely riddled with machine gun blasts.[90]

There was also graphic film footage shot by a journalist living in Cité Soleil,[91] which MINUSTAH acknowledged that it had seen but dismissed as 'lies' without sending a team to the neighbourhood to investigate.[92] Under-Secretary-General for Peacekeeping Operation, Jean-Marie Guehénno, publicly acknowledged, in filmed footage that is available on the UN's own website, 'I have to be honest with you, there may have been some civilian casualties'[93] but no one from the UN has visited the neighbourhood, then or at any time since, to talk to the community and investigate what happened.[94] Local lawyers and NGOs jointly filed two complaints to the Inter-American Commission on Human Rights.[95] Amnesty International published two statements, the first noted that:

> MINUSTAH officials recently admitted that an internal investigation concluded that a number of unarmed civilians may have been killed during a UN operation in Cité Soleil on 6 July 2005. Amnesty International urges UN officials to make public its findings.[96]

---

[88] Report of Philip Alston, Special Rapporteur on Extrajudicial, summary or arbitrary executions (n 46), 324–325.

[89] 'Haiti Post-Dread Wilme' Cable Number 'Port au Prince 001829' (n 78).

[90] Donnelly, 'Eyewitnesses Describe Massacre by UN Troops in Haitian Slum' (n 77).

[91] The journalist has since died but the footage has been used in Pina (director) *Haiti* (n 78).

[92] Report of Philip Alston, Special Rapporteur on Extrajudicial, summary or arbitrary executions (n 46), 330.

[93] UN Haiti/Guéhenno, United Nations Audiovisual Library (28 July 2005), available at www .unmultimedia.org/avlibrary/asset/U050/U050729b/. (accessed 30 April 2020).

[94] McLaughlin and Wills (directors) *It Stays With You* (n 79).

[95] Two Petitions to the Inter-American Commission on Human Rights both titled *Urgent Request for Provisional Measures Based on Grave Threats to the Lives of Civilians in Port-au-Prince*, one against the Federative Republic of Brazil and the other against The United States of America, November 2005.

[96] Amnesty International *Haiti / Dominican Republic: Deaths continue as MINUSTAH fails to protect civilians* AMR 36/004/2006, 16 January 2006.

The second Amnesty statement reported that there were allegations that a demonstrator had been killed during protests in February 2006 and called for a full and impartial investigation:

> The man's death has been attributed by protestors to members of the United Nations Stabilisation Force in Haiti (MINUSTAH) who they have accused of firing at the crowd of demonstrators ... The UN has previously been implicated in civilian deaths during policing operations in July 2005 and January this year.[97]

The UN did not respond publicly to either of these calls. Two months after Iron Fist, in the midst of an outcry over the scale of casualties incurred, General Heleno resigned. According to some reports Heleno was removed from office at the request of the UN.[98] Yet no one from the UN went to the Cité Soleil neighbourhood to speak to survivors.

Approximately six months later, on January 4th 2006, Heleno's successor, General Bacellar, refused requests from the US Embassy in Haiti and Dr Reginald Boulos, President of the Haitian Chamber of Commerce and Industry, to conduct an operation similar to Iron Fist because too many people would be killed: he said that his job was to defend the Haitian constitution not to fight crime.[99] However, two days later MINUSTAH's civilian head of mission, Juan Gabriel Valdés, insisted that UN troops would soon 'occupy' Cité Soleil: 'I think there'll be collateral damage but we have to impose our force, there is no other way'.[100] The following morning General Bacellar was found dead in his underpants on the balcony of his hotel room: apparently he had shot himself.[101] Bacellar's deputy, Eduardo Aldunate, who subsequently took over as interim force commander, reported that 'the press exaggerated the danger on the streets' and we 'were under heavy pressure' including from a 'top official of an important country' to go into Cité Soleil and clean up the gangs but we 'knew that civilians would take more casualties than the gangs if we did this'.[102]

---

[97] Amnesty International *Fear for safety/Possible excessive use of force* AMR 36/007/2006, 14 February 2006.
[98] L. Fernandes, 'Ghosts of Massacre in Haiti Haunt Bolsonaro Government Generals', *Brasil de Fato*, 19 March 2019, www.brasildefato.com.br/2019/03/19/ghosts-of-massacre-in-haiti-haunt-bolsonaro-government-generals/ (accessed 30 April 2020).
[99] P. Davison, 'UN's Chief Peacekeeper is Found Dead in Haiti Hotel', *Independent*, 9 January 2006, www.independent.co.uk/news/world/americas/uns-chief-peacekeeper-is-found-dead-in-haiti-hotel-6112275.html (accessed 30 April 2020).
[100] K. Ives, 'WikiLeaks points to US meddling in Haiti', *Guardian*, 21 January 2011, www.theguardian.com/commentisfree/cifamerica/2011/jan/21/haiti-wikileaks (accessed 30 April 2020).
[101] Davison, 'UN's Chief Peacekeeper is Found Dead in Haiti Hotel' (n 99).
[102] Aldunate, *Backpacks Full of Hope* (n 68), 143.

7.4 'Collateral Damage' Caused by Minustah in Cité Soleil

Following Bacellar's death there was a pause in large scale military operations until almost the end of the year. But between December 2006 and March 2007 MINUSTAH carried out fifteen heavily militarized operations in Cité Soleil. The largest, Operation New Forest, which the UN said was undertaken 'to fight crime and insecurity',[103] took place on the night of 21/22 December in Bois Neuf a Cité Soleil neighbourhood in which many people live in corrugated metal shacks – and MINUSTAH fired 10,00 bullets.[104] The Bureaux des Avocats Internationaux documented 31 people killed in the operation, among them children and the elderly, 33 wounded and 238 people displaced.[105] The president of the Haitian Senate's Human Rights Commission described the operation as 'a crime against humanity'.[106] MINUSTAH's civilian head of mission Edmond Mulet stated 'there has been collateral damage definitely'[107] – yet no one from the UN, or from the Haitian government, visited the neighbourhood after this, or after any of the other operations during this period, to investigate the number of casualties and whether there was anyone in need of medical care.[108] Use of the term collateral damage in a law enforcement context is inappropriate since it implies a different (and looser) approach to the proportionality equation than is permitted under IHRL. Despite this, MINUSTAH officials – including both Juan Gabriel Valdès, the 2004 to 2006 UN Special Representative of the United Nations in Haiti, and his successor Edmond Mulet – routinely referred to both anticipated and actual deaths and injuries of people that were not directly targeted as 'collateral damage',[109] which apparently did not warrant investigation, apologies, or compensation. Several survivors said that they tried to report the deaths of their family members but were repeatedly turned away.[110]

[103] 'Clarification on the joint PNH/MINUSTAH operation in Cité Soleil Port-au-Prince' UN statement by Direction Centrale de la Police Judiciaire (DCPJ) at 250–3630 and MINUSTAH (Je Wè Bouch Pale) at 244–3503, 26 December 2006, www.ijdh.org/2006/12/ar chive/institute-for-justice-democracy-in-haiti-home-437/ (accessed 30 April 2020).

[104] Dorn, 'Intelligence-led Peacekeeping' (n 80), 814.

[105] Buncombe, 'Civilians Caught in Crossfire During Port-au-Prince Raids' (n 84).

[106] Dr Armstrong Charlot, interview with Siobhán Wills at 33 Relief Clinic Hospital, Delmas, Port-au-Prince, 29 January 2018; The Red Cross said UN troops 'blocked Red Cross vehicles from entering Cité Soleil', Y. Engler, 'The Haiti Occupation Continues', *Counterpunch*, 7 February 2014, www.counterpunch.org/2014/02/07/the-haiti-occupation-continues/.

[107] 'Half-Hour for Haiti: Tell The Times to Tell the Whole Story', Institute for Justice and Democracy in Haiti, 14 February 2007, www.ijdh.org/2007/02/topics/law-justice/half-hour-for -haiti-tell-the-times-to-tell-the-whole-story/ (accessed 30 April 2020).

[108] Survivors' testimonies in McLaughlin and Wills (directors) *It Stays With You* (n 79).

[109] United Nations Juridical Yearbook 2009 (New York: United Nations 2010), 429; R. Fatton, Jr., 'Haiti's Crisis of Governance' in J. Heine and A. Stewart Thompson (eds.) *Fixing Haiti and Beyond* (United Nations University 2011), 41, 61; C. Lynch, 'U.N. Peacekeeping More Assertive, Creating Risk for Civilians', *Washington Post*, 15 August 2005.

[110] Survivors' testimonies in McLaughlin and Wills (directors) *It Stays With You* (n 79).

7.5 RULES OF ENGAGEMENT FOR UN PEACEKEEPERS

The UN Guidelines on ROE 'provide simple and informative direction, which will not only expedite the production of ROE for UNPKO but may also be used for generic purposes', with the aim of ensuring consistency of ROE across UN peacekeeping missions. Annexed to the Guidelines is a list of sample ROE:[111]

Rule 1.1 Use of force, up to, and including deadly force, to defend oneself and other UN personnel against a hostile act or a hostile intent is authorized.

Rule 1.2 Use of force, up to, and including deadly force, to defend other international personnel against a hostile act or a hostile intent is authorised.

Rule 1.3 Use of force, up to, and including deadly force, to resist attempts to abduct or detain oneself and other UN personnel is authorised.

Rule 1.4 Use of force, up to, and including deadly force, to resist attempts to abduct or detain other international personnel is authorised.

Rule 1.5 Use of force, up to, and including deadly force, to protect United Nations' installations, areas or goods, designated by the Head of Mission in consultation with the Force Commander, against a hostile act is authorised.

Rule 1.6 Use of force, up to, and including deadly force, to protect key installations, areas or goods designated by the Head of Mission in consultation with the Force Commander, against a hostile act is authorised, **OR**

Rule 1.7 Use of force, up to but excluding deadly force, to protect key installations, areas or goods designated by the Head of Mission in consultation with the Force Commander, against a hostile act is authorised.

Rule 1.8 Use of force, up to, and including deadly force, to defend any person who is in need of protection against a hostile act or hostile intent, when competent local authorities are not in a position to render immediate assistance is authorized. When and where

---

[111] United Nations, *Guidelines for the development of ROE for UNPKO*, UN document MD/FGS/0220.0001, May 2002 authorized by Major Tim Ford, Military Advisor, Department of Peacekeeping Operations from 2000–2002. The Guidelines are based on those promulgated in 2000 by Jean Marie Guehenno, Under-Secretary General for Peacekeeping Operations from 2000–2008 published in T. Findlay, *The Use of Force in Peace Operations* (Oxford: Oxford University Press 2002), 425.

7.5 Rules of Engagement for UN Peacekeepers 135

> possible, permission to use force should be sought from the immediate superior.
>
> **Rule 1.9** Use of force, excluding deadly force, to prevent the escape of any apprehended or detained person, pending hand-over to appropriate civilian authorities, is authorized.
>
> **Rule 1.10** Use of force, up to, and including deadly force, against any person and/or group who limits or intends to limit freedom of movement, is authorised.[112]

The UN's ROE Guidelines and annexed sample rules provide a template for drafting mission-specific ROE but they do not restrict expansion if the drafters believe that the mandate requires such expansion. Troop contributing states may also, and often do, introduce caveats narrowing the ROE as applied to their troop contribution, usually in order to comply with their own domestic laws or to avoid becoming drawn into an armed conflict.

Commander Dale Stephens, writing about his experiences whilst serving with the UN Transitional Administration in East Timor (UNTAET), commented that the 'UNTAET ROE were expressed broadly and, prima facie, did permit the use of force in order to perform necessary duties, though this was necessarily "read down" to permit lethal force only in situations where lives were directly threatened'.[113] UNTAET's numbered ROE on use of force,[114] which Commander Stephens considered to have been 'expressed broadly', were almost identical to those set out in the Sample UN Rules of Engagement annexed to the 2002 UN guidelines. In the intervening years, UN peacekeepers' ROE have diverged significantly from the 2002 sample rules and are much broader than the UNTAET ROE that Commander Stephens thought were 'expressed broadly' and therefore needed to be read down so as to permit use of deadly force only when lives were threatened.

---

[112] The UN *Guidelines for the Development of Rules of Engagement and Sample ROE for UN Peacekeeping Operations*, 1 December 2000 also contain an additional rule '**Rule 1.11** Use of force, up to, and including deadly force, to resist armed forceful attempts to prevent peacekeepers from discharging their duties is authorized'. T. Findlay, *The Use of Force in Peace Operations* (Oxford: Oxford University Press 2002), 425.

[113] *Law and Military Operations in East Timor Feb 2000–May 2002: Lessons Learnt for Military Officers* (Melbourne: Australia Defence Force Military Law Centre and Asia Pacific Military Law Centre 2003), 48.

[114] Rules of Engagement for the Military Component of the United Nations Mission in East Timor, 2000, published in *Law and Military Operations in East Timor Feb 2000-May 2002: Lessons Learnt for Military Officers* (Melbourne: Australia Defence Force Military Law Centre and Asia Pacific Military Law Centre 2002) Annexures X and Y.

136 *UN Peacekeepers' Use of Deadly Force to Maintain Law and Order*

Mission ROE for responding to civil unrest are illustrative of the problem. The sample rules on reaction to civil unrest annexed to the 2002 UN guidelines:

Rule 5.1: Action to counter civil unrest is not authorized.

Rule 5.2: When competent local authorities are not in a position to render immediate assistance, detention of any person who creates or threatens to create civil unrest with likely serious consequences for life and property is authorized.

However, MINUSTAH's ROE, drawn up in 2004, explicitly authorized the mission to use force, 'up to and including deadly force in order to put a stop to acts of civil unrest'.[115] Civil unrest is defined in MINUSTAH's ROE as 'the commission, perpetration, or instigation of acts of violence that affect public peace and order'.[116] There is no requirement that the violence affecting public peace and order must pose an imminent threat to life. The provision in MINUSTAH's ROE for dealing with civil unrest contrasts with a similar provision in the ROE drawn up in 2009 for use by the UN Mission in the Central African Republic (MINURCAT), which authorized use of force, 'up to and including deadly force to prevent or put a stop to acts of civil unrest that are a threat to life or of serious bodily injury'.[117] Neither sets of ROE make any reference whatsoever to IHRL.

It is not just the numbered ROE setting out the circumstances in which deadly force may be used, that are of concern. The sections in mission ROE dealing with permissible Weapon States also raise questions with regard to compatibility with IHRL. For example, under MINUSTAH's ROE the Force Commander may authorize 'as he believes operationally appropriate', without need for consultation with UN headquarters, that:

---

[115] Rules of Engagement for the Military Component of the United Nations Stabilization Mission in Haiti, 28 June 2004, signed by Jean-Marie Guehenno, Under-Secretary General for Peacekeeping Operations (confidentially on file with author). MINUSTAH's mandate does not refer to civil unrest. Resolution 1542 (UN Doc. S/RES/1542 30 April 2004) does state that the mission is mandated under Chapter VII 'in support of the Transitional Government, to ensure a secure and stable environment within which the constitutional and political process in Haiti can take place'. Resolution 1542 also mandates the mission 'to assist the Transitional Government in extending State authority throughout Haiti and support good governance at local levels' but this provision is in Part III of the mission's mandate: only Part I is adopted under Chapter VII.

[116] Ibid.

[117] Rules of Engagement for MINURCAT Troops, annexed to Rules of Engagement for the Military Component of the United Nations Mission in the Central African Republic and Chad, February 2009 (draft copy, awaiting signature of Alain Le Roy, confidentially on file with author).

7.6 Conclusion

Helicopter-mounted guns and missiles may be deployed. Guns may have a loaded magazine or belted ammunition inserted in or attached to the weapon. They may be cocked and ammunition inserted into the breach and fired. Missiles may be prepared for immediate firing.[118]

Given that MINUSTAH's mandating resolution and relevant Secretary-General's reports confirmed that the main problem in Haiti was not armed conflict but 'the existence of challenges to the political, social and economic stability of Haiti' – and that the main source of armed violence were the gangs based impoverished densely populated neighbourhoods – an authorization to use helicopter mounted guns and missiles without the need for further consultation or higher authorization, seems extraordinary.

7.6 CONCLUSION

Questioned about Operation Iron Fist in 2005, General Heleno stated on Haiti's Radio Metropole, 'We carried out an operation to show that the forces of order are powerful and that we have the means to impose the law . . . We will carry out operations, exert pressure, kill and arrest bandits'.[119] Neither IHRL nor IHL permits the killing of bandits in order to impose the law. More than fourteen years have passed since Amnesty International called on the UN to publish the results of its internal inquiries into deaths caused by UN fire in Haiti 2005 and authorize an impartial investigation – but nothing has been done.

Currently the Brazilian government is openly asserting that it is implementing in Rio de Janeiro in 2020 militarised law enforcement tactics honed by Brazilian commanders and troops during their thirteen years of service with MINUSTAH. In his current capacity as Brazil's Minister for Security, General Heleno frequently cites MINUSTAH's ROE as the ideal for model Brazil's military police, whom he says must be permitted to use snipers to fire from helicopters at favela gang members; Heleno says that he operated under similar Rules of Engagement in Haiti.[120] At the time the UN insisted that it

---

[118] Provided that the weapon state does not exceed the authority of Security Council 1542 and subsequent mandating resolutions: Rules of Engagement for the Military Component of the United Nations Stabilization Mission in Haiti (n 115) Annex D Weapon States

[119] General Augusto Heleno Ribeiro Pereira, Radio Metropole 'Forces of Order Have the Means and the Will' 17 July 2005, https://haitipolicy.org/2005/07/forces-of-order-have-the-means-and-the-will (accessed 30 April 2020).

[120] General Heleno participating in a debate about military intervention in Rio de Janeiro, *GloboNews*, 17 February 2018 (Translation J. Forlani) https://globosatplay.globo.com/globonews/v/6512023/ (accessed 30 April 2020); G. Stardgarter, 'General Behind Deadly Haiti Raid Takes Aim at Brazil's Gangs', *Reuters*, 28 November 2018.

138 UN Peacekeepers' Use of Deadly Force to Maintain Law and Order

only used helicopters for surveillance and never fired from them.[121] Heleno now claims that

> Our rules of engagement in Haiti were highly flexible. They gave the commander of the scene, not the commander-in-chief, the power to injure and lethally wound anyone who had a hostile action or intention. This means that a guy armed with a rifle assaulting or stealing cargo becomes a target whom I can eliminate it. Is it hard? It's hard, but that's the way it has to happen.[122]

This might explain the comments made by eight MINUSTAH soldiers interviewed by Folha in 2006, who said 'the name "peace mission" gives the wrong impression of what is happening in Haiti ... In fact there is no day when UN troops do not kill a Haitian'.[123]

On 7 January 2006, General Bacellar was found dead, apparently from suicide following his refusal to conduct an operation in Cité Soleil that he believed would result in many civilian deaths. Two days after Bacellar's body was found Dr Boulos, Head of Haiti's Chamber of Commerce, angrily criticized MINUSTAH on Radio Metropole:

> We really do not care about what certain international human-rights-defense groups may say ... You cannot make an omelet without breaking eggs. We think that MINUSTAH's generals need to make plans to limit collateral damage. But we in the private sector are ready to create a social assistance fund to help all those who would be innocent victims of a necessary and courageous action that should be carried out in Cité Soleil.[124]

Clearly the number of deaths and injuries resulting from MINUSTAH's operations was a matter of such public concern that it may have led to a commander's suicide and was discussed on Haiti's main radio station, yet survivors of Operations Iron Fist and New Forest claim that no one from the UN or from any state agency has ever visited their neighbourhood to speak to

---

[121] Clarification on the joint PNH/MINUSTAH operation in Cité Soleil, *Port-au-Prince*, 26 December 26, 2006, Direction Centrale de la Police Judiciaire (DCPJ) at 250–3630, MINUSTAH (*Je Wè Bouch Pale*) at 244–3503; Buncombe, 'Civilians Caught in Crossfire During Port-au-Prince Raids' (n 84); B. Terrall, 'Haiti: A Coup Regime, Human Rights Abuses' *Global Policy Forum*, 26 January 2006, www.globalpolicy.org/component/content/a rticle/186/34461.html (accessed 30 April 2020).

[122] General Heleno, *GloboNews*, 17 February 2018 (n 120).

[123] L. Capriglione, 'Soldados revelam o horror da vida no Haiti' *Folha de Sao Paulo*, 29 January 2006.

[124] Dr Reginald Boulos, Radio Metropole, 9 January 2006 quoted in B. Terall, 'UN's Deadly Legacy in Haiti 'Peacekeepers' *Global Policy Forum* 7 February 2007, www.globalpolicy.org /component/content/article/186/34483.html (accessed 30 April 2020).

7.6 Conclusion

them or to view the bullet holes in their homes and hear their stories in situ. As Cité Soleil resident Evelyn Myrtil said 'it's as though you're worthless'.[125]

In June 2018, in response to survivors' filmed testimonies sent to him detailing the deaths of their children and parents, Under-Secretary-General for Peacekeeping Operations, Jean Pierre Lacroix, stated that the UN was 'closely examining this matter' and would respond as soon as possible.[126] But to date, at the time of writing December 2020, there has been no response and no one from the UN has yet visited the Cité Soleil neighbourhoods where MINUSTAH's most intense operations took place. NGOs and churches have also written to the UN Secretary–General and the Under-Secretary-General for Peacekeeping – but the UN has not responded to any of their calls for an investigation.[127]

[125] Testimony of Evelyn Myrtil in McLaughlin and Wills (directors) *It Stays With You* (n 79).
[126] Email from Jean-Pierre Lacroix *Re: Inquiry into investigation into collateral damage by UN peacekeepers in Haiti*, 23 June 2018.
[127] Copies of letters and emails on file with authors.

8

Conclusion

8.1 INTRODUCTION

The law on global governance that emerged after the Second World War 'was grounded in irrefutable trust in international organizations' and an assumption that their subjection to legal discipline would not only be unnecessary but 'detrimental to their success'.[1] Eyal Benvenisti has observed that:

> The law that evolved systematically insulated international organizations from internal and external scrutiny and absolved them of any inherent legal obligations – and, to a degree, continues to do so .... Today, although a 'culture of accountability' may have taken root, its legal tools are still shaping up and are often contested.[2]

UN peacekeeping is one of the areas that has been most resistant to demands for transparency and accountability. Whilst major advances have been taken to ensure that UN peacekeeping operations are better equipped to tackle war crimes and human rights abuses committed by armed groups, there has been comparatively little action taken to ensure that host state residents are protected from abuses by the mission itself. In this book, we have examined UN peacekeeping practice in Haiti through the lens of international human rights law (IHRL). This chapter draws together our conclusions and recommendations for the future. Many of the challenges MINUSTAH faced are similar to those faced by other twenty-first century peacekeeping operations; but the fact that there was no armed conflict in Haiti during the entire time that MINUSTAH was deployed (and therefore IHL was not relevant to any of

---

[1] E. Benvenisti 'Upholding Democracy Amid the Challenges of New Technology: What Roel for the Law of Global Governance' (2018) 29 (1) *European Journal of International Law* 9.
[2] Ibid.

8.2 *Peacekeeping Expands to Protect Human Rights but Fails* 141

MINUSTAH's activities) makes Haiti highly suited to a case study of peacekeepers' IHRL obligations.

This book has focused on three aspects of MINUSTAH's human rights responsibilities: (i) accountability for the outbreak and spread of cholera, (ii) sexual exploitation and abuse by peacekeepers, and (iii) the use of deadly force against non-combatants. In all three studies the mission's practice has been found wanting. We argue that MINUSTAH's failure to uphold human right standards, together with its lack of transparency and poor accountability, are problems that are likely to arise again in future missions unless Department of Peacekeeping Operations (DPKO) commits to applying IHRL standards to its own activities, changes its practices to reflect this, and puts in place effective measures to ensure transparency and accountability.

8.2 PEACEKEEPING EXPANDS TO PROTECT HUMAN RIGHTS BUT FAILS TO INCORPORATE INTERNATIONAL HUMAN RIGHTS LAW STANDARDS INTO ITS PRACTICE

With the notable exception of the UN operations in the Congo in the 1960s, Cyprus in the 1960s and 1970s, and Lebanon in the 1970s, early so-called traditional peacekeeping missions largely involved observation and protection through interposition, but since the 1990s the United Nation (UN) has expanded its field operations to include large-scale highly interventionist missions mandated under Chapter VII of the UN Charter.[3] The inability of UN troops to prevent genocide in Rwanda and Srebrenica in 1994 and 1995, and the UN's subsequent failure to address atrocities committed by government forces in Sri Lanka in 2009, is one of the reasons behind the routine adoption of mandates under Chapter VII. Most Chapter VII missions explicitly authorise the use of 'all necessary means' or 'all necessary measures' to carry out all or some of the mission's mandated tasks, although MINUSTAH's mandate did not. However, even without a Chapter VII mandate or an explicit authorisation 'peacekeepers are authorized to use force … to execute their mandated tasks in appropriate situations'.[4] Peacekeeping missions' authority

---

[3] United Nations website https://peacekeeping.un.org/en/our-history (accessed 30 April 2020); NATO, *Allied Joint Doctrine for the military Contribution to Peace Support Operations* AJP 3.4.1 Peace Support Operations 2 December 2014 https://assets.publishing.service.gov.uk/government/uploads/system/uploads/attachment_data/file/624153/doctrine_nato_peace_support_ajp_3_4_1.pd (accessed 30 April 2020); A. Roberts 'The Crisis in UN Peacekeeping' (1994) 36 (3) *Survival* 93, 99.

[4] United Nations Department of Peacekeeping Operations/ Department of Field Support Ref: 2016.24 Guidelines: *Use of Force by Military Components in United Nations Peacekeeping*

to use 'all necessary means' is not without limits: mandates must be construed in accordance with applicable international law, including IHRL. This is only possible if the UN adopts clear guidelines on implementing its IHRL obligations, including those obligations relating to transparency and accountability, and ensures that mission personnel are trained to apply them.

Since 2004, with the deployment of MINUSTAH, the tasks assigned to peacekeeping missions have further expanded to include assisting governments to extend their authority to all parts of the state, and if necessary to assist governments to maintain law and order through the use of military force – a process commonly known as 'stabilisation'.[5] Since stabilisation routinely involves intense use of force in support of the host state government and entails intervention on wide ranging scale, it necessarily challenges the core principles of peacekeeping: missions should be impartial, should use a minimum of force, and should have the consent of the main parties to a conflict.[6] In addition to MINUSTAH, three other UN missions have been formally designated as stabilisation missions. The United Nations Multidimensional Integrated Stabilization Mission in Mali is mandated inter alia 'in support of the transitional authorities of Mali, to stabilise the key population centres, especially in the north of Mali and, in this context, to deter threats and take active steps to prevent the return of armed elements to those areas'[7] and the United Nations Multidimensional Integrated Stabilization Mission in the Central African Republic is mandated inter alia to 'adopt urgent temporary measures on an exceptional basis . . . to maintain basic law and order and fight impunity' in support of the transitional government of the Central African Republic.[8] Most notable, and most controversial given peacekeepers' traditional protected civilian status, MONUSCO's Force Intervention Brigade has been mandated since 2013, to undertake targeted offensive operations to 'neutralize and disarm' groups considered a threat to 'state authority and civilian security'.[9] But UN stabilisation activities are not limited to missions that have stabilisation in their title – tasks aimed at stabilisation are now a common feature of Chapter VII peacekeeping

---

Operations, effective 1 February 2017, https://info.publicintelligence.net/UN-PeacekeepingFo rces-2017.pdf (accessed 30 April 2020).

[5] A. Gorur, *Defining the Boundaries of UN Stabilization Missions* (Washington: Stimson Centre 2016), www.stimson.org/sites/default/files/file-attachments/Defining-Boundaries-UN-Stabiliza tion-Missions.pdf

[6] United Nations Peacekeeping Operations Principles and Guidelines ('the Capstone Doctrine'), approved by J.-M. Guéhenno, USG/DPKO, 18 January 2008.

[7] Security Council Resolution 2100 (UN Doc. S/RES/2100), 25 April 2013.

[8] Security Council Resolution 2149 (UN Doc. S/RES/2149), 14 April 2014.

[9] Security Council Resolution 2098 (UN Doc. S/Res 2098), 28 March 2013.

8.2 *Peacekeeping Expands to Protect Human Rights but Fails* 143

mandates. One result of this expansion of mandates to include stabilization is that in many parts of the world 'the primary enforcers of order are not police officers or government soldiers but the blue-helmeted troops of the United Nations'.[10]

Since international humanitarian law (IHL) is only applicable to peacekeepers when they are engaged as combatants in an armed conflict, it does not play a significant role in peacekeeping; the international law regime most relevant to peacekeeping is IHRL.[11] Peacekeeping operations should not only be formally regulated by IHRL but conceived and implemented through an overall IHRL prism particularly where missions are deployed to undertake highly interventionist multi-dimensional operations that deeply impinge on the lives of the host state population, and therefore potentially on their human rights. The OHCHR views the UN's multifaceted roles, including its peacekeeping operations, as being situated within an overarching goal of protecting human rights and is working to bring about a human rights oriented change across the entire UN system. In its 2014 Aide-Memoire to the Human Rights Up Front Plan of Action, the UN acknowledged that a re-orientation of all UN activities so as to bring them within a human rights frame, in both theory and practice, would entail a change in the UN's institutional culture;[12] but changing institutional culture is not easy.[13] To view new mandates and previous practice through a prism of human rights is a challenge, since it entails interpreting past practice differently than had been envisaged at the time the mission was deployed. In some cases, peacekeeping operations that have been considered a success may have to be reassessed in light of the UN's human rights obligations. It would also require adopting unfamiliar approaches to ongoing and future missions that might be a challenge for mission personnel that have worked all their lives according to different standards.

---

[10] S. Auteserre, 'The Crisis of Peacekeeping: Why the UN Can't End Wars' (January 2019) *Foreign Affairs*, 101.

[11] N. D. White, 'Peacekeeping and International Law' in J. A. Knoops et al. (eds.) *The Oxford Handbook of United Nations Peacekeeping Operations* (Oxford: Oxford University Press 2015), 43, 53; T. Gill et al. (eds.) *Leuven Manual on the International Law Applicable to Peace Operations* (Cambridge: Cambridge University Press 2017), 150, 152; ICRC, *Violence and the Use of Force* (Geneva: ICRC 2015), 37 www.icrc.org/en/publication/0943-violence-and-use-force (accessed 30 April 2020); D. Murray et al., *Practitioner's Guide to Human Rights Law in Armed Conflict* (Oxford: Chatham House Royal Institute of International Affairs and Oxford University Press 2016), 260.

[12] United Nations, (2014) Aide-Memoire to the Human Rights Up Front Plan of Action, on file with authors.

[13] W. Vandenhole and P. Gready 'Failures and Successes of Human Rights-Based Approaches to Development: Towards a Change Perspective' (2014) 32 (4) *Nordic Journal of Human Rights* 291, 311.

The UN's peacekeeping strategy tends to favour top-down deals struck with elites rather than 'embracing bottom-up strategies that draw on local knowledge and letting the people themselves determine how best to promote peace'.[14] Despite the fact that UN troops are now heavily involved in law enforcement and are often the primary enforcers of order within the host state, mission activities are largely opaque and distant from the population. Often the majority of the mission's personnel do not speak the local language. Residents cannot easily access mission bases to report their concerns and there tends to be very little public information provided as to how to seek redress for death, injury, or loss. Often there is no effective means of bringing a complaint because of the broad scope of UN immunities and the UN's failure to provide alternative processes by which people can bring claims and secure a remedy where these are upheld. Consequently, peacekeeping, even when it is aimed at promoting democracy and human rights, itself poses serious challenges for democracy and human rights – especially when it involves deployment of a large number of military personnel over a long period of time.

Today UN troops make up the second-largest military force deployed abroad.[15] In most cases their mandates are drafted by the 'penholder states' – the United States, the United Kingdom, or France – with very little discussion among the Security Council as a whole since members tend to be reluctant to risk upsetting the careful balance of negotiation achieved between the Permanent Three, unless their own interests are at stake.[16] Host state parliaments have little or no say in the deployment of the mission or its activities, since host state consent, if it is obtained at all, is usually only the consent of the executive. In 2011 and again in 2013, the Haitian Senate unanimously passed resolutions demanding that MINUSTAH leave Haiti.[17] The then Secretary–General, Ban Ki Moon, acknowledged the Senate's demands but determined that MINUSTAH should nevertheless remain.[18] The mission did not draw down until October 2017.

Commenting in 2016 on the UN's response to the cholera epidemic that MINUSTAH created, Special Rapporteur Philip Alston described the UN's

---

[14] Auteserre, 'The Crisis of Peacekeeping' (n 10), 101–102.

[15] Ibid.

[16] Note by The President of the Security Council (UN Doc. S/2014/268) 14 April 2014.

[17] K. Ives, 'Haiti: Uruguay will Withdraw from MINUSTAH President Says' *Haiti Liberté*, 30 October 2013; www.globalresearch.ca/haiti-uruguay-will-withdraw-from-minustah-president-says-beginning-of-end-of-un-occupation-of-haiti/5356424 (accessed 30 April 2020).

[18] Report of the Secretary-General on the United Nations Stabilization Mission in Haiti 19 August 2013, S/2013/493 para. 8; Ives, 'Haiti: Uruguay will Withdraw from MINUSTAH President Says' (n 17).

8.3 *Conclusion*

'existing legal approach of simply abdicating responsibility' as morally unconscionable, legally indefensible, politically self-defeating, and unnecessary.[19] Several individuals within the UN have attempted to take survivors claims seriously, but abdication of responsibility through prolonged delays, ignoring of letters and emails, and denial of responsibility has been a common feature of the UN's overall institutional response to human rights violations by MINUSTAH. Haitian lawyers and NGOs have encountered strong resistance within the UN departments and sectors with whom they have sought to raise awareness of the human rights violations committed by MINUSTAH. As researchers and human rights advocates we too have experienced resistance from the UN Secretary–General, the Under–Secretary General for Peacekeeping, DPKO, and MINUSTAH, despite our sustained efforts to draw to the UN's attention the violations that our three case studies reveal. MINUSTAH's successor, MINUJUSTH, did make some effort to respond but rapidly disengaged and advised that survivors should pursue their claims with New York. Three separate sources – from DPO, the UN Office of Legal Affairs, and MINUJUSTH – informed us that after MINUSTAH drew down in October 2017 all the documents relating to it were placed unlabelled in sealed shipping containers and sent to New York – and that the keys to these containers have since been lost.

8.3 CONCLUSION

Given that DPO already requires UN peacekeeping police to comply with IHRL, including when they are engaged in robust operations, it should not be too much of a challenge for the Secretary–General to promulgate a document affirming that IHRL obligations apply to all aspects of peacekeeping operations, except to the extent that they are displaced by IHL under the terms of the Secretary–General's Bulletin on the Observance by United Nations Forces of International Humanitarian Law.[20] One reason the UN might be reluctant to formally acknowledge peacekeeping troops' IHRL obligations is the weight of past missions. Acknowledging the applicability of IHRL to peacekeeping operations brings with it a potentially significant reputational challenge for the UN and for the states that contributed troops to the missions, as well as being costly in terms of compensation. But failure to address past

[19] Report by Special Rapporteur on Extreme Poverty and Human Rights, Philip Alston, A/71/367, 26 August 2016.

[20] U.N. Secretary-General's Bulletin, Observance by United Nations Forces of International Humanitarian Law, (U.N. Doc ST/SGB/1999/13) 28 August 1999.

violations and to commit to upholding IHRL in future will not only perpetuate the suffering of survivors, past, present, and future but will cause long lasting damage to the UN.

These are difficult challenges but they must be addressed if OHCHR is to succeed in its mandate of mainstreaming human rights throughout the UN organization and bring UN peacekeeping into line with its legal and moral obligations. UN peacekeeping missions should not, and legally must not, provide support to host state governments that commit serious violations of human rights – but the mainstreaming of human rights requires more than that. It requires DPO to bring UN peacekeeping practice in line with international law and formally recognise the applicability of IHRL to all UN operations and recognise that outside the conduct of hostilities all decisions and actions that affect the rights and well-being of human beings should be governed by IHRL – not IHL. It requires that UN missions be accountable to the people directly affected by their operations – such as the people living in the mission's area of operations – and not just to host and troop contributing states and their political elites.

Index

Afghanistan, 9, 29
African Charter on Human and Peoples' Rights, 59
African Commission on Human and Peoples' Rights, 59
Agamben, Giorgio, 20, 21
Ahmed, General Maqsood, 124–125
Aldunate, Eduardo, 132
Al-Skeini case, 39
Alston, Philip, 78, 80–81, 123, 144, 145
Amnesty International, 137
Annan, Kofi, 7, 16, 37
Aristide, Jean-Bertrand, 21, 24, 25, 27, 28, 72, 85, 126

Bacellar, General, 132, 133, 138
Banković and Others v Belgium and Others, 39
Benvenisti, Eyal, 140
Birmingham Initiative, 78, 81, 82
Bodin, Jean, 19
Bosnia and Herzegovina, 37, 89
  Stabilisation Force for, 9
Boulos, Dr Reginald, 132, 138
Brazilian Bar Association, 130
Bulletin on the Observance by UN Forces of International Humanitarian Law, 37, 38, 40
Bureaux des Avocats Internationaux (BAI), 72–74, 78, 115, 133
Burundi, 57

Cambodia, 56, 57, 89, 105, 110
Capstone Doctrine, 46, 118
Carroll, John, 130

Case Concerning Armed Activities on the Territory of the Congo, 38
causation logics, 8
Cédras, Raul, 24
Center on International Cooperation, 127
Central African Republic, 3, 9, 29, 57, 89, 93, 136, 142
China, 84
cholera
  outbreak of, 11, 66–68
  sanitation, 69–71
  UN responsibility for, 72
Clinton, Bill, 22, 70
Colwell, Rita, 69
complexity theories, 8
Concanon, Brian, 78
Congo, 141
consent
  principle of, 5
Convention on the Privileges and Immunities of the United Nations (CPIUN), 2, 43, 49, 50, 51, 52, 74, 95, 97
Cruz Report, 9
Cruz, Carlos Alberto dos Santos, 9
Cuba, 70
Customary Human Rights Law, 60
Cyprus, 141

de Albuquerque, Catarina, 80
Democratic Republic of Congo (DRC), 3, 30, 57, 89
Dominican Republic, 15, 22, 131
Donnelly, Seth, 131
Dorn, Walter, 129
Doyle, Michael, 4
Duvalier, Jean-Claude, 15, 24

147

Index

Edkins, Jenny, 23
Einsiedel, Sebastian von, 14
Eliasson, Jan, 80
England, 19
European Convention on Human Rights, 39, 60
European Court of Human Rights, 39

Fatton Jr, Robert, 16
Forces Armées d'Haïti, 25
Former Republic of Yugoslavia, 56
  genocide in, 66
Foucault, Michel, 20
France, 9, 19
  colonial regime in Haiti, 16
  recognition of Haitian sovereignty, 21
Freedman, Rosa, 63, 81

Ghali, Boutros-Boutros, 85
Group of Friends of Haiti, 78, 85, 88
Guehénno, Jean-Marie, 131
Guinea, 89
Guterres, António, 10

Haiti
  colonial history of, 15
Hammarskjöld, Dag, 4
Hampson, Francoise, 39
Heleno, General, 130, 137
Heller, Leo, 80
Heyns, Christof, 123
Hobbes, Thomas, 19
Hoffman, F, 41, 43
Honoré, Sandra, 86
Hovell, D, 63
humain terrain system (HTS), 9
Human Rights Committee, 39
Human Rights Council
  resolution 9/9,38
Human Rights Due Diligence Policy, 46
Human Rights Up Front, 46
hybridity, 22–23

impartiality
  principle of, 5
Indonesia, 15
Institute for Justice and Democracy in Haiti (IJDH), 72–74
Inter-American Commission on Human Rights, 58, 131
Inter-American Court of Human Rights, 58

International Committee of the Red Cross (ICRC), 119, 121
International Court of Justice (ICJ), 36, 38, 42
International Covenant on Civil and Political Rights, 36, 39, 60
international crimes, 56–57
International Criminal Court (ICC), 56
International Criminal Law (ICL), 56
International Crisis Group, 127
international human rights law (IHRL), 11, 12, 34–41, 44, 60, 61, 62, 117–119, 121–126, 130, 133, 136, 137, 140, 141, 142, 143, 145, 146
international humanitarian law (IHL), 36–37, 46–47
Iraq, 9, 29, 56, 57
Issa and Others v Turkey, 39
It Stays with You: Use of Force by UN Peacekeepers in Haiti, 129

Jean-Jean case, 109
Justice and Democracy in Haiti (IJDH), 72

Kenya, 57
Keohane, Robert, 19
Ki-moon, Ban, 4, 11, 27
Kolbe, A, 110
Kosovo, 14, 22, 44, 57, 60, 89
Krasner, Stephen, 17, 18, 19–20, 45

Lacroix, Jean Pierre, 139
Lavalas coalition, 24–25
Le Roy, Alain, 68
Lebanon, 56, 57, 141
Legal Consequences of the Construction of a Wall in the Occupied Palestinian Territory, 38
Legality of the Threat or Use of Nuclear Weapons, 36
Lemay-Hébert, Nicholas, 81
Leuven Manual, 121
Liberia, 57, 89, 105, 110
Lindstrom, Beatrice, 73
Lynch, Colum, 78

Maguire, Robert, 16
Malaysia, 87
Mali, 142
Malone, David, 14, 83
Manderlier v Organisation des Nations Unies et l'Etat Belge, 50, 62

Médecins Sans Frontières (MSF), 70, 130
Medical Support Manual for United Nations
    Peacekeeping Operations, 68
Medrano, Pedro, 80
Mégret, F, 41, 42
Ministry of Public Health and Population
    (MSPP), 70
Model Memorandum of Understanding
    between the United Nations and
    personnel contributing States, 44
Mudgway, C, 112
Mulet, Edmond, 133
Myrtil, Evelyn, 139

Nepal
    UN troops from, 67–69
Neto, Lt-General Peixoto Vieira, 127
New Zealand, 85, 87
non-use of force
    principle of, 5
Nuremberg Trials, 55, 57

Office of the High Commissioner for Human
    Rights, 58
Onuf, Nicholas, 13, 19
Operation Iron Fist, 130, 137, 138
Operation New Forest, 133, 138
Organisation of Americas States, 87
Oxfam
    allegations against, 108, 111

Pan-American Health Organization
    (PAHO), 70
Paust, J.J., 50, 55
Pereira, General Augusto Heleno Ribeiro, 127
Piarroux, Renaud, 69
Pin-Frat, Véronique, 23
Police Nationale d'Haïti (PNH), 25
Power, Samantha, 104
Préval, René, 21, 25, 33
Pūras, Dainius, 80

Rana, General Kishore, 68
Responsibility to Protect doctrine, 17
right to truth, 59
Rights Up Front Action Plan, 63
Risse, Thomas, 18
Rome Statute (1998), 56
rules of engagement (ROE), 3, 28, 40, 119, 124,
    126, 134–137
Russia, 84

Rwanda, 37, 56, 57, 141
    genocide in, 66

Save the Children UK
    report on child abuse, 89
Schmitt, Carl, 20
Schuller, Mark, 71
Searle, L, 106–107
Sengupta, Somini, 78
sexual exploitation
    UN definition of, 105
Sierra Leone, 56, 57, 89, 105
Somalia, 37, 57
South Sudan, 57, 89
Sri Lanka
    allegations against UN troops from, 31
Status of Forces Agreements (SOFAs), 102, 119
Stephens, Commander Dale, 135
Sudan, 57
survival sex, 112

Taiwan, 15
Tharoor, Shashi, 5
The Chatham House Practitioners' Guide to
    Human Rights Law in Armed
    Conflict, 125
Timor-Leste, 14, 44, 57
troop-contributing country
    obligations of, 54

UN
    Convention on State Immunities, 49
    Department of Peacekeeping Operations
        (DPKO), 35, 37, 47, 118, 119, 121, 122, 124,
        127, 141, 145, 146
    Dispute Tribunal (UNDT), 101
    General Assembly resolution 57/306, 90
    Human Rights Council, 58, 60, 87
    Independent Panel of Experts on the
        Cholera Outbreak in Haiti, 70
    Mission for Justice Support in Haiti
        (MINUJUSTH), 1, 27, 33, 104, 145
    Mission in the Central African Republic
        (MINURCAT), 136
    Multidimensional Integrated Stabilization
        Mission in Mali, 142
    Office of Legal Affairs, 74, 77, 78, 125
    Office of the Coordinator of Humanitarian
        Affairs, 71
    Office of the High Commissioner for
        Human Rights, 34–35

UN (cont.)
 operations in Mali (MINUSMA), 3, 9,
  29–30
 operations in the Central African Republic
  (MINUSCA), 3, 9, 29–30
 Refugee Agency (UNHCR)
  report on child abuse, 89
 Security Council Resolution, 1542, 13
 Security Council Resolution, 2467, 93
 Stabilization Mission in Haiti
  (MINUSTAH), 4, 9, 11, 13, 15, 25–33, 48,
  69, 74–75, 83, 85, 88, 104, 107–108, 116,
  144–145
 Transitional Administration in East Timor
  (UNTAET), 135
 Victim's Rights Advocate, 2
UN Charter, 42, 50
 Article, 56, 42
 Chapter VI, 4
 Chapter VII, 1, 3, 7, 27, 30, 36, 37, 116, 120,
  125, 128, 141, 142
UN Guidelines for the Development of Rules
 of Engagement, 126
UNEF, 5
United Kingdom (UK), 84

Universal Declaration of Human Rights, 4, 34,
 60, 62
University of Maryland, 69
Up Front Plan of Action, 143
Uruguay, 87, 88, 108
 allegations against UN troops from, 32,
  107–109
*Use of Force by Military Components in United
 Nations Peacekeeping Operations*, 47

Valdès, Juan Gabriel, 132, 133
Vatellian sovereignty model, 17–19
Venezuela, 85, 87

Weber, Max, 18
West Africa, 89
Westendorf, J.K., 106–107
Westphalian sovereignty model, 17–19
World Health Organisation (WHO), 70

Yugoslavia
 International Criminal Tribunals for, 57

Zeid Report, 91, 100
Zero Tolerance policy, 89, 90, 105

CPSIA information can be obtained
at www.ICGtesting.com
Printed in the USA
LVHW021220030821
694401LV00003B/269